Borgo Bioviews
ISSN 0743-0628
Number One

Starclimber
The Literary Adventures and
Autobiography of Raymond Z. Gallun

by

Raymond Z. Gallun
with Jeffrey M. Elliot

Edited by Paul David Seldis
and Mary A. Burgess

BORGO PRESS / WILDSIDE PRESS

www.wildsidepress.com

Library of Congress Cataloging-in-Publication Data

Gallun, Raymond Z., 1911-
  Starclimber : the literary adventures and autobiography of Raymond Z.
Gallun / by Raymond Z. Gallun with Jeffrey M. Elliot ; edited by Paul
David Seldis and Mary A. Burgess.
    p. cm. (Borgo Bioviews, ISSN 0743-0628 ; no. 1)
  Includes bibliographical references and index.
  ISBN 0-89370-348-6 (cloth). — ISBN 0-89370-448-2 (pbk.)
  1. Gallun, Raymond Z., 1911- —Biography. 2. Authors, American—
20th century—Biography. 3. Science fiction—Authorship. I. Elliot, Jeffrey
M. II. Seldis, Paul David, 1958- . III. Burgess, Mary Wickizer, 1938- .
IV. Title. V. Series.
PS3557.A4167Z475 1991   89-82175
813'.54—dc20   CIP

SECOND PRINTING

CONTENTS

ILLUSTRATIONS

For Annie, Frieda, and Bert,

With Love

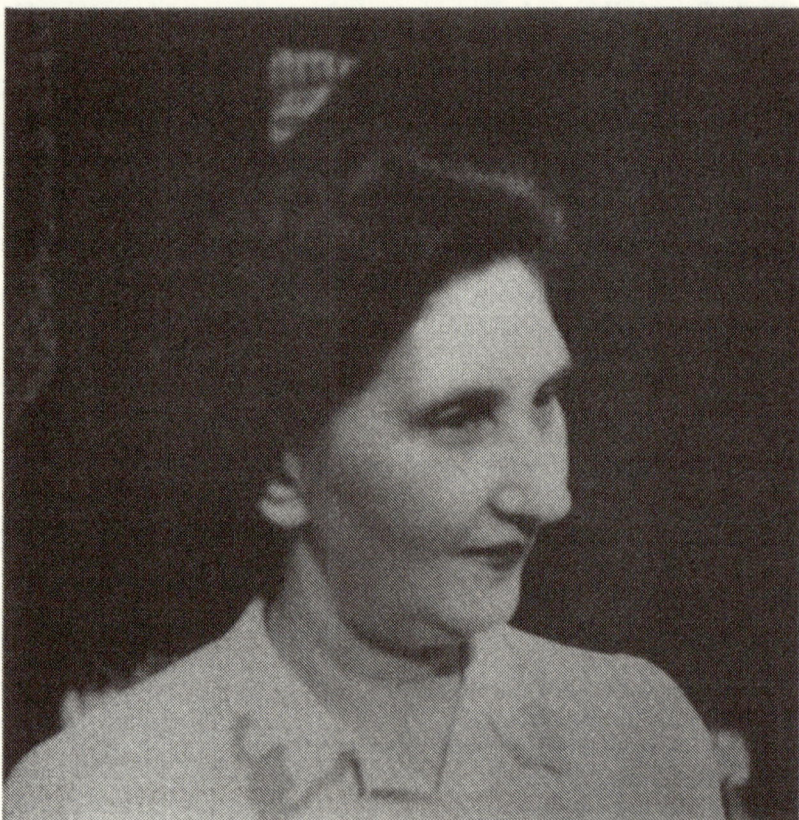

Frieda Talmey Gallun
(died May 19, 1974)

INTRODUCTION

In his introduction to *The Best of Raymond Z. Gallun*, author John J. Pierce states: "Few today appreciate the importance of his [Gallun's] role in the creation of modern science fiction. Few realize he was one of three men—along with John W. Campbell and Stanley G. Weinbaum—who did most to set in motion the evolution of science fiction from crude pulp fiction to a form increasingly imaginative and literate." Despite his achievements, however, Gallun has somehow failed to win the recognition that such contributions would seem to warrant. This is attributable, in large part, to the fact that he has steadfastly eschewed publicity, preferring instead to let his work stand on its own. Fortunately, Gallun's work has begun to be rediscovered by a new generation of science fiction enthusiasts, who are paying increasing attention to the literary accomplishments of this "Quiet Revolutionary."

Born in Beaver Dam, Wisconsin in 1911, Raymond Gallun received his early education in the Beaver Dam public schools. Upon graduation from high school in 1928, he attended the University of Wisconsin, Madison, for one year, before he was hit by "horizon fever." As a youth, Gallun held "lots of knocking around jobs," including working as a canner, seaman, English instructor to refugees from Nazi Germany, telephone solicitor, boatyard worker, and farmhand, among others. By then, except for language and literature courses at the Alliance Française, Paris, France, and San Marcos University, Lima, Peru, his formal education was ended. Marrying late in life and in a somewhat more settled mood, Gallun lost his first wife, Frieda Talmey, to cancer in 1974, and, with her, his "best friend." Four years later, in storybook fashion, he married his boyhood sweetheart—Bertha Erickson—and set sail for a honeymoon around the world. Sadly, she passed away in 1989.

Penning his first two science fiction tales at the age of sixteen, Gallun broke into print in 1929 with "The Space Dwellers" in *Science Wonder Stories* and "The Crystal Ray" in *Air Wonder Stories*. In 1934, he began publishing regularly in F. Orlin Tremaine's *Astounding Stories*, and winning reader praise for his still popular "Old Faithful" series, which includes "Old Faithful," "The Son of Old Faithful," and "Child of the Stars."

Gallun's first book-length novel, *Passport to Jupiter*, appeared in *Startling Stories* in 1950. *People Minus X* was a Simon & Schuster hardcover in 1957. This was followed in 1961 by *The Planet Strappers*, which explores a group of young adventurers of various personalties who join the rush to pioneer the solar system. *The Eden Cycle*, published by Ballantine, appeared in 1974. This novel, which

Gallun considers his best science fiction work, is a close examination of the dream-sequence idea which he first presented in the earlier *Passport to Jupiter*.

From about 1940, Gallun's science fiction appearances became less frequent, due to other interests and concerns, with long hiatuses during World War II, the mid-1950s, and from 1961 to 1974. During the course of his sporadic career as a science fiction writer, extending back more than fifty years, Gallun has published 120-odd stories and books, many of them long ago. A prolific writer during his intervals of activity, his work appeared in virtually every science fiction magazine of those times, among them *Astounding Science fiction, Amazing Stories, Marvel Tales, Wonder Stories, Startling Stories, Planet Stories,* and *Galaxy Science Fiction.* His pseudonyms include "Dow Elstar," "E. V. Raymond," "Arthur Allport," and "William Callahan." In 1979, Gallun received the First Fandom Hall of Fame Award and, in 1985, the Lifetime Achievement Award.

Asked to assess the pulp era, and its contributions to the science fiction genre, Gallun writes:

"*Amazing, Astounding, Wonder, Startling, Marvel*—there was a magical innocence even in the old names of the mags, and a Charm of the Improbable, much of it lost now, it seems to me, though there is, of course, also a vast gain in sophistication.

"To me, being of a generation that can look back to when they were only wild dreams to most folks, moon journeys, atomic power, etc., remain rather miraculous to this day. I hope that those born nearer to such accomplishments can still feel some of that, instead of merely accepting them.

"In the old days we dreamed free, with few guidelines. Relatively little speculative fiction was yet written. So the field was wide open for our own gropings and yearnings to know about the hidden things in time and space. Literary quality wasn't of very great importance. We couldn't profit so much from what others had done. But we could get a new idea a lot more easily.

"Science fiction didn't have much recognition. If you read it or wrote it, quite a few people thought you were nuts. And you could feel sort of guilty and ashamed.

"Myths that we loved as substitutes for unreachable realities have since, sadly, been smashed. We are now told that Percival Lowell was mistaken—that there are no canals on Mars. Nor is there any Barsoom or Pellucidar.

"But maybe the reality, or the dream nearer the reality, has an improved romanticism. And the job of writing isn't so very much changed.

"I still opt for a positive approach to the future. I still think that advancing science and technology—under control by good and broad judgment—offer the best means for making the centuries to come good ones. Though there are many incomplete areas to be filled. Even in just our solar system, there is surely not yet any shortage of energy or materials, if we can find ways to reach and handle them, and the spiritual acumen to keep ourselves and whatever we touch in balance. I like simple living, with no over-emphasis on material possessions. But I do like to think that, before so very long, Mars and Venus will be made habitable, and that a two century lifespan will be the regular thing. I even hope that somebody will actually set off for the stars.

"I suspect that—granting the application of good sense as much as possible—there is no need to retreat, and close doors, either externally or inside ourselves."

Raymond Gallun is of medium height, thin, and has an unnaturally pale complexion—owing, by and large, to recent medical problems. He possesses a warm, strong voice and very quick eyes. Everything about Gallun is casual and easy—although his questions are pointed and direct. He boasts a hearty laugh. His mind is sharp, quick, and incisive. Gallun is open and accessible—eager to make himself understood and to understand others. He is sincere; nothing in him betrays a shrewdness or cunning. Even if one is not in agreement with him, his politics, or his ideology, one cannot help but respect him, admire him, like him. I know I do. And I think you will, too.

Yes, Gallun has his critics—those who fault his often "clumsy and primitve" fiction, his "awkward and ungrammatical" style, his "gaudy and overwritten" prose. Yet, these same critics are quick to admit, as does Donald M. Hassler, that his "treatments of several of the more sophisticated problems facing modern man are often exciting and provocative to read." Clearly, Gallun is a vintage science fiction pulp writer. His fiction, like his mind, is rich in contrasts; Gallun delights in mining the vagaries and complexities of human existence. His images are powerful, poetic, and provocative. In final sum, as one critic puts it: "A genre that can retell the most profound human dilemmas in what are often such rough forms is indeed sturdy and growing, and Gallun was one sturdy and often rough writer who contributed greatly to its growth."

—Dr. Jeffrey M. Elliot
Durham, North Carolina
October, 1990

Raymond Zinke Gallun-1943

I.

BACK TO BEAVER DAM

I've seldom tried poetry writing. But I've just retrieved these verses from among some old papers. Their content is revealing:

The Temple

It was a hut of turf and mud
Built in a Wisconsin marsh—
But really in a dream—
That tried, for fancy's groping
In the reaching mind
Of a twelve-year-old,
To bring home to the farm
Impossibly—
From time-sealed space and books,
A glimpse and feel
Of Babylon...
Or Thebes...
Or terraces of Ur...
Or North Star gropings...
Or even yet the smoky smells
Of Neanderthals stalking mammoths...

The project was unfinished;
It ended in the summer fading
Of a vision,
And supper-calls,
And weariness, and shrugs, and petulance...
And mud-caked overalls and scoldings...
And some successive bright and vagrant
Interest, long since blurred out of memory...

Cows trampled the uncompleted edifice...
Grass grew, but forty years were kind;
The man returned and found—
Faint but there—

The tufted rectangle,
And chuckled to himself...

The chuckle, too, was incomplete...
Or touched with aches
Beyond the simple scope
Of humor at one's own
Pre-adolescent foolishness;
It fumbled at enchantments
That were ever here, and sought—
In manhood too—
But never held for more
Than instants in the years...
Being less graspable than quicksilver,
Or the bright, warm feeling of a star...
With yet a hurt and yearning.

For one more moment
In the summer dusk
A magic lingered,
Braced by the ruin,
And the twilight's red,
And a startled heron's squawk
And fleeing magesty...

What could not be kept
Rested there,
Cupped in the man's chuckle
And his heart—
Tangible for then,
And like all beauty
And all love
Among all minds
That grope, and try to touch—
Infinity...

—Raymond Z. Gallun,
January 11, 1963

The first part of the above occurred in the early 1920s.

In a sense, the second part—the return—occurred, too, though in 1963 I was never very near to Beaver Dam, Wisconsin, where I was born on March 22, 1911. Yet far from my beginnings, I evidently experienced a vivid surge of nostalgic sentiment. It might have been real, and in a way it was.

10

More recently than 1963, and closer to the scene, I could have tried to locate the actual site. But the shaggy woods where I used to wander around as a youngster, had become largely a collection of neat, one-story dwellings, smooth-lawned, flower-bedded, and I suppose more sophisticated. The world had moved on. And a new street had been put through the spot where the odd old house in which I grew up had stood.

Some of the marsh was still there, not far off. I could have tramped into its bogginess, but I didn't. Failure in the quest was too likely. Besides, I had to see some people, and move on. So why should I yield that much to an aging romantic's ego trip? Let the old memory be, green, golden, cattailed, and murmuring. At least the ageless sounds of wind in trees, and of water lapping at the shores of Beaver Lake, were unchanged, as was the bright sunlight.

So I went away, making good-humored noises, though wryly saddened too, and thinking that maybe someday yet I may go look....Which probably will never occur as a physical event. I guess it doesn't matter.

Though that twelve-year-old was I, I feel detached from him as though he were somebody else—which of course he was. Recognition of this truth produces no identity crisis. He was eager, impatient, scared, and full of wants and doubts; I am much more easy-going. I can look on him with indulgent sympathy.

However, let me again become our joined earlier selves. I suppose everybody sometimes fumbles backward toward those oldest, mistiest memories. Let me see what I can dig up:

Scattered impressions. Light and dark. A day seeming very long, then.... Something soft and tickly stirring against my ear. Though I like cats, and am not allergic to them, even now, hearing or even thinking the sound of the word, "kitty," produces a faint, sneezy sensation inside my nose—I have no idea why.

There is some confusion between what I actually remember, and what was told to me. I can't recall yelling out "Anna!" instead of "Ma-ma!," the supposedly instinctive first word of babies—because my mother was sick, and a younger sister of hers was a stand-in for a while. Nor can I actually bring back from my own mind the later occasion when, being left to poke with a stick into a barrel of "ground feed"—oats and barley intended to be mixed into the swill for hogs, while my mother looked after our one cow, I somehow managed to topple face first into the powdery stuff, and narrowly escaped suffocation by inhaling it. Nor do I clearly recall rambling off to the back pasture, and hugging a rear leg of our sorrel horse, Tony, doubtless to express affection to the only part of him that I was then big enough to reach. As the story goes, Tony reciprocated sensibly by not kicking or moving, until poor ma again rescued me from my impulsive and cautionless ignorance. Ma was too busy to watch me every minute; so subsequently she tied my middle with a clothesline.

If I was accident-prone, this condition wasn't hard to understand; I was fuzz-headed, curious, precipitous, and dreamy; lessons in hard reality didn't stay with me very well. Thus, by the mystery of just what trait-shaping genes come down unpredictably to everybody from the ancestral pool, maybe I was already on the way toward involvement in science fiction?

I guess my people were considerably an individualistic lot anyhow—unless most families are a bit like that? Pa's father, and several of pa's father's siblings, came from Osterwieck, a tiny German town, midway between Munster and the Dutch frontier, which was only about twenty kilometers farther west. This may explain my Dutch rather than German name—pronounced "Galloon," though I readily accept "Gallon." Sometime back, there must have been a migration from Holland. The Galluns were tanners by trade. The elder of my grandfather's brothers, and one elder sister, arrived in Milwaukee, Wisconsin, early enough to have the advantage of providing leather for the Union Army in the Civil War.

My paternal grandmother—née Henrietta Bruett—was born in Holstein, also in Germany, in another little town whose name I have forgotten. She was a clergyman's daughter. But she had a mind and a will of her own. Migrating to the States very young, she married Wilhelm Rueping, who had started a small tannery in Beaver Dam. After his death she married my grandpa, Wilhelm Gallun, who thus became stepfather to five children. Kids were considered an economic asset in those days, along with an established business. And grandma evidently liked younger men; anyhow, she produced five more offspring, not counting non-survivors.

Grandpa Gallun died at age thirty-two of pneumonia, contracted while fighting a bad blaze on a wintry night, as a member of the volunteer fire department. Grandma then tried, not very successfully, to run the tannery herself. Also, she was briefly married again, then divorced. Meanwhile, though, she opened a saloon in Beaver Dam, and made a go of it. It was her sort of thing.

Her fourth husband, Walter Schlaebitz, was an immigrant carpenter who often sent verses he had written back to Germany, extolling the wonders and attractions of the United States. Grandpa Schlaebitz was fifteen years younger than grandma, and managed to outlive her from the fall of 1912 till early 1919—so he was the only grandparent I halfway got to know—a nice, quiet, sickly old gent.

As a tiny tot I had been scared of my father's mother, on the few occasions that I saw her. She was gruff and hard and semi-invalid; her legs had pretty much given out. My image of her is dim: sitting in her big, leather-backed chair, with a little white apron across her ample middle. Her house was large, old, and mysterious. There was a square piano in a room separate from the parlor. Perhaps the last time I saw her alive—a chilly autumn day—I believe I can remember a hard coal fire already glowing red, and with tiny blue flames, behind the isinglass windows of the big parlor heater stove. From earlier I recall that in the main kitchen there was a dumbwaiter, with cords and pulleys, by which food could be brought up from the *kellerküche*, the utility kitchen in the basement, where most of the cooking was done. Once pa had put me between the shelves of the dumbwaiter, and rode me up and down as in a miniature elevator.

When grandma gave an order, her tone compelled instant obedience. This particularly concerned the girl who was acting as a housemaid, a niece of Grandpa Schlaebitz.

I didn't care too much for my grandma, though she fascinated me. The only thing I really did like about her were the big, soft sugar cookies she baked, some brown and gingery, some pale, with a taste of anise.

On her final afternoon—the Dodge County Fair was in full swing in the fairgrounds about a half-mile away—I was put out in her side yard to "play" in a pile of sand, intended, I think, for repairing the walks. There I was left alone and out of the way, while a swarm of relatives older than me were congregated within the house, at her bedside. I was too uninstructed then even to have any idea of how to play in sand. All I knew was that something terrible and solemn was going on, and that in my total dummy's incompetence, I was expected to meet the unknown with no support from anybody. Of course I wound up howling in complete woe and panic....

About my maternal grandparents, what I do know of their origin was that they came from a village near Stettin, then in Germany but now in Poland. They were Julius Zinke—his family name is my middle name—and née Emmalina Huth. Grandpa Zinke had served in Bismarck's war with France, and came to the U.S. to get away from the military tradition. They brought with them their baby daughter, Matilda. The others of their numerous progeny were born in the States. Grandpa, being a broad, muscular type, switched from the tailoring he had learned in the old country, to more appropriate railroading, which was expanding all over America. First he located in Portage, Wisconsin; then in Beaver Dam.

Of course, there were frontier stories. For instance, grandpa had been away, laying track in the direction of St. Louis. Arriving home in the wee hours of the morning just after there had been a noisy Indian powwow outside of town, he decided, through misplaced prudence over how many drinks he had had, to creep into the house through a window. All that saved him from getting his head split by an axe in the hands of my grandma was that he had squeaked out, "Lena!"

My mother, Martha Emmalina, was, I think, their fifth child.

II.

ANNIE—AND OTHERS

Of the whole lot, the eighth, Anna Dorothea Zinke—Annie—was the unique one. To think of her as a maiden aunt in any sterotyped sense would have been preposterous. She was a genial individualist who went her own good-natured way, until too insistently commanded, or obstructed. Then rebellion. She would do housework sketchily when there was pressing need. But my recollections of her are of another sort. Once, while she was pitching hay up in our small barn, she spat out of the high-placed loading-door of the haymow; what landed on my young head was a generous splat of tobacco juice. Ma said that when a young man—thinking that Annie would make a fine helpmate on his farm—had proposed marriage, she had blackened his eye. In winter time—and in this I was sometimes along with her when I got big enough—Annie would be in the frozen marshes, clad in a long sheep-lined coat, red stocking cap, and flat-soled galoshes with heavy socks inside, and with a .22 rifle and a burlap sack of traps over her shoulder, catching muskrats for their pelts, or else she'd be spearfishing through a hole chopped in the lake ice. To me, Annie was a kind of distaff Paul Bunyan. Unlike my ma, she had black hair which she wrapped around her head in two braids.

Ma had another tale about her—a joke?—to wit, that Annie wasn't really one of the family, but that Grandpa Zinke, then a section foreman, had found her as a tiny papoose, along the railroad tracks, after a band of Indians had passed through.

Annie sang all kinds of Irish songs that she had picked up from the trainmen. By association and osmosis, she seemed more Irish than German. Once when I was quite small she hoboed out to Montana; she wanted to be a cowpoke. The results of that all-summer adventure remained obscure, but seem to have been not all to her liking. Yet, undaunted, she remained much the same Annie. On one occasion, out of a bag of oranges she had brought for my sister and me, she impishly pulled a pearl-handled revolver. Ma was horrified. Annie loved guns.

She didn't live with us most of the time, but in town; I never found out just where, and got over hinting. Yet she hiked out to our place nearly every day. She tended our corn patch and garden. In summers and early autumns while I was growing up, usually she had a young fighting rooster—just one at a time, since two together would have murdered each other!—boarding with our hens, and to give it range. I have memories of placing a cockrel in the center of an old bed sheet, Annie holding a pair of the sheet's corners, and I holding the other pair. Thus we'd flip the bird into the air, and let it land repeatedly back on the sheet—to improve its footwork.

Meanwhile I was learning a lot about these rather fascinating fowls. When they are about eight-weeks-old their combs and wattles are "dubbed"—snipped off with a scissors. Back in those days the stumps were then dabbed with fresh wood ashes, to medicate them and to stop the bleeding. The reason for this dubbing is two-fold: large, undubbed combs and wattles would bleed a lot in a cockfight; more importantly, taking off the heavy comb reduces the inertia of the cock's head, enabling him to dart his beak much faster, and to be generally much quicker and more agile.

Sometimes Annie brought a second bird out to our place, to act as a sparring partner for the first. For this purpose, little socketed knobs of plush—"muffs"—were tied over the natural spurs with attached strings, to keep the contestants from hurting each other too much.

But in a real cockfight—*sub rosa* in various countryside places, and I never saw one while I was living in Beaver Dam—the razor-sharp steel "hooks" were socketed over the spurs. Then truly the cock became an armed, aggressive warrior!

Of course, cockfighting was illegal in Wisconsin. Though, considering the attitude of the cocks themselves, I have sometimes wondered why the SPCA and the lawmakers insist on this. I hope I don't make myself out to be a heartless monster by saying this! Let me explain: Without qualms, most people eat chickens that, one supposes, have been humanely slaughtered, as is the natural destiny of these poor, passive creatures. But a fighting cock is something else! The gleam in his fierce alert eyes, his swaggery walk, his whole character, are focused on battle. Weighing maybe three pounds, he's always looking for something to fight. Don't turn your back on him, or he'll be slashing at your heels. Keep small children safely out of his reach....At our strange, five-acre homestead we also had a succession of Boston terriers—excitable, persistent little dogs. So, inevitably, dog and rooster would be at each other, to the point of exhausting the dog, but eventually making him wary, with his back hairs abristle, before charging the rooster, who might turn tail for a bit, before reversing abruptly and jumping over his opponent's head and slashing down with his spurs and claws, making the pooch yelp in pain and surprise.

But one of these roosters found a more formidable kind of enemy. He'd go out by the road and attack passing automobiles, flying at the spinning wheels. For this, he eventually came to a sad end. But lying broken in the ditch, he could still manage to struggle up and try to crow his defiance. The SPCA should acknowledge that the *real* cruelty to these birds is to keep them from what they most want—to fight.

As a kid, Annie had been a trial and a cutup at school, particularly to another legendary character in Beaver Dam, Miss Mary Ann Spellman, a tough Irish teacher who taught most of my aunts and uncles, my parents, my sister and myself, and numerous cousins. On her retirement, a grass-roots movement started, so for two terms she was elected mayor. Most of the aldermen were former pupils of hers, so, in a nostalgic way, it was school all over again.

Annie had escaped early from the rather straightlaced control of her parents—my grandparents—though I guess they learned to tolerate her as she was, well before they both died, not far apart in time, within a year ahead of my birth.

Generally, Annie didn't care for a regular job. But in addition to gardening, she papered and painted rooms for hire. And she was the town gadabout, dispensing local news and gossip, going from one friendly house to the next. She told fortunes by palmistry and cards. And every once in a while she got boisterously drunk on home-brewed wild grape, elderberry or dandelion wine, or on hard apple cider. And she arranged charitable aid for poor families. One of my early recollections is of a little kid yelling shrilly at her, when I was riding with her in town in our one-horse trap: "Hey—Annie Zinke! That bed you got for us was all fulla bedbugs!"

What money she acquired that she didn't spend on small gifts for my sister and me, and otherwise being similarly disposed of elsewhere in other families, she mailed away to acquire dubious gold-mine stock. She was that sort of nebulous, romantic dreamer, needing a someday-vision. She was a flawed, often exasperating, yet lovable individualist....She's long gone now; I'm not sure quite how, and I've never felt free to ask—or even to want to know—specifics. Somehow, though vastly different in many ways, we had a likeness in the vibes to which we responded. She is perhaps my most fondly remembered family member...and, in some subliminal way, she helped shape me, whether toward an interest in science fiction or not.

I'll forego writing down any more anecdotes about her. Yet she led me to some that involved other persons, which may be worth recounting.

Often riding into town behind old Tony the horse when I was about five-years-old, she dropped me off several times at the grain elevator across from what we called the "Old Depot," while she drove on somewhere else. In charge at the elevator was an old Irishman—I'll call him Pat, which was his real name. His buddy Mike—again, truly named—was a flagman at the railroad crossing, and was often present in the grain-dusty, cubbyhole of an office. My impromptu babysitters were an incongruous pair. Mike was a small, prim, no-nonsense sort. One arm was off just below the crook of his elbow, on which he could still hang his signalman's lantern. Pat was big and jolly, and he liked to sing. One of his favorite songs was a ballad called "When Pat Malone Forgot That He Was Dead." Incidentally, Annie had learned it from him, and soon I learned it complete from Annie. Get me a little high some time, and feeling good in happy company, and I can still be persuaded to give forth with my own rendition!

In his dinner pail, Pat usually had baloney-on-rye sandwiches, and he'd give me part of one, which I'd nibble with diffident dignity and appreciation.

One day Pat showed me a tack hammer, the magnetic-headed kind to which a tack would stick for easy pounding. Then he pulled up his overall leg to display his artifical underpinning, rather well and naturalistically designed, articulated, and made, even in those primitive olden days.

I was in wonder of the device.

16

"Go ahead, Raymie," Pat urged. "Hammer in a tack or two! They'll help hold up my sock!"

In awe at a marvel and a privilege, I complied happily.

Both of these old gents were Civil War vets. Yes, I'd heard vaguely of Abraham Lincoln, and even of Lee and Grant. But they seemed as remote in time as Moses—though I am aware now that they were scarcely fifty years away!...Fifty years?...To me, then, that was already not much less than eternity. But now, groping back across more than seventy years toward those two old codgers who have long since vanished into the mists, I find myself straining to hear their voices, and to recapture the smell of grain, horses, and wood smoke, and the feel and mood of that particular rural summer day.

* * * * * * *

Besides Annie, one other of my ma's siblings also stood out for me. He was Julius Zinke, Jr. The name, by the way, has two syllables; to point this out, it was sometimes spelled Zinkey.

When I first met Uncle Julius, the best I could do at addressing him was to call him Unca Doody. He was a Navy pharmacist, who had been around the world with Admiral Dewey and the fleet, after the Spanish-American War. He appeared only briefly on occasional furloughs; this was an occasion for great excitement in our household. But he kept me at a reserved distance; he was my mother's youngest brother, number nine of a family of ten, and I guess he didn't care much for pesky small fry.

But even when he was away he remained a legend. Hanging in our cramped kitchen was a photograph of the USS *Virginia*, the battleship on which he had served, and stowed away upstairs was the small, wicker-covered trunk, full of surplus belongings, that he had left with us: photographs of strange places, dried snakeskins, Navy pennants, portions of uniforms, exotic shells, a tin box for Murad cigarettes containing foreign coins, a Filipino bolo....

Ma said that Uncle Julius had been everywhere with the Navy. For a while this assertion got mixed up in my head with her explanation of what the stars at night were: "places where other people live." So, my notions of geography and cosmology being rather hazy and illogical then, I naturally assumed that Unca Doody had sailed to the stars with the Navy, too! Without even realizing it, I had found for myself my first thought of an interstellar fleet.

III.

AN ECCENTRIC HOUSEHOLD

In laying the groundwork for this write-up, I have so far skipped around considerably as regards chronological sequencing. However, I have intentionally delayed mention of an important event which happened before my earliest memories. I have done this because I was at first unaware of it, and then, for a considerable time, it meant little to me.

You see, soon after my birth, my father, Adolph Gallun, had moved us from a house near the center of Beaver Dam to a place at its northern edge, which, with the financial help of a cousin of his, he had purchased for a low price. Doing this was part of his occupational ramble. He had been a bartender, store-clerk, laborer, and insurance salesman. Now he intended to raise chickens, and this five-acre spread was ready-made for that purpose, including a large sign: The Highland Poultry Farm.

Its creator had been an evidently rather eccentric and reclusive science teacher and inventor, from another region. He must have had an overburdening of novel ideas, but couldn't quite find The One. In his way he was surely a very bright man, even though he wound up a suicide.

There was a long, tree-lined driveway, flanked by a large garden. The chicken coops were to the rear of the high-peaked house and small, white barn, which was connected by a passageway. In Wisconsin this was indeed an unusual architectural feature that, in a Midwestern, small-town conformist society of those days, tended to cause eyebrows to elevate. In my mature years, though, I have since seen older constructions of the same kind in the state of Maine; and it was from there that the builder seems to have come—this indicated also by addresses written in some of the books he had left in the attic.

Separately, my folks were both good, well-intentioned people. Yet together they were a mismatch; their personalities differed; they couldn't communicate with each other, or cooperate, very well. So there was mutual, and somewhat destructive, confusion.

Our new home had novelty characteristics that seemed to have grabbed pa's enthusiasm for up-and-coming things in the young twentieth century. Yet his perceptions weren't very deep. In the barn, in what we called the Engine Room, a two-and-a-half-horsepower gasoline engine was mounted, and was belted to an overhead shaft that had extra belt pulleys that might run various appliances—washing machines, corn shellers, etc. A geared-down power shaft ran along the passageway to where it could turn a rotary pump for "soft," cistern rainwater,

18

and a standard, upright pump for well-water. The latter pump was fitted with a system of torsion springs intended to equalize the upward and downward strokes of the well-rod, and thus reduce uneven strain on the engine. The tanks for the hard and soft water were mounted on top of each other in the big attic of the house, to establish gravity pressure.

So of course pa had been intrigued: it was a complete, forward-looking water system! Yeh—maybe—except that in Wisconsin winters, in which temperatures of twenty degrees, Fahrenheit, below zero were common, it inevitably froze up! The bathroom became largely non-functional, and, in the worst of weather, the standard outdoor, rural plumbing—fortunately, also provided—came back into its own.

Ma had undergone an operation in a hospital in Milwaukee while the purchase and move were made. Possibly, pa wanted to give her a pleasant surprise.

Anyhow, at first sight of the place, she seems to have taken instant exception to pa's delight with it. Her initial reaction must have been bitter indeed. Yet, with time, this mellowed down to multiple complaints, not constant, but recurrent and frequent:

"This crazy house!...All the rooms too small! And hooked together in such a peculiar way that you hardly know which one is supposed to be what.... Kitchen sink set in the darkest corner, where you can hardly see to peel potatoes! Hot water tank stuck behind the heater stove in the parlor, and blocking the way so that you almost have to squeeze past to get into the bathroom—and what's *that* doing *here*, anyhow?...The upstairs not even finished—just bare rafters! And does your pa finish it? No!...Barn joined to the house! Who ever heard of such a thing! What if there's a fire?...That loony inventor who built this place! When we first came there were batteries and burglar alarms even on the hen coops!...And some kind of magic lantern screen was hung up in what we used as the dining room!...Anyhow, what do we want stranded way out in the country, away from everybody? Five acres isn't enough for a real farm!...I'm ashamed of this nutty house! It's not a farm, and it's not a town! It belongs to nothing! It's odd! It makes us odd!..."

Poor ma. She was high-strung, industrious, conscientious, the best. She wanted herself and her family "to be somebody." She liked poetry, and sometimes she wrote verse. She often sang cheerfully as she worked—songs in English and German. A favorite of hers was that one that reaches its climax in the line, "The chisel, the pen, and the palette shall be held in those little brown hands...." Aimed, hopefully at her kids, of course. And she wanted to be *with* people. Only, I think she was a little afraid of them. She didn't want to be "different." Yet, without realizing it, I guess she was.

It isn't hard to see that contact between my parents wasn't particularly smooth. Pa was a mild man, though his judgment wasn't always sound, and at a certain point he was excitable. The exact time of day didn't mean too much to him, while ma kept our clocks set fifteen minutes ahead of the correct hour—by the six o'clock morning whistles of the factories in town—for fear that somebody might be late for something. Getting pa out of bed to go to a job was her daily trial. Predictably, the chicken farm fizzled as pa's mainstay employment, so again he was taking whatever jobs he could get: moulder in a foundry, salesman, store clerk. Meanwhile, though, being locked in by a firm choice—and by inertia—we continued to live where we were. Often, we were broke.

Yet, in my remembered time, my folks had gotten over most of their fighting; they just went their separate, rather dutiful ways. Evenings, pa would wander back into Beaver Dam to be with his friends.

During my early, small-fry years, ma's complaints about our house, and the lonesome isolation from the mainstream of the local population that it imposed on us—except for my gregarious, beer-drinking dad—passed largely over my head. Ma tried to be responsive to my numerous questions about the broader, physical world; also I learned to get along well by myself—except for my penchant for blundering into bad situations. On a social level, I was still simple and insensitive, and didn't feel particularly excluded from contact with anybody.

I remember that very early the blazing ball of the sun drew my attention. What *was* it? I don't recall ma's unclear answers to my pesky queries about it; but I *do* remember one declaration that I made—related to some playtime spent with an older, half-Irish cousin of mine, who was on a butterfly-catching kick with a long-handled net: "Ma, next time Kathleen comes out I'm gonna make her give me her net! Then I'm gonna reach up and haul down the sun and see what it is!"

Yes—indeed an ambitious, *super* science fictional enterprise!

Of like kind, though of a mundane insignificance which allowed me to be actively destructive, was an episode involving a Christmas-gift drum from an aunt and uncle. In the presence of these guests, I tore open the wrapping paper and was somewhat disappointed. I was then told that if I tapped the drum with the sticks, it would make music. I tried, but this didn't work to my satisfaction. So I figured that whatever musical mechanism must be inside the thing was malfunctioning. Further, I wanted to find out what it looked like. So, when adult attention drifted quickly away from my small and abrasive presence, I scampered to the kitchen, procured a knife, and used it to rip open a pasteboard head of the drum. Well—what a swindle! There was nothing at all within! I howled out my further disappointment. But I howled louder when ma, horrified and embarrassed almost to tears at my unconcealable mistreatment of a gift in such proximity to the givers, cuffed me soundly. I suppose that that drum was one of the most promptly destroyed Christmas presents ever heard of.

I don't think that I was entirely so impossible a brat, though. It couldn't have been very long after that that ma had me standing on a chair, helping her wash dishes. She believed in enforcing the work ethic, and in this I was pliable and proud. I recall that ma and I laughed a lot together. So I seem to have been often of a cheerful disposition.

One thing I especially have to point out about that house: up in its big attic were shelves and boxes of books that had belonged to its builder. Nobody ever came to get them, even after we moved in. I found my way to them early, though I don't think that any of them were intended for children. There were two sets of encyclopedias. And books on astronomy, geology, paleontology, biology, physics, chemistry, mathematics, history....Most of these were college-level textbooks. There were also books on mechanics and carpentry, and illustrated pamphlets of birdlife. And books about archeology—more specifically Egyptology....If I couldn't yet read, I could at least look at the pictures.

One of the first books I lugged downstairs for closer attention was one by the famous Egyptologist, Sir William Flinders Petrie. Somehow—I don't know quite why—my attention became focused on one strange, flat-styled picture in it, of a shaven-headed man standing in a voluminous robe, and with a triangular device leaned against his shoulder, while his long fingers touched parts of the object.

"Ma—What's this?" I demanded. "What's the guy doing?"

She read me the explanation under the picture. That the man was an Egyptian harpist, Eighteenth Dynasty, circa 1450 B.C.

My questions multiplied. I knew nothing of harpists or harps. Ma tried to give explanations....To this day I don't entirely understand the processes of fascination. Just what is it about any subject that grabs at a person, and holds on? What common force is there that draws different people toward, say, collecting stamps, climbing mountains, or laboriously gluing together towers of matchsticks? To some, a particular pursuit can be an excitement, to others a total bore. Explanations, of course, are easy, and valid: a thing of individual spirit—how a certain topic impinges on how an individual person is made, thinks, dreams, and feels. Beyond that answer, though, are more elusive conundrums....

Anyhow, way back then, I think I tried to grab at all that time. Ma got across to me some of the idea that "more than three thousand years" was an awfully, awfully long while behind us. Still, in that different, once-upon-a-time region, it seemed that I could almost hear that ancient harp twanging away, the tune it played just beyond the range of my ears. I felt pleasant, chilly, scary tingles.

A real harp of any sort would have been an impossible luxury in our household. It was years before I actually saw one. Yet had there been a harp around in my early youth, I might have become a fairly competent harpist. Till now the ripply, elfin quality of harp music takes hold of me. We did have an old piano in our parlor, or front room, given to ma by her elder brother, August, when he moved to Kansas City, Missouri. Under ma's instruction, I pingled at it sometimes, but it wasn't the same thing at all....However, something did stay with me from looking at that picture of that ancient musician: I have been an Egyptology buff ever since.

* * * * * * *

My recollections of my earliest years are a scattered jumble, often vivid, but not always clear as to chronological sequence: Fourths of July, in which, not too closely supervised, I was allowed to light firecrackers. For one Christmas, pa bought me an alcohol-fired toy steam engine by mail order from Montgomery Ward in Chicago; if I remember correctly, it cost ninety-eight cents, plus shipping charges. I loved it, but I think he played with it more than I did at first; and it kept him at home evenings for awhile....In the early autumns there were the Dodge

21

County fairs, at which, with pa or ma or sis or Annie, I had my first merry-go-round and Ferris wheel rides. There I also watched balloon ascensions. These took a couple of hours of preparation in the late afternoon. The balloon was suspended limply over a furnace consisting of a large sewer pipe section imbedded vertically in the ground, with a firepit underneath. The pipe was crammed with kindling wood, liberally doused with a mixture of gasoline and kerosene, which was then ignited. Through the canvas fabric, you could see the flames shooting up inside as it gradually filled with hot air and smoke, swelling to a firm, tall, pear-shape that not only pushed at the overhead cross rope that supported it between two upright poles, but also strained at its other tethers.

Of course I didn't yet understand the Archimedean principle of the balloon—the hot, expanded gases inside this one being lighter than ordinary air, and hence buoyant. Still, all that was happening was mightily marvelous to me. At last the restraining ropes would be cast off, and the balloonist would go aloft, usually head downward with his boot-toes hooked inside a large ring attached to the shrouds of a parachute, which wasn't packaged like the chutes of fliers of a later date, but hung, full-length, down from the balloon. On his way into the sky the balloon man would perform fearsome acrobatic tricks on the ring. When he was no more than a black speck against the firmament, he would start drifting down on his parachute. Presently the balloon, shrunken to tiny size, and left deserted up there, would tip over, spilling black smoke from its open bottom end, and crumple into a fall.

There soon came a fair when an open-structured, pusher-type biplane was added as an additional featured attraction. Ma, sis (Charlotte), and I saw it for the first time from our own porch. It was way up over Beaver Dam, and very tiny; often I couldn't be sure in what direction it was moving as it performed stunts. Loop-the-loops and wing-overs, sis said they were. She was getting to be a nut about airplanes—and fliers. She already knew the name of the pilot of this plane. So, pretty soon she gave the same name to a pert and saucy young pullet hen whose neck feathers were flecked with tawny gold: Jimmy Ward.

In the fall I had many buckets of potatoes to pick up for storage in the cellar, as soon as they were dug. Likewise carrots and beets. And apples from our few trees.

And in the buggy, behind old Tony, there'd be a final visit of the season out to Oakwood Cemetery. Ma always paid special attention to a small grave with a modest headstone, on the top of which there was a tiny, crouching lamb. Ma was bitter when she saw that somebody had knocked the stone ears off the lamb. That grave belonged to my brother, Arnold, who had died of a combination of children's diseases, topped off by peritonitis, a year before I was born. He had been eighteen-months old. Maybe I was his replacement.

* * * * * * *

Somewhere along the line there came a summer day when I did something truly abominable. It involved another kid, too, but maybe I provided the inspiration. I had been brought into town to somebody's house. Fooling around, the other kid and I got to chewing lawn grass. Then we spat the green juice on all those nice clean bedsheets flapping on the clotheslines.

That was the one time that ma truly whopped me good!...

I think that that incident influenced ma's decision about her simultaneously precocious and retarded youngest—me. I was husky, and pretty good-sized. So one damp, quiet morning in early September, she walked the mile-and-a-half with me, and managed to enroll me in kindergarten of the Third Ward (Lincoln) School in Beaver Dam. For months she had been refusing to talk German to me anymore; I had to improve my English. I was then four-years-old. I guess ma was glad for the prospect of getting rid of me for a few hours a day. Thereafter, for a while, I trotted alongside my sister, every weekday morning.

For the first couple of years, I got along all right in school. But when I was in second grade, ma was in the local hospital with pneumonia for a month. The United States had entered World War I. Pa was working long hours as a moulder in the foundry; even Annie had a job there as a core maker. Sis, now in high school, usually went in the late afternoon to see how ma was, and didn't hurry home. Arrangements about me were slap-dash and vague. Today I guess I'd be called a neglected kid. I didn't eat very well, and was inattentive about warm clothes. It was chilly autumn. After school I'd trot that mile-and-a-half. Even when there was a visible sunset, the red rays would glint lonesomely on the windows of our peculiar house, looking small and lonely across the fields. When I got to it, the chances were that I wasn't strong enough to turn the key—by traditional custom stashed under the stoop—in the cold-stiff lock. So I'd go into the warmer chicken coop and talk to the hens.

Meanwhile, at school, I got beaten up as an oddball. Further, in one of my solitary late afternoon rambles into the woods, I fell out of a tree, and hurt my back. Besides that, I slipped while running in loose gravel along the road, and skinned my knee, and it got infected. Misplaced prudence—being so dumb as to hurt myself—made me keep mum about my injuries.

So when ma got home from the hospital, I was already a bit sick and feverish....

IV.

A NEW BEGINNING

There seems to be a similarity in the histories of many writers: often an early homelife quite different from the average, perhaps including a difficult, yet someway culturally aware, lack of affluence. Often, too, a period of serious illness, restlessness, alienation. A fierce urge to get away, to get past obstacles and maladjustments.

I don't think there is any star-marked mystery here, since all these factors challenge and help develop and direct imaginative and romantic young minds by inhibiting and restraining them toward working at their endowments in a special way, without letting either the person or his aptitudes get lured too easily and too soon by more regular, more attractive—and maybe more sensible!—paths of least resistance.

I can make no analysis of the incomprehensibly intricate process by which a particular set of genes—with good and bad effects—is handed down from ancestors to everybody, including myself. Otherwise though, my own case is as suggested above—with the inevitable difference of detail.

Now I had the spell of illness indicated in the formula.

Within a couple of weeks after ma's return, I was much sicker. My left, lower belly was bulging, and it ached. Dr. Krahn drove out to our place twice in one day. By kerosene lamplight that evening at my downstairs bedside he spoke to my ma, and in my presence. Maybe I wasn't supposed to understand any of what he said, or he thought that I was grown enough to accept whatever I could make of it. Anyhow, I was keyed up; it was one of those tense occasions when, in spite of fever, attention is keen, and memory is firmly impressed:

"If Raymie has what it must be, we don't have much time. The walls of the thing might be thin, and if they are stretched further and break, that means another case of peritonitis in your family. Not good...."

So the next morning Dr. Krahn drove out in his Model-T Ford coupe, and rode me, bundled in ma's arms, to the big, refitted house that served Beaver Dam as a hospital. Luckily, no blizzard obstructed the surgeon from coming down from Fond-du-Lac. His spectacles gleaming, he poked lightly at the bulge in my belly.

"All we can do is try a drainage," he remarked laconically.

Again I had that concentrated, memory-engraved attention. It was very hot in the operating room. The table felt as if I were lying on a padded ironing board. On a side table, mysterious, ominous surgical instruments gleamed in trays of steaming hot water. Above and around me were grave adult faces. Three elderly doctors; all younger physicians had been drafted into the armed forces. But then,

24

somehow, I had come to trust old people more than the young. And there were nurses, and ma and pa, and a couple of aunts besides Annie. Back then—a thing unthinkable today—such intrusion into an operating room was still permitted.

Then I was looking up into the gauze ether cone, and could see nothing else except the moistening drip of the liquid ether—the common anesthetic of then—into its fabric. And I smelled that sweetish, sickish stench; it's a thing you don't ever forget. I groped at the bulge in my belly, wondering just where the surgeon would cut...or maybe he'd just stab, the way I'd heard that boils were sometimes lanced. Ma had told me that what I had was like a big boil. Being urged to breathe deeply, I kept checking for signs of "going to sleep," which it began to seem would never happen. So far as I know, those signs never came....Oblivion sneaked up on me.

As has occurred to me not long ago, I am the only one left alive of all those people who were gathered in that hot room that afternoon. Of course, I was much the youngest; but nobody there would have bet much on my chances then.

Our hospital didn't even have an x-ray machine. So I was opened up in front to do "an exploratory"—to find out what-was-what. Then I was turned over and cut open again. According to the talk I heard later on, two quarts of pus were drawn from a large perinephric abscess around my left kidney. Where the pus came from remains somewhat of a question. "Maybe from a spinal injury," Dr. Krahn once speculated later on. There never has been a clear answer.

As an anesthetic, ether had a bad side effect; you came out of it in a terrible agony of thirst. And you were allowed only an ounce per hour of drinking water, because more might cause vomiting, which would strain your disturbed insides and the surgical sutures. Having been told that I would remain out cold for a while, ma and pa had gone forth for a bit of supper. But I woke up sooner than expected. The nurse left to watch me let me suck on a piece of wet gauze.

Not long after I was again conscious, church bells began to ring and factory whistles to blow. Talk about timing for a new beginning! It was January 1, 1918.

* * * * * * *

Back then, there were no wonder drugs—antibiotics. Nor were there any of the precise, modern diagnostic and therapeutic procedures. Physicians worked much more by insight and what might even be called intuition. And who had ever heard of vitamins? The closest anybody came to them was in cod liver oil. But there were tonics which gave you an appetite for some pretty good food—hence fairly well-balanced nutrition. Also, there was a sufficiency of what we now call TLC—Tender Loving Care. It didn't need a label then; it was just something that was expected and present. It made up for a lot of the relative primitiveness of medical know-how.

I was in that little hospital for twenty-seven days, sheltered from a memorably snowy, windy, frigid Wisconsin winter. I behaved rather well, except that when I began to feel good again—for a couple of very early mornings, way before the nurse came around to wash me up and it was still black of night outside—I would start to sing at the top of my lungs, waking everybody up. Of course I had to be straightened out about that, though some kindly folks said they didn't mind.

When I was finally taken home, the "Round Oak" heater stove in our front room was stoked up good to shed plenty of warmth. Though the incision in my back was still draining a little, I was feeling fine. The only problem was that when I tried to stand up it was as if needles were stabbing into the soles of my feet. That was another shortcoming of medical custom of that era: on the theory that to recover you needed complete rest, they kept you in bed. So, from inactivity, your bones lost calcium and you forgot how to walk, and had to learn how all over again. Nowadays, they get a patient up on his feet again as soon as possible.

My convalescence was rapid enough so that ma sent me back to school by the end of March. She wanted me to pass, in spite of my long absence. One thing she impressed on me was that I had had a very narrow squeak, and had better appreciate, and make good use of, the boon of my continued existence. I tended to agree. So my illness had left its beneficial mark, though, in the end, physically I wasn't much the worse for wear, either. Still, I had to take things slow for a while.

Raymond Z. Gallun (1928 High School Graduation)

V.

BOOKS—AND MORE BOOKS

So I got more into books—not just those from our attic, but from the public library as well. There was self-identification with heroes, explorers, fliers of aircraft, searchers for treasure, builders and users of submarines....Yeh—Tom Swift....And the thought: What to make of myself? Ma pushed me some—that's for sure. But what she said was pragmatic: "learn a good trade or profession." That sounded sort of dull to me. Meanwhile, she enforced her work ethic: chickens and pigs to tend, garden weeds to pull out, strawberries and raspberries to pick in season, and bugs to knock off the potato plants with a piece of roofing shingle, into an old bucket with kerosene at its bottom. Not totally uninteresting activities, but hardly inspired.

Another thing about ma: she was a sucker for itinerant book salesmen, especially if they offered heavily illustrated, educational books for young people A lot of the money she got from selling our berries went into the purchase of such volumes. And they were my meat.

Further, ma's disgruntlement about the oddities of our house, and its isolation, began to rub off on me, as my sensitivities increased. Likely, I would have become ashamed of it on my own, without any help from her. And I was becoming a little ashamed of myself. Whether from within or from without—or both—I felt myself getting more and more different. Or so it seemed to me.

I suppose that all people have an instinct for compensation; what you think you lack in one direction, you try to make up for in another. If I couldn't catch a baseball worth a darn—and, deep down, wasn't particularly interested in learning how—I was gripped by the vivid and fascinating imageries that came out of books, including the rather esoteric ones that an otherwise never-known builder had left in the house in which I was forced to live.

I began to hate that house; it seemed to exclude and push me further away from the nebulous things I half wanted, always deepening my separation. Yet it was a hate-love relationship because, when there was time, that house was a wonderful place to curl up alone with a book and my romantic imaginings. All around was the ageless sky and the countryside, and the death and rebirth of the changing seasons, to give the contents of the books real substance....Yes, there were star charts, too, in those books from the attic.

For quite awhile my vision, normal at first, had been going myopic. So, rather belatedly, when I was in fifth grade, I became "four-eyes." But I took this minor insult from my classmates with good nature. My gain far outweighed any loss; with glasses I could read what was written on the blackboard again, and all the more distant scenes around me cleared up to pristine perfection!

For quite awhile too I had been rugged enough to warn any wise guys off my back.

Also, when I was in the fifth grade, our teacher, Miss MacLean, had a nice custom of reading to our class for half-an-hour right after lunch. One novel she read to us was *Tarzan of the Apes*. So she found Tarzan for me. When I mentioned him at home, my sister said that Edgar Rice Burroughs had written books about Mars, too; she had read one of them from the library. We hadn't had a cow since I was little, but an ex-racehorse had replaced Tony. Sis loved horses, and I suppose it was John Carter's thoats that had grabbed her attention—since thoats were a particularly bizarre and fierce kind of steed.

So I read *A Princess of Mars* myself, and being already very susceptible, I was hooked. Almost without any thought, or even awareness, another problem was solved for me: what to try to become? What job, what profession? Astronomer? Geologist?...Once I had even wished to become a harpist. All these glamorous goals had seemed remote and hard to get at—at least right now....Besides, in succession, and bunched together, there had been so many that I had imagined applying myself to. It wasn't practical to have them all!...Except maybe in one way—each for a while—inside my skull. Write! That way I could be anybody I wanted to be, for as long as I liked....Then somebody else....Nothing lost....Not tied down to any one line. And be always a hero, of course....You could shape destinies....

I can say now that Edgar Rice Burroughs was surely a man for his time. I don't think that there was a science fiction writer of my generation who wasn't influenced by his yarns. Even the flaws and crudities in his novels helped young heads toward thinking critically and constructively while they developed their own skills.

For instance, consider John Carter mating with Dejah Thoris, a Martian princess who laid eggs as a bird does, to successfully produce a son, Carthoris. What strange biological improbability was this?...So, a defect, among others, marring the wondrous background of an exciting and fascinating yarn with something hard to accept as real. Couldn't I do better?

Anyhow, I got started writing very soon, putting myself on a schedule—one hour every evening. No, I wouldn't be a science-fictional spaceman right away; instead I'd be what gripped me more just then: an Egyptologist, looking for treasure, of course, led on by a kind of desert mirage—the image of an ancient ship.

The Phantom Dahabeyeh was never finished, though I scribbled on and on, doggedly and with increasing disgruntlement, through several massive notebooks and about three years. I strung together all the vivid adjectives and adverbs I could find, trying to say how marvelous and exciting it all was, till most of the action was hopelessly bogged down in over-long, over-pressurized descriptions.

It was during this interval that I tried building that hut in the marsh. I guess it was supposed to embody all the book-lore I had gathered and added to imaginatively, about Egypt and Mesopotamia and Stone Age stuff to which I wanted to give some solidity beyond just make-believe. I planned to beam the roof with willow branches, to which I would fasten marsh grass thatch. And there would be a place for fire—a kind of altar?...

Well, the effort never got farther than the rectangular base of gathered stones, and the first three tiers of grassy bog-lumps for the walls. I suppose what stopped me was not so much ma's complaints about how grubby I got, but more the pathetic triviality and lopsidedness of the thing, in contrast with my imaginative concept. It—and I—had failed .

That summer at least, I expect I looked like the shyest, messiest, most untaught kind of rural kid—a sort of towheaded woods elf who, on being sighted, might scamper away into a thicket. To a degree, this was all true. But there was an incongruity and contrast which now adds to my belief that the most intense drama isn't easily visible, since it happens inside people. No matter my external aspect; I was well into smatterings of the major sciences, and my particular interest just then was in learning to read and write Egyptian hieroglyphics, and I had made some progress; in our attic I had long ago found E. A. Wallace Budge's grammar book.

And, no, I didn't set fire to the marsh the next time it burned—as some people suspected. Over the years, its autumn-dry grasses flamed up quite often. Maybe careless hunters lit it, or other kids, or, as easily, the cause could have been spontaneous combustion in the underlying layers of peat.

My sister, Charlotte, went away to a small college farther north. Pa had a job in the battery factory, and was able to help her out with money.

Meanwhile I got deeper into that particular and peculiar pang of early adolescence: being left out of things, not belonging among my peers, far behind them in social growth, it seemed to me, with no idea of how to get "in" with the crowd, or catch up.

Still, I couldn't say that I was at all unhappy—except now and then. I enjoyed what I did; there was a richness to it. I kept to my own course, in part because I didn't know what else to do. I hadn't learned how to play, in the regular sense, but I didn't lack for exercise. Work; first around our place; then over to the neighbor's farm. Every time I mowed his lawn—bigger even than ours—I got a dollar. And I shocked grain for him at harvest time, and helped him whenever I could, otherwise. I hung around with him, as if he was my second father; his wife and he had no children of their own, and I've said that I was drawn to older people.

True, I was somewhat split inside. Part of this was that I was defiantly and secretively proud of being different in my ways and interests. And I liked to wander alone.

Just now I recall a winter afternoon, very cold and bright. I had climbed over the ice hummocks at the shore and had walked a long ways on the frozen lake. I came to a little forested island, so densely overgrown—doubtless because no people or large animals ever intruded there to break any paths—that it was literally impossible to set foot on it through the barrier of interlocked twigs. Annie had told me about that island, and walking around its edges now, I mused about it with cold, pleasant, soaring thrills. It was a small, closed, barricaded world, all to itself! And my musings rambled on, linking it with the friendly neighbor's casual collection of Indian arrowheads, and the stone axe head—relics he had plowed up in his fields over the years. Even centuries and millennia back, had no Indian warrior intruded on that island either?...Somehow the question had a haunting elusive beauty to it!

But what truly made me remember that afternoon was that a big, white snow owl flew soundlessly out of that thicketed, ice-locked, almost arctic island, and went skimming low over the frozen lake....

****

When I got into high school my adolescent sensitivity had tightened up further. Had certain members of my class, whom I considered better-favored, somehow come into my house, I am sure I would have paled and quivered with emotional shock and denial, though I could accept certain others readily enough. There was, for instance, a ham radio operator, very skillful at putting complicated devices together, who was my good friend.

Otherwise I remained pretty much a loner. And a grind. Sure—I shone in science and English classes, and even somewhat in Latin, the only other language offered, but I stayed away from social functions, feeling unable to cope. As for athletics, I did take a crack at the wrestling team; I had the muscles, but I wasn't very apt. Summers I worked in the local pea cannery—a fifteen-and-upwards-hours-per-day deal for everybody there, at the height of the pea pack. Once I worked for twenty-seven hours at a stretch, packing cans still hot from the cookers into boxes—thirty-five cents an hour, time-and-a-half for overtime. Not bad for then.

The last couple of years at Beaver Dam High School, I subbed for pa, Wednesday and Saturday evenings, as sweep-up man and fire tender, because pa could do better on those nights clerking at the J. C. Penney store. At the battery factory my standing-in for pa this way was somewhat outside of the rules, but it was tacitly allowed by the night electrician, and by the plant manager, too, when he saw that I was conscientious and interested, and knew what I was doing. I didn't have a separate timecard; I just punched-in for pa, who would show up just after midnight.

It was a spooky, "science fictiony" place to work, with almost nobody else around. There was that pervasive pungence of acid, and the eerie sixty-cycle-hum of the rotary converters, from beyond the rows and rows of vats where the newly lead-pasted battery plates were being "burned in" by the passage of DC current through them in their acid bath. You could hear the sleepy roar of the oil fires heating the plate dryer room and keeping metallic lead for casting the plate frames molten in the big crucibles. Those furnaces were a worry; the fuel oil, imperfectly strained, often contained sediment; and the burner nozzles would become partly clogged, causing malfunctions. Burning oil could flow out onto the floor.

Yes, several years after my time there, the factory finally did burn down. A fully loaded fuel tank, mounted high on the wall, broke its wooden support bracket, and came crashing and splashing down on a hot crucible. And— whoosh!—tall flames and black smoke were through the roof in a couple of minutes.

VI.

BEGINNING LINES

Looking back, it seems to me that every circumstance had ganged up to shove me toward writing science fiction. Early, I discovered Farnsworth Wright's magazine, *Weird Tales*, and therein, of course, "World Saver" Edmond Hamilton's yarns, which I loved! However, my own attempts to write such stories weren't doing too well. And from my abortive struggle with *The Phantom Dahabeyeh*, I retained a fixation on the Middle East, and the Orient in general. I even had a phase wherein I perfumed our front room by burning Vantine's Temple Incense. Somehow all this, since my attitudes were rather lyrical, *did* lead me into a brief go at verse. So here are the beginning lines of something called "Caravans":

> *Ebony black 'gainst the morning gold—*
> *A picture that long has been mystic and old:*
> *Caravans...*
> *Arab bands...*
> *Loaded with stuffs from the Sunrise Lands!*
> *You can hear their song*
> *As they jumble along*
> *Over the sands...*
> *The camels sway*
> *And their shadows play*
> *Like stilted genii far away*
> *O'er dune and rill...*
> *And each rock and hill*
> *Glares with the heat of the new-born day....*

Most of the rest I have forgotten. Anyhow, my English teacher, Miss Minneftawa Lampert, sent the poem to *Magazine World*, a magazine for high-school students published by the Atlantic Monthly Company. If not for other reasons as well, I suspect that my poem was considerably too long for them to print.

But I wrote others. Maybe the editors appreciated my dogged efforts, or sensing despair, even feared the worst about me. In any case, sometime in 1928, they *did* publish the following:

Defeat

He rears above me, leaden, chill—
A great gray Titan swathed in gloom,
And all around, the world is still
As some, long buried, dusty tomb.

I see his face; his awful eyes—
They bore within my inmost soul.
My last faint dream of Future dies,
Stamped out by this inhuman ghoul.

Printed out for anybody to see, these lines struck me all wrong. It was as if the most secret part of my innards had been exposed. And I started to try to live those verses down. But some perhaps well-meaning girl of the class that would graduate after mine, took it upon herself to memorize them, stop me in the hall, and recite them to my face. Possibly this was a gesture of admiration; but, considering how I felt, I took it as an attempt to get my goat—which it did! Of course these verses have long since become a joke to me of my strained adolescence. But it was different back then.

I reddened to my gills, muttered some virulent expletives, and stalked away. In those days, though I was usually cheerful enough, I did some rather lurid cursing on occasion—a defense against being addressed as "Hey, Prof!" and some other conditions, including how damnably cherubic and young-for-my-age I looked.

I also received a bronze medal for some verse that was put into an anthology of writings by Wisconsin kids, sponsored by the *Milwaukee Journal*, and sent to our then-first lady, Mrs. Calvin Coolidge. But that was the end of my spasm of versification.

Not long thereafter, I overheard one of the teachers remark that she thought I was developing dementia praecox—an older term for schizophrenia. And I was scared she was right! This inadvertent prompting didn't help; it only brought on a black mood in which I felt bitterly sorry for myself—a thing which I have seldom done—and how miserably life and the world had treated and *warped* me! For a short while I brooded over every painful recollection—the bad qualities of *that house*, and how fuzz-headed and prone to get into mishaps that I used to be, and one incident which I have previously failed to mention, where I was hit by a car on the road while I was daydreaming, smashing one of its headlamps with my head, and scaring everybody by being brought home bloody and unconscious.

Further, I recalled how unfairly I had been imposed upon. Somehow, my attention settled on the last horse we had had, till it dropped dead a couple of years before; a racing mare named Polly, retired from the track because she had developed "heaves," a form of equine asthma. Sometimes I had thought that that flighty beast was my friend! It was my duty to feed her, bed her down, and shovel out her stall. But hitch her to a potato patch cultivator and she'd try to take off as if she was rocket-propelled! It was exhausting labor just to hold her between the potato rows....Then pa had a habit of staking her out, on a halter and a rope, along the highway, where there was plenty of grass for her to stuff herself with. If she wasn't watched every minute, she was likely to pull loose from the stake, and ramble off. As it was my job to catch her, I was sure she had a perverse sense of humor. She'd let me get within a couple of yards of her. No gift-apple would entice her to be good. For a short ways she could still run like the devil. But, more commonly, she'd just snort out a derisive negative, swish her tail, and trot in leisurely fashion further down the road, and start cropping grass again. This procedure was repeated again and again, until she decided for herself that it was time to go home. One summer evening she led me on like this for about seven miles—half-way to Waupun—before she let me bareback her, in the near-darkness, and ride her back to our place. Her end came, I suspect, in part from some irate person's stabbing at her ribs with a pitchfork after she had gotten into his cornfield. Anyway, there were marks on her side, though they could have been from a barbed wire fence.

That darned, exasperating nag! But maybe thinking about her at last had a reverse effect against my morbid bitterness, undoing it somewhat by retrospective humor, affection, and sympathy. Quite soon I recovered from my inner misery.

* * * * * * *

During the hot months of 1926 I made a truly important discovery. I saw a large-sized magazine displayed in the window of the local book and stationery shop. There was a picture of an enormous housefly on the brightly colored cover. And there was the name of the publication spelled out in letters of declining size, large-to-small: *Amazing Stories*.

I bought that issue at once, fairly gobbling its contents. I did the same with succeeding issues. "Station X" by G. McLeod Winsor really grabbed me. I think it was a reprint. It was about a Martian invasion of Earth accomplished by radio contact—a transfer of mind, intellect, and know-how, to the bodies of living Earthlings. It was as spooky as all get-out; you never knew which of your friends had been transformed into super-intelligent Martian monsters, who had left their alien forms back on Mars. You could only tell an invader by the amazing speed, efficiency, logic, and precision with which he worked, using the big guns of battleships far more effectively than the trained human crew ever could; and improvising super-advanced equipment from parts of terrestrial devices. But these invaders—originally from the moon—were a decadent, robber-kind; ages ago they had stolen the forms of the native Martians, and now they were bent on making another switch, to Earth forms. They had to lose. Another gentler kind of beings from Venus, who had not corrupted themselves into loss of the capacity to improve, defeated them in the end.

And there were other excellent yarns in *Amazing Stories*. By Edmond Hamilton. By A. Hyatt Verrill....Soon to come would be David H. Keller....And Edward Elmer Smith of the *Skylark* yarns.

Anyhow, these were tales that groped into the future, into the yet-unknowns, into impossibilities that might someday become possible, and into all manner of what-ifs. Though I had not always known it, there was the sort of ambience, work-stuff—or whatever anybody wanted to call it—that I must have been preparing all along to get involved with—to do! So, at least, I felt.

I patterned "The Crystal Ray" from the shorter yarns in Hugo Gernsback's original *Amazing Stories*. Clearly, he wanted some scientific idea to predominate; the writing, the people, and even the story plot were secondary. Though I was hardly aware of these things then; I just wrote much as the others wrote.

Part of my reason for buckling down and finishing something was that everybody in junior English was expected to write a short story. As for scientific thought, I don't now quite remember how I picked it; it was almost a random choice, the first one of which it seemed I could make something—the refractive and other light-modifying properties of transparent crystals seem to have been the basic spark. So, by a little mental juggling....What if some exotic, natural crystal could transform normal sunlight passing through it into a death-ray? Violence is a pivotal element of adventure fiction, and perhaps, to at least a subliminal extent, of human nature. So was the germ of a superweapon which, to make a story, required a war to be won against terrible odds. And where does our hero discover this crystal? Color the answer up romantically: flying over the Andes in an exotic sort of aircraft that can do better than a thousand miles per hour—of course this is in an era beyond 2,000 A.D. At the edge of an extinct volcanic crater, a natural mass of crystal juts up. At the center of the crater floor there is a barren spot, a place where a primitive tribe of Indians has been practicing human sacrifice for ages, once a year, and when the sun is low, and its light gets transformed, becoming lethal as it passes through the outcrop of crystal. The hero has heard about this. So he lands, collects a trove of the stuff, takes it home, and technologizes a natural phenomenon and a primitive rite into a weapon that wins the war. Hooray....

My teacher gave me only an A-minus for the story. But then, of course, she didn't understand science fiction. Besides my effort had turned out three times as long as the top length-limit allowed by her assignment to us, her pupils. I had failed to find a way to compress my story that much. And my chicken-scratch handwriting, even when I tried to make it as legible as I could, wasn't the easiest to read.

For my senior-year English-class yarn, I worked well ahead of the need, and was more ambitious, idea-wise. I had become almost lyrically and defiantly fascinated by the ruggedness of biological life. You see, some scientists had, for instance, insisted that the planet Mars was too cold, too dry, and with too thin an atmosphere for any biology to have developed on its surface—a negative attitude which my romantic heart didn't want to accept. I knew the counter-arguments, among them that even on the bottoms of Earthly oceans, cold, lightless, and under a pressure of three tons per square inch, there were living creatures. Besides, I myself had often tramped through snow and wind and twenty-below-zero temperatures during Wisconsin winters, and had survived vigorously enough.

I decided to set aside Mars—under whose sign, Aries, I had been born—entirely. Why not go the limit—dream up a natural biology that could be native to outer space itself? I spent a lot of happy hours mulling the notion over. It was like intruding into the farthest distance to some yet-unperceived natural marvel there, which many would deny as impossible! But why?...If they said that water—the liquid basis of all known life—would either be frozen solid in the spatial cold or be turned to tenuous gas in the pressureless ambience, why not answer that maybe somewhere here was a liquid that would neither be so volatile or so easily congealed? If they insisted that the most common energy source for keeping known biological processes active came from the combustion of food by inhaled oxygen—which was surely absent in space—I could reply that the required power could be of a different origin. After all, even on Earth, there were anerobic bacteria that could be killed by exposure to free oxygen; their energy came from a fermentive process. But that was nothing compared to what I needed.

I solved my dual problem by imagining a liquid that would be an element above uranium in its atomic number. It wouldn't boil away easily, and it wouldn't freeze, except perhaps near absolute zero, a temperature which it could never quite approach, because it would *naturally be radioactive*, as was likely for very massive atoms. It would constantly be producing heat and other energy by atomic decay!

So, there I had the whole idea together: a liquid that, first, would serve all the motile requirements of biology, comparable, that is, to blood circulation. And second, *within itself*, it would contain a mighty energy source. Why couldn't this be used to energize all metabolic and bodily activity in another, entirely different life-form, to which it would be intrinsically harmless, because it was in that liquid that the other biology had evolved?

I had no idea then of what yet-unperceived ground I was treading. Exobiology, an acceptable college-level subject today, didn't exist as a word, and I suspect was scarcely a gleam in the eye of any serious biologist.

Let's try to put that whole, rather remote era into perspective: in 1927, the year before, Charles A. Lindbergh had made the first solo flight across the Atlantic. We had radios. The Model-A Ford had pretty much replaced the Model-T. There were tractors around, but with most farmers, the chief pulling power was still horse teams. Television? It was still a "science fictiony" vision—being worked on, yes, but still far in the future as a workable household device. Had there been any such thing within my range, I would have run to it puffing, not primarily to enjoy the latest educational television program, but to behold the sheer, intrinsic miracle.

And a particular hero of mine, Dr. Robert H. Goddard, was experimenting with primitive, liquid-fuelled rockets, with which he hoped to reach "high altitudes." He didn't quite dare to say that the goal could be the moon—though that was implied, to the laughing scorn of many, who had read about Goddard in the *American Weekly*, which came out with the Sunday papers. Thus they, and the believers and potential believers, were at least kept informed, thanks largely to the forward-looking editor, Abraham Merritt, who also wrote excellent fantasy and science fiction, including *The Moon Pool*.

American Weekly also featured articles about the possibility of releasing atomic energy—"A glass of water contains enough power to drive the largest ocean liner across the Atlantic." And there were articles suggesting that interplanetary communication would be possible with massed searchlight beams. A. Merritt must have been quite a guy.

Yes, radioactivity was known of, and considerably understood, special thanks for this going to Madame Marie Curie, discoverer of radium. But there was a long way to travel to get to true nuclear physics, and its bad—and good—effects.

So there I was with my concept for nuclear biology. One of the best ideas I've ever had? Maybe....It has been said that a person's best, and most sweeping notions, come early in life, before mental inhibitions on the inventive capacity set in, and when the eager, groping drives are at their height.

So now, how to make a story of it? Here, I was not too able. But considering Gernsback's emphasis on scientific concepts, literary niceties such as realistic character development, etc., were not very important, and might even be superfluous to the science-oriented readership of *Amazing Stories*. Better to stick to forms already familiar to them, like a young scientist working alone in his remote, woodland laboratory. So far not hard for me to visualize, when I *really* lived in a house that had been designed and built by an eccentric inventor who seemed to have sought rural seclusion!

Though it wasn't strictly necessary for the exobiologically-based plot, I couldn't restrain myself from the temptation to stick another related idea of mine into the beginning of the yarn: my hero was trying to release atomic power, and I had a method for his approach—he wanted to duplicate the conditions by which it was probably being freed at the sun's center: enormous pressure and heat.

In this I was also on new and uncertain territory. The old notion that the sun's energy came *solely* from its gravity-induced contraction had only in recent times begun to seem ridiculous; over only a few million years, the solar bulk, squeezed together, would have diminished beyond any cosmologically and geologically acceptable possibility. So physicists were just getting at the truth: hydrogen atoms combining—fusing—to form helium?

Whether my notion was right or not, my hero ran into the obvious defect in his method: the press he devised, a super-hard metal rod to be forced slowly into a socket bored into a great metal ball, broke down long before anything like the kind of pressure needed could be reached. There were no materials known or conceivable that could withstand such strain without breaking. The gravity-sustained pressures that occurred naturally deep in the solar mass could never be matched in an Earthly laboratory by the means attempted. So my hero was brooding miserably over his failure.

What must follow was almost obvious. Though I didn't quite see it consciously that way, it was time for the Good Genie to enter, bring cheer, take control, provide more satisfying alternatives and thoughts to the unhappy young scientist.

Out of the night and the woods, comes a great, dark humanoid, his huge muscles glistening with frost caused by the chill within them, though the weather is warm and humid. Thus appears Othaloma of the Stars. He has learned Earthly languages, and he tells my hero about his people: far away and long ago, they were once of an entirely terrestrial type, with air-breathing, water-based biology. But their world was dying, and soon would not be able to support them. Searching long and hard for a solution to their difficulty, they had at last come upon a very remarkable thing, on a small airless planetoid: primitive, natural creatures of the radioactive biology that I have already described.

Wise men from among Othaloma's ancestors had taken specimens of these creatures back to their home world. After long study and experiment, they had finally achieved a means of converting hydrogen-oxygen-carbon-based life to this different and far hardier life form. So Othaloma's kind had been freed from almost all limitations. Cold could not hurt them, and they were resistent to heat below incandescence. They needed no air to breathe. They were practically immortal. They could wander far and wide throughout the universe, needing no space suits at all. And didn't my hero want to drop his petty playing along with atomic energy, come join them in their star-spanning ship, be transformed too, and go soaring off into true freedom? Of course he agrees.

In thinking up and writing "The Space Dwellers," it may be that I was acting out, symbolically, my intended escape from the strange home that I hated and loved, and reassuring myself that I would get away from it eventually. Nowadays, though, I wonder idly whether, by some deeper, more universal instinct that commands all biology to propagate itself as widely as possible, I wasn't also acting out an arcane urge, innate in our human species, to extend its presence even to the stars?

Well, I had forewarned my teacher, Miss Mary Johnson, that this story would be about twenty pages long—a bit longer, even, than the earlier yarn. But, with the help of my ham radio buddy—better at the scribble machine than I—I took it down to the commercial studies department for a couple of evenings after school, and got the script typed up. I had doubted the chances of "The Crystal Ray" for being printed, but now I thought, what the heck—so we typed up that one, too.

Maybe because I was considerate about her eyesight, Miss Johnson did give me an A for "The Space Dwellers," though she seemed somewhat miffed at me for writing this wild kind of story, while refusing to do more verse.

Nope, when I graduated from Beaver Dam High School in June 1928, I didn't get top honors; I was down on the list by at least half-a-dozen, in a class of seventy-three students. In the sciences I had done okay, and not too badly in Latin; elsewhere I had a couple of incompletes which I had been slow to make up....Ah, well—a relief. I would have been a disaster as a valedictorian. Stage fright. To this day getting up in front of a lot of people makes me nervous.

* * * * * * *

I was back in the cannery again. Then, for a year, in the shoe factory, learning to be a cutter, paying my board and saving my money. Sis had finished college, and was away. Without any tremendous enthusiasm, I agreed with ma that I should go to the university. I scribbled at quite a few stories, but didn't finish anything. One of my distractions was that I was wondering what had happened to the two scripts I had sent to *Amazing Stories*.

I felt that the central idea in "The Crystal Ray" was faulty; a death-ray would probably have to have high power. Just passing sunlight through an exotic crystal couldn't give it that. Like perpetual motion, such a phenomenon would defy the law of conservation of energy; there was no source from which the boosting power could come.

But for the idea of life compatible with extreme, radioactive, conditions—a premise central to "The Space Dwellers"—I not only had considerable hopes, but insistent, passionate belief! And my increasing worry was that Gernsback wouldn't be able to adjust to such a novel—though, to me, a perfectly *sound!*—scientific notion.

Yet I didn't dare write and ask about my yarns, fearful that I might upset some tenuously balanced apple cart!

Lo, early in 1929, I guess in gloomy February, I got two letters from Gernsback by the same post. Their text was identical, except for separate yarn titles. Both letters said that Gernsback very much liked the story referred to, and wanted to publish it.

Wow! Today I can't quite recapture my innocent young triumph of then. *Two* science fiction yarns of mine, the first I had ever completed and submitted, were in! And with the great Gernsback!...

But then the dark side, the flaw that made it all a Pyrrhic victory. Gernsback went on to say that, due to involuntary bankruptcy, he was no longer connected with *Amazing Stories*. He continued by declaring that he was in the process of setting up some new magazines, and that of course I had sent my manuscript(s) to his private home on Riverside Drive, and not to *Amazing Stories*, but that I should send him a letter so that he would be sure of this.

Naive Honest John—me. I couldn't quite grasp that this was a legal tactic to establish my agreement to his right to print the yarns. One thing I felt I lacked was some older person worldly enough to guide me in unusual quandaries like this one. But who was there?...Imagine my situation: I was a young guy, suddenly lifted up about as high as I could go, yet, in the same moment plunged into the brambles of a bankruptcy, and of extended uncertainties.

Taking care with my penmanship, I wrote to Gernsback, hinting as much as I could that he should be my adviser. I told him that I very much wanted him to publish my stories, but that *truly* I had sent the scripts to him as editor of *Amazing Stories*, and what should I do?

Promptly, I got the manuscripts back. With them was a short, curt note, stating that I was now free to submit them wherever I wanted. I returned them to Gernsback at once. So another agonizing wait, seeming longer than it was. The stories were accepted. I suppose no real difference was made, except that they might have been printed a couple of months sooner. "The Crystal Ray" and "The Space Dwellers" appeared simultaneously and respectively, in the November 1929 issues of *Air Wonder Stories* and *Science Wonder Stories*. And I had two crisp checks—for twenty-five and thirty dollars. Considering inflation since then, that would be the equivalent of about four hundred dollars now. Not too bad, I thought.

VII.

HIGHER EDUCATION

By then I was at the University of Wisconsin in Madison, rooming with a lusty, noisy, and somewhat boozy family. My embarrassments about where, and in what sort of house I had lived, in Beaver Dam, were removed. Now was my first escape, and I meant to make good use of it, to catch up, if I could, on so much that I had missed! As I entered my cramped little room, I could snap on a switch and have electric light, like regular town-folks. And my narrower bed wasn't under bare rafters in our unfinished upstairs any more! Nor would I have to edge my toes gradually down under the heavy but icy covers before I could go comfortably to sleep on frigid winter nights; there would be artifical heating all around me!...But this much was only the start. My aims were less on performing the tasks of the curriculum than on living. Is this a common attitude of many who go away to school?...I had a tentative schedule figured out. I had hoarded quite a little money over the years. So I could afford to take it easy and find my path for a couple of months, before I did like the other students working their way, and got a part-time job washing dishes or busing tables in some restaurant.

These intentions went awry to a certain extent. Having been inhibited for so long in other directions, I tore loose with a bit more zeal than I had expected. There was Prohibition "hootch" around. That had been readily available in Beaver Dam, too; in fact pa had peddled the stuff, sometimes even leaving bottles in rural mailboxes. But there such "likker" had meant nothing to me one way or the other. Now, though, it had an appeal brought on by readily available companionship, some of it feminine, town-girlfriends of my new family. Set free in my fresh environment, good-natured, eager grins came out on my face readily enough. And after a couple of shots, my outlook got even better. Likely as not, I'd start to sing, feeling that I was everybody's good guy. A few times I got good and drunk, and passed out.

Losses and gains? Well, I'd call it all gain. Technically it could be argued that I had lost my virginity to a pair of older girls from the neighboring countryside, back when I was five-years-old. It seems this often happens to small boys when distaff persons reach the age of curiosity and experimentation, and look for somebody too young to threaten them. So, who's to complain? That's part of the natural flow of life. To find out is self-improvement.

Between then and the university, though, there had been nothing much of that for me. So I did some casual catching up. I might have entangled myself in something truly stupid and sentimental; but I was lucky, and I was wary at the right points....And over all I didn't go really hog-wild all that much, about anything.

I didn't shine much as a scholar at the University. There were a few students still around with the high-raised and flopping hand—the teacher-I-know thing. Worth an indulgent smile. Past my first year in high school I'd gotten over that much emphasis. Now I felt that I was still more blasé. Let those eager-beavers give their answers.

I liked the physics lectures and the lab work. The physics math bugged me somewhat. French was all right, but it was book-French. History had its merits, but footnoting every bit of your source material while writing your term paper was a pain-in-the-neck. English Lit was spoiled by a dullard of an instructor. Composition? Mildly entertaining, but not much to it that I could seriously relate to. Stories from *The American Mercury* as models? I tried, but it was hard for me to bend my wits in their direction.

Remembering my old debt to physicians for saving my life, I had often thought that I should become that sort of useful citizen myself. Biology, in all its forms, had always fascinated me. Besides, I was a rather kindly soul. So I made friends with a couple of medical students. One morning when I had a free period they invited me to come along to the stiff-lab. There I watched them cut into part of a cadaver to trace out such things as nerves and blood vessels. I wasn't particularly squeamish. Back home I'd butchered quite a few chickens for Sunday dinners. But there in that stiff-lab were zinc-lined chests containing assorted pieces of human bodies, gray from pickling in formaldehyde: arms, legs, lengths of viscera, fingers....And there was the severed head of what seemed to have been a Filipino boy of about fifteen years. The expression on his face looked as though he was crying....

I didn't feel very much disturbed.

"Time for lunch!" one of my companions chuckled agreeably.

I went into the washroom and scrubbed my hands thoroughly with strong soap, and then rinsed them with lots of water. But when I came forth I sniffed them again. Somehow, beneath the disinfecting smell of soap, I detected the pungence of formaldehyde, and beneath that another ghost of an odor, like that of an old fried hamburger that had been left lying for a day or two in a garbage dump.

I clowned up my discovery with an exaggerated grimace of distaste, charged back into the washroom, and scrubbed my hands again. My medical friends followed me and watched, amused.

"Eating a nice limburger cheese sandwich with raw onion topping will fix you up, Ray," one declared solemnly. "In cases like this, that always works."

I took him at his word as well as was possible, except for that particular cheese. The coffeeshop where we went didn't have any limburger.

A first encounter with a stiff-lab shouldn't stop anybody with serious intentions toward becoming a medical doctor. In fact, the challenge ought to increase his determination. I thought so, too. I felt my jaws tighten grimly. When a particular drive really gets hold of me, I can usually stick to it pretty good. But this one

was a bit short on intensity. Maybe it wasn't quite me?...I couldn't be sure....
Anyhow it was much too soon to decide.

Where the passing time went, I hardly knew. I never did get that part-time job as I had intended. I just sort of drifted comfortably along, as if I had lost something, or was making believe, without any tangible evidence of it, that I was a rich fraternity brother, or perhaps, more appropriately, that I was some kind of Oriental mystic, disguised as an indigenous kid from rural Wisconsin gone to the University, and observing, in critical detachment, the customs of the Western World.

With my physics lab partner, who truly was a rich kid and a nice guy, I had long, involved discussions about philosophical and scientific topics. He taught me to play chess—at which I've never become very good, or even very interested. At his urging, we tried collaborating on some stories. To me they were half-assed almost from the start, but somehow I didn't care much, as if I were concentrating on being lazy; as if everything was a big joke, anyhow. So that was the rather nebulous state I had gotten into....Well, for anybody who basically wants to write, nothing is ever a total loss. Without ever hurting myself very much, or getting, in any serious sense, out of control, maybe I was intuitively counterbalancing some of my inner incongruities after all.

And, separate from my activities at the place where I lived, there was a girl whom I liked very much. In adjacent rooms in Bascom Hall, we had similar French classes during the first period, five days a week. Our vibes must have matched. Anyhow, out in the corridor, we got to talking. We'd been born a mere twelve miles apart. She was interested in psychology, and in someday seeing the world. So, particularly on the latter point, we clicked right away; besides, we were two country youngsters. So, nearly every day, we met after French. It was a unique relationship and ritual, all very platonic. Yakking away largely about our shared mutual interest, we'd amble down Bascom Hill to the beautiful, new Memorial Union building. There, in the quiet, oak-paneled lounge of the library, sitting on a luxurious divan, we'd talk some more, and each have a cigarette; I might never have become a smoker if it hadn't been for her. And we'd pronounce numerous magical words, such as Fez...Isfahan...Hong Kong...Singapore...Rangoon....

I never got forward or fresh with her, like I'd come to do where I roomed. Nor did I speak to her with easy, free-flowing vulgarities. There were simple and/or complicated reasons for this: though we liked to think of ourselves as *avant-garde* persons, we were deep-down, grimed-in, corn-patch old-fashioned kids, in which a serious intentioned young man was supposed to be, um, honorable. She didn't seem the sort for anything else. Especially when I was getting a few someday-visions about her, like even imagining pushing a pram...

Yet that wasn't the entirety of my attitude. For one thing, I seemed to have somewhat different personalities, each fitting different places and situations, and I sensed that there would be a jolting confusion about who I was if I didn't keep them separate. But the bottom line element was a wariness which warned: beyond a certain point, the closer one got to a person with whom a serious involvement was likely, the more one stuck his neck out. Self-protection, yes. Yet wasn't it considerate shelter for the other party as well? We were both very young, and I, in particular, had had scant time to get myself sorted out.

However, with her, I kept tiptoeing along a thrillingly reckless edge, saying:

"I got away from home, Bert, and I don't want to go back....Though maybe I will....The University is okay, I guess....But I keep thinking that it's kind of a bust....For instance, I could have spent the same amount of money—and the same time—going a lot farther, and to better advantage...."

What I actually spent getting through that 1929-30 interlude at the University of Wisconsin was between five and six hundred dollars, a fairly frugal level, yes; though it may startle some students used to much higher costs nowadays. But, with my casual, shrugging lack of providence in not getting a part-time job, my bankroll was going to drop below two hundred bucks.

Though she had worked, her attitude toward the University resembled mine.

So, kiddingly—we were often in that nebulous region of "maybe"—she would respond with a teasing smile:

"We could buy an old car for a few dollars, Ray....Then—west?...Toward San Francisco to start?...They must need maids on big passenger liners...."

That enchantment of distant places—enhanced now by the charm of feminine companionship! Don't think I didn't sweat with temptation and indecision!...Yet I suppose the outcome was inevitable. I couldn't rely on my befuddled head. So I had to drift along, and let my guts—or my reality-chilled, deep-down intuition—guide me. I was too scared. What she suggested was too fast, too soon. I felt inadequate, unready. Doing what I wanted to do would be like stepping into an abyss, and losing control....When there were certain things I *had* to do, and *must not* mess up!...I was already way behind in following up the printing of my first two yarns with effectively writing any others....Besides, there had been a stock market crash, and predictions about getting jobs weren't good....Further, letters from my mother indicated between the lines that she was coughing a lot, and not feeling very well.

Excuses, excuses....

So along came springtime, late May, and the end of the term.

"I can't, Bert....The timing is wrong....The notion is kind of cockeyed, anyhow....Maybe next year...."

We parted rather coolly. I was still neurotic about where I lived in Beaver Dam, and she was a special person whom I couldn't accept in that ambience. So I made no mention of seeing her over the summer. But I suppose what influenced me most in my negative decision was feeling the beat of my own, old, private drummer pulling me back to where I could respond best. True, names like Delhi, London, and Cairo were exciting incantations; but others, much farther out of reach, had a stronger pull: Mars, the moon, the stars....

Looking backward seventy years, I still have to admit that that star-crossed pair of kids probabaly wouldn't have made it, then. I would have messed up....Old sensible plans shouldn't be spoiled. I needed to work and wait.

VIII.

A MILESTONE STORY

Back home, the chirp of sparrows and the cluck of chickens gave me a kind of relief. So did the rattle of cans at the cannery; nothing was changed there—yet. Business slump or not, the pea pack had to go on—same sweaty, somehow uplifting challenge to the muscles, same wages, same fifteen-to-twenty hours a day. Helping around home on rare days off. And trying to get something together enough to write....

There were a few contacts with my used-to-be-girl by phone. We both said maybe we'd go back to school in the fall. Otherwise, in addition to working, she seemed to be having a good time. Then, in early September, there was another phone conversation. More cheerful kidding. She said I hadn't given her any moral support, and that she was getting married, and taking off for Texas. I wasn't very startled; I only felt somewhat hollow, and wrong-way. So, more seriously, I added that I hoped she knew what she was getting into. But I ended, quite earnestly:

"The best of luck, Bert. My hand is on my heart...."

Over the next several difficult years we exchanged some letters, and I saw her a few times, mostly by chance. Then silence and forgetfulness.

But that same September of 1930, just a couple of days after I had talked with her, something drew me back to Madison. Though I was still ten percent thinking I might continue as a university student, it was mostly nostalgia. Curiously, one of the things that I latched onto was remembering how our ancient history professor, Alexander Alexandrovich Vasiliev, from Kiev in the Ukraine, used to begin all his lectures: "Ve heff seen thet..." He was a bemused, studious old gent, a very old-school, European-type scholar. But it had been rumored that he could play the piano marvelously.

I stayed in Madison only a couple of days. Then, a stick in the mud, I went home. One excuse—ma was not getting healthier, so I'd better be around.

It was back to the shoe factory for quite a while. And I turned out several new yarns: if, in some far-off, future age, the fires of the sun waned, couldn't the dead moon be similarly ignited to supplement them, and keep the Earth from freezing up? (Nobody knew for sure then that that was impossible.) That was "Atomic Fire," in the April 1931 *Amazing Stories*. That September, *Amazing* also published my novelette, "The Lunar Chrysalis." What if, before the moon had gone airless and dead, it had spawned an advanced culture that had put itself into suspended animation to wait for ages till the Earth had cooled enough to receive these non-humanoid Lunarians? But what if their time-clock had gotten stuck, so that it remained for the first Earthmen who reached the moon to unknowingly release these monstrous beings from their extended sleep? *What then?* Ultimate friendly agreement, compromise, and mutual benefit, of course! In 1931, we terrans were trying hard to remain idealist-optimists.

Ma had been off at a state sanatorium for some time; tuberculosis was still a major killer back then. But toward the last she was transferred to the Wisconsin General Hospital. So I returned to Madison to be with her for a few of her final days. She died on September 4. She was fifty-four years old, and her birthday was the same as mine, March 22. Me—Her gift to herself? A poor, conscientious, intensely well-meaning woman, she deserved much better than she got—maybe including yours truly.

A number of my co-workers at the shoe factory had been sent to the sanatorium, too. Several didn't come back.

But, for the living, life doesn't stop. With some of the money for "The Lunar Chrysalis," I bought myself a new portable typewriter. So, without renting a machine, I could type up a long novelette that I had been working on through the summer—"The Revolt of the Starmen."

I'd come quite a ways in learning how to handle mystery, fast-action suspense, and even characters. As for the scientific part, I took what I had used in "The Space Dwellers"—hardy, radioactively energized, outer space-compatible life, and added another parallel notion: if there could be fierce, quasi-humanoid warriors native to space itself, why couldn't they also have natural, living mounts of the same unique metabolism as themselves to ride?...No, nothing like actual horses in form—but flattish, radially-ridged disks of exotic, rubbery flesh, rather! And, from their ventral surfaces, why couldn't they project propulsive energy, perhaps corpuscular? Thus, wouldn't this allow them and their primitive riders to go charging off into whatever interplanetary or interstellar distance as nomads of the universe?...I had these starmen under the control of a slick humanoid at first—a Martian nobleman who plotted to use them to help him gain control of Mars and Earth....Till the starmen rebelled....

I was proud of that yarn. I sent it to Gernsback, and he accepted it promptly. Payment would be due, as usual, on publication. Elated by my success, I hastened eagerly to write more for Gernsback.

What if a ship came from deep space, but instead of landing, on Earth, just went mysteriously into orbit around it? No contact was attempted until a strange radiation came down. Though humans remained entirely conscious, they discovered, to their horror, that they had lost control of their bodies, and directed by a will outside themselves, they were compelled to build mightily for the alien invaders. That was "Waves of Compulsion."

Then I wrote "Moon Mistress," a novelette involving terran adventurers with an ancient lunar cult.

Gernsback was always running contests to attract readers to his science fiction magazines. So now he sent me a prize-winning story plot cooked up by one John B. Michel, an up-and-coming fan who was destined to gain considerable importance. The result was "The Menace from Mercury," which got us a Frank R. Paul cover illustration on the Summer 1932 *Wonder Stories Quarterly.*

Meanwhile though, before Gernsback had yet published any of my new yarns that he had accepted, I began to have some doubts. For one thing, he offered me a contract, agreeing to pay me three-quarters of a cent per word, *on acceptance,* if I agreed to send all my stuff to him for "first refusal." And why was he doing that for his writers? Now, belatedly, I found the probable answer—in *Writer's Digest:* W. M. Clayton's *Astounding Stories,* edited by Harry Bates, was paying *two cents per word on acceptance,* and—innocent, bemused me—I hadn't even known! It was fairly clear that Hugo was trying to counter superior competition with his contracts.

I read through the current issue of *Astounding.* Shoot—I didn't mind about the other yarns of mine so much, but in pace and tone, and novelette-length too, "The Revolt of the Starmen" seemed exactly the thing for Harry Bates. And I hadn't even shown it to him.

Well, a deed done was a done deed, and I'd have to live with it. But I wrote to Gernsback, saying that I preferred to remain strictly free-lance.

It seems I was sort of hung up just then on lunar yarns. I wrote another novelette called "Moon Plague"—not a bad one, I believe even now. It was about sentient, mobile vegetation, adapted for living under harsh, lunar conditions. Bates' letter, when he sent it back, seemed to have some vaguely ominous interlinear signals in it. He said that Mr. Clayton had gotten to it first, and so there was no good in his reading it himself. Had somebody, under the strains of a business in trouble, blown his stack?

But I meant to get into *Astounding,* or bust! My determination was almost desperate. I had yet another—but very short, and I thought neat—moon story in mind. To save time I began composing it, and memorizing the paragraphs, while I set dies on hides spread on the block of my "clicking machine" at the shoe factory, and cut out leather vamps, tips, and quarters.

You can't win 'em all. Sometimes it seems you can't win any. "The Flight of the RX-1"—only 3,500 words long—in which a man flew the first rocket to the moon, but found he had no chance to return, won me an apology from Harry Bates: "A story I really liked...." But he was out of a job. *Astounding Stories,* and the whole string of Clayton magazines, had folded. The Great Depression was biting deep, at last.

Not being entirely the best cutter in the world, I was laid off at the shoe factory.

"The Flight of the RX-1" eventually wound up in the July 1933 issue of *Amazing,* which was also struggling to survive. "Moon Plague" made it even later, in Gernsback's January 1934 *Wonder Stories.* But both of those dates were not only far ahead of the times, but also out of sight of any prediction.

What to do now? So far I hadn't gotten any new money at all from Gernsback. And sis was home again, too. No—we Galluns weren't in any unusual boat of calamities. In fact, I suppose we were luckier than many. We didn't have any rent to pay, and pa and I both got jobs at the hempmill, where the regular working season lasted through the winter months. The hempmill was a half-mile across the fields from our place. The wages were seventeen-and-a-half cents an hour. Don't laugh or sneer; the little company, marginally alive, couldn't have paid much more. The job was a miserable one, but in a ten-hour day you earned about two bucks, and there weren't any deductions. Two bucks bought a lot of groceries then. No—I wouldn't want to go back to that kind of economics, but there were advantages.

"The Revolt of the Starmen" came out in the Winter 1932 *Wonder Stories Quarterly*. Its appearance put me actively in a category with guys such as Stanton A. Coblentz, P. Schuyler Miller, Clifford D. Simak, Lloyd A. Eshbach, Nathan Schachner....I was very pleased.

Seeing a yarn of yours for the first time in print is always a heady experience. The opening words were just as I had made them....Okay....But then I looked at Paul's illustration. Sure enough, there were my starmen, swooping along in space, looking right enough. Maybe I glanced back at the picture of me, in the midst of the opening text; it was no worse than when it had fronted for "The Crystal Ray" and "The Space Dwellers"—that damnable, cherubic, high school graduation picture of mine—I had had no other—brutalized by being roughly copied as a drawing. Well, no sweat....Vanity, vanity—and shame on you....

But then my attention jumped back to Paul's illustration of the story. Something wrong?...What were those peculiar, mechanical-looking, flat, round things that my starmen were riding on? With control levers yet?!

My fingers scrambled through the pages as I searched out the significant place in the text. And, sure enough, an abominable alteration!

Very soon thereafter, and without any prompting from me, I got Gernsback's letter of explanation. I don't remember the exact wording, but the substance was this: I must realize, if I thought the matter through carefully, that living creatures that could propel themselves through space were impossible. Therefore, changes had been necessary.

I'd suspected that something of this sort might happen. In honor to the great man of whom I was then in awe, I admitted, even through my bitter, inner denials, that maybe he was right.

However, at this much later date, my attitude is somewhat different. Poor Hugo! Had he looked forward into the marvels and enigmas of the universe, and the miracles that Man would achieve in it, until he couldn't see? Had he missed my major point entirely? Was he so hung up on the power of human, mechanical invention, that he couldn't grasp the fact that Nature was a worthy, and often far superior, competitor? Yes—even today?...There were winged reptiles and birds and fish millions of years before there were airplanes and submarines. Stars like the sun burn on for ages, their nuclear energy output fairly well stabilized by a built-in, natural regulating system, and no thanks to Mighty Man. And mightn't Nature also devise a different biology with another fluid and energy source basis other than the familiar water and chemical one? And going that rather slight distance in natural ingenuity, mightn't Nature also devise a necessary, space-effective propulsion system—for instance, with streams of ions—ions also being things fundamental to Nature?...Nuts!

46

Yet maybe, on another level, Hugo was right to make the change. To keep his magazines halfway viable, he had to consider what his humanly proud readership would believe.

To me, almost the worst thing about the change was on the level of story-mood. My starmen were intended to be simple, primitive nomads of the universe, relying on natural circumstances for all their needs. So, take away their living, vital, natural mounts, their starfish-shaped space-horses, and put them on silly, complicated mechanical platforms, which they probably lacked the technology to invent, or build, anyhow? What clumsy, incongruous meddling was this?

I didn't even write a letter of protest. What was done was done, and so be it....I waited for Gernsback's check for the story. It didn't come. About that, I *did* write. Where was my money? I seem to remember he *did* send me something—"on account." I think it was fifty dollars. With further prodding from me, he made a couple of other partial payments. Eventually, by writing to a well-known authors' agency, I got the name of an attorney named Ione Weber, who originated in Wisconsin but was practicing in New York. She could nudge Gernsback more directly. For a contingency fee of fifteen percent, she got Gernsback to settle up for all my stories that he had accepted and published, at the rate of fifteen dollars a week, an arrangement which he stuck to fairly well. I wrote a letter to *Writers' Digest*, giving Mrs. Weber's name and address, and I believe other writers who had had trouble collecting from Hugo also availed themselves of her help.

I never met Hugo Gernsback personally, but there is no doubt he was quite a fellow, with much to admire. The contacts I did have with him, though, were pretty specific, and I've gotten the backlash of other people's experiences with him. He liked to send out gaudy, futuristic greeting cards. In one—I think, for New Years—he characterized himself as a "Philanthropic Deadbeat." It is almost a puzzle whether that is a contradiction of terms or not. About being very slow at paying his writers, he did have the legitimate excuse of hard times, though he seemed to play it to the hilt. He hung on to a nickel with the passion of a Scrooge....

* * * * * * *

Back to that January of 1932....My splurge of writing science fiction novelettes hadn't yet gotten me a dime. The best market had died. The remaining ones were shaky, slow, and poor-paying—hardly worth the effort to try for. Maybe I should tackle *True Story* or *True Romances*?...But science fiction was the only kind of writing that was then seriously part of me. Conditions being what they were, why do any writing at all? Those ten hours a day at the hempmill were about enough for my bodily endurance, even though I was a considerable distance from being feeble.

I've told about this interlude, and its results, in other, shorter scribblings before this one. That job was in a corrugated sheet iron structure immersed in a Midwestern winter. Big sheaves of hemp were brought in from outside, where they had been laid in conical stacks in autumn to age. Now they were put on a slow-moving conveyor system over steam pipes, to thaw out the frost and dry them. Being young and agile, while most of the other employees were rather elderly, I was stationed with those at the other end of the "dry-kiln," where you had to keep moving fast. So I was trotting back and forth, lugging bundles of hemp from the hot dry-kiln to a frigid place near the wall, where I broke the bundles apart and fed the hemp stalks in bunches between spinning steel rollers that crushed them, preliminary to separating the fiber from the dry stalk pulp. The air was full of thick, blackish dust. Everybody was coughing. Considering the alternate hot-cold situation, too, it's a wonder we didn't all get pneumonia.

The job was physically straining, noisy, and entirely monotonous. It put me into a kind of somnambulistic state; my rapid motions continued, but they were zombie-like. My mind had to go somewhere—into escape.

I began to imagine, according to some patterns already set. Mars, my red star, was my favorite getting-away region, back then. Going to work and coming home, both in the dark, there were realistic hints in the grimed snow of the fields, as revealed by my flashlight beam. Mars, near its polar caps? Sure, it would be far harsher there, climate-wise, but the likeness was sufficient to suggest what was lacking.

Pa was usually with me, crossing those fields, but we weren't very talkative company for each other. And I needed a special friend. So...a Martian? All day, struggling with bundles of hemp, I'd try to dream him up. I wasn't trying to compose a story for sale; I was disgruntled about doing that; this was just for myself, and maybe my companion on Mars. No—he wouldn't be anything like an Earthly person, physically. The chance that another chain of evolution would produce similar beings on a rather dissimilar world was, after all, very remote. And I wanted to make him as real as I could; I was getting onto a basic drive of mine: *that an important function of whatever I imagined should be an interim substitute for mysterious realities not yet revealed—to respond a little to a burning urge to know.* I think I've usually favored realities about other worlds well above any imaginings about them; they're generally more satisfying, and at least as wonderful.

My Martian wouldn't have any conception of smiles or frowns or tears. But, being alive, he would have to have similarities to us. Though I *did* make the reckless assumption that he would have a mind. Having physical needs, and being subject to injury, he would probably know hunger and thirst, distress and comfort. Needing to defend himself, he would probably understand fear and courage. Needing to reproduce, and to look after his young, he would probably have the equivalent of love. And, possessing a mind, he would probably have intense curiosity, a yearning to find out.

So what if he wanted to learn more about Earth, just as I wanted to know more about Mars? Here was a solid likeness, to contrast dramatically with all the differentness! A basis for sympathy that would stand out! Something beyond the rather tiresome story motivation of conquest and defense, common in many yarns, including mine. Instead, just to learn—to find out! The scientist's fundamental drive....

I constructed my Martian and his world from all that I read that was considered fairly solid, scientifically, about Mars back in those days: thin air, dryness,

48

cold, plus Percival Lowell's—proven fanciful now—ideas about "canals." I borrowed a few touches from H. G. Wells' *War of the Worlds*—much more convincing than anything in Burroughs's Mars books. Adding a sense of struggle and obstacle came easily, direct from the job I was doing: my Martian, his efforts—and thus him also!—condemned as useless and worthless by his own, hard-pressed-to-survive kind. But he goes on, trying to make use of what little he has managed to learn of terran methods of communication by his studies of messages in Morse code flashed in telescopic light signals from Earth by attempting to compose an understandable message in the same medium. He tries to hitchhike his way to Earth from Mars, on a comet that will pass quite close to both. And so, before he perishes in the effort, he at last achieves a little of his fondest intention: seeing Earth at ground-level range.

That was how I cooked up "Old Faithful," which was to become my best-remembered story.

But maybe there was another factor in the process, which I'll recount again almost as a joke.

You see, the large variety of hemp, grown for its fiber is a close relative of marijuana. It, too, is *cannabis*; the leaf forms are the same; no doubt the alkaloids it contains are very similar. And at the hempmill, the dry, waste pulp of the stalks was used to fire the boiler that produced steam for the engine and the dry-kiln. The smoke that poured from the smokestack had exactly the pungence of burning pot. So maybe "Old Faithful" came out of a drug-induced mind expansion?...As for myself, I'm more inclined to think that my vision was more from auto-hypnosis, caused by my need to get away, mentally and emotionally, from a dull, uncomfortable task.

Though dog-tired, I continued the escape in the evenings, painfully penciling out the story by kerosene lamplight on the dining room table. Then I typed it up. I kept thinking that the yarn was just for me—without any comformity to any editor's requirements or taboos. But what should I do with it when it was finished? I responded to habit, and I mailed the script to the only remaining market that I respected: T. O'Conor Sloane's *Amazing Stories*.

After a long time he got around to sending it back to me—I believe just with a printed rejection slip.

No, "Old Faithful" didn't find its way so easily into print.

* * * * * * *

1932, and till nearly the end of 1933, constituted a rough stretch for most everybody. We Galluns managed to stay off the relief rolls. Pa and I were old hands at the cannery; we had that in summer. Now there was a new president on the scene—Franklin Delano Roosevelt—FDR. So what would happen now?

During the past year I'd tried something I had always wanted to try—in memory of Uncle Julius. So my ham radio buddy, myself, and three other guys got together, drove down to Milwaukee, and took a crack at joining the Navy. I was exed out at once for my shortsighted eyes. But I was sure some of the others would make it; they had an excellent know-how of radio, which the Navy ought to find very useful. Uh-uh. For one reason or another, we all came back saddened—five goose-eggs. The Navy was very picky, then. It was no easy refuge for jobless and frustrated young men.

But in 1933 light appeared on my horizon! A solid old publishing house, Street & Smith, had bought *Astounding Stories*, and was bringing it back! I lost out in a couple of shots at it. Feeling briefly depressed, I even tried to join the CCC—the Civilian Conservation Corps—recruiting for public works projects, including forestry, etc. They shelved me on a waiting list.

Well, it didn't matter, because I cracked into *Astounding* with a little story, "Space Flotsam." There was no letter at all from F. Orlin Tremaine, the new editor. Just a Street & Smith check with a notation of what story it was for on it. Thirty-five bucks—payment at the bottom rate, a cent a word. But I'd never gotten that rate before!

"Space Flotsam" was about a young crewman shoved out of his big space ship by intruders who had dominated it. He was left to drift toward smothering death in his space armor. His problem was to turn the tables on the enemy.

I was already into other yarns: what if, on a frozen moon of Saturn, a native culture of another, cold-compatible life form had sprung up? What if a friendly contact, by radio—and by a kind of teleportation, allowing an exchange of artifacts—was established between those beings and Earth? What if the atmosphere of their world was mostly hydrogen and methane, while much of the snow underfoot was frozen oxygen? What if, though their technology was advanced in another mode, fire was unknown to them in their super-cold environment, though they were curious about it? What if an Earthman, in control of the teleportation equipment, as a friendly gesture, though not thinking quite straight, teleported to them *a lighted candle?*...That was "The World Wreaker."

"The Wand of Creation" was about what the title implies: the riddle of how the spark of life first got started on Earth. That was long before the concept of "primordial soups," generated by lightning flashing through an atmosphere of methane, ammonia, carbon dioxide, and water vapor, and containing DNA and RNA, took hold among biologists. Instead, I visualized a transient catalytic agent, a mineral, still existing deep in the Earth's crust. My explorer had a vehicle with a great, high-speed drill at its front end, in which he bored his way downward and found the stuff.

In "The Machine from Ganymede" the human plans for a new and terrible weapon were mysteriously stolen by a small, weird robot-device from outer space! Everybody was scared, fearing that strange entities would be using the weapon against Earth. But, as the plot twist, there was some relief, when, through telescopes, tiny streaks of yellow light were seen flashing in the vicinity of Jupiter. The color identified the weapon—being used to win a local war among Jupiter's numerous satellites! Here were huge and violent events only hinted at across enormous distance! What was it all about? What kind of bizarre beings were involved? And would they next attack Earth?...On the theory that to reveal mysteries entirely is to destroy their appeal and dramatic effect, I gave no answers.

50

I got this far in my renewed burst of writing, before I reread "Old Faithful." I had thought it too much my own thing—too out-of-formula for any editor. But when I mentioned the word "formula" in a letter to Tremaine, he came back at me swiftly with a terse note to the effect that, in *Astounding*'s new thought-variant policy, he wasn't interested in formula stories. This was a good, guiding comment, characteristic of Tremaine. So I thought—what the heck!—I'll show him "Old Faithful."

Several weeks passed—no problem, no answer yet. Then, from an extraneous source, a fan, Julius Schwartz, later to become my agent, with whom I was in contact by mail, I got the word: Desmond Hall, Tremaine's assistant, had said that "Old Faithful" was very much liked....I had a nice check very soon after....

And when it was published, it *did* make quite a hit, judging from readers' letters in *Astounding*'s "Brass Tacks" department.

Here, at this late date, shall I pause to speculate just why? People academically interested in the history of science fiction have applied agreeable terms to it, such as "a milestone story." The advance commonly pointed out was a new approach to aliens. Old Faithful himself was a monster physically, by human standards, totally unlike us outwardly. I was intentionally quite vague in describing his appearance; I gave only rather spooky hints. *But I let myself—and other folks—see inside him.* Though he wasn't strictly a benevolent creature, *he dreamed, he wanted, he struggled and tried*—as we do. Therein, I think, was the novel sympathy that readers felt toward him, as I had felt for him myself. That he wasn't just a horrible enemy bent on conquering the Earth, as so many aliens before him had been, was rather new, too; but this, I think, was more or less incidental to his main impact.

Besides, my yarn about him touched on what I believe is a big, instinctive, and maybe rather terrifying question and curiosity in the minds of many of us terrans: *what will those first other-world entities that we ever meet be like, and how will the meeting go?*

H. G. Wells' *War of the Worlds* was an effective, realistic, convincing, *first encounter* story. And perhaps "Old Faithful" was another. First encounters fascinate me. I've done quite a few yarns of that kind. The recent novel by Carl Sagan, *Contact*, tends to prove what I've just hinted: that the subject of first encounters can draw a lot of instinctive public attention.

IX.

A POISED INTERVAL

Things were looking a lot better for me in 1934. No, my way of life didn't change so much outwardly. I still worked at the cannery, during the pea-season, and was on call to label and pack up shipments now and then during the rest of the year. And there were other odd jobs. I like the sweaty relief of physical labor, and I remained a country type of young fella, not visibly very different from any other, except that I grinned genially a lot more than I used to, though I didn't usually explain why. Blending in, I kidded and joked around some on a job, like anybody else.

Generally, I kept my science fiction magazines out of sight of other folks. In a small, Midwestern city of then, those vivid covers could incite some disapproving glances. Though SF was the center of my existence, I was secretive and somewhat embarrassed about this. Yet even while I toiled at something else I was busy stewing up yarns to write out as soon as I could: "Mind Over Matter," "Telepathic Piracy," "N'goc," "The Son of Old Faithful...."

I was pretty much a private person. I had never met any real science fiction fans—much less any writers. Somehow, I never even sent any letters to "Brass Tacks." I guess I figured I should leave doing that to the readers. My part was to write yarns that ought to be able to speak for themselves. Though, of course, I read the letters. Some of those were very perceptive. But there was a kind often seen that typically began something like this:

Dear Editor:

Though I am only eleven years old, I have been reading science fiction for more than a year....

Then there was the matter of opinions about various stories by certain scribes. Some judgments were nicely, calmly balanced, citing pro and con factors. But then there was a class of correspondent that went always for superlatives:

...Though I know you won't dare print my letter, such-and-such (story) by that so-and-so (writer) reeks! It makes me want to vomit!...

*Such-and-such (story) is wonderful!   A work of sheer ge-
nius!...*

Yeh—raw youngness, boasting proudly of its youth, and shouting to make
its presence and opinions plain. In such words there were shadows of myself, as I
had been, and perhaps basically, still was, though with a smoother surface. So tolerance, tolerance....Let them grow....

Of course I looked through these letters for approval of my stuff, and I
found enough of it to make a reasonable balance. Still, I knew I'd better take even
the best of it with a grain of salt. I'd have to keep figuring out, and writing, stories
as well as I could, or I'd slip backward and lose. Every script submittal was a gamble—another separate contest against a lot of competition....

No—I hadn't met any of the other scribes; nor did I yet write to any of
them; I wouldn't have known quite what to say, but I was surely aware of their existence, and proud in my separate, loner's way, that I was one of them. Besides the
others that I have mentioned before, there was Stanley G. Weinbaum, with deep,
human feeling in his stories, and Jack Williamson, who wrote both long space
epics, and fine, sober pieces of lesser length, with philosophical overtones. I can
quote, verbatim, the beginning of one early short story of his, to this day, though I
have forgotten its title:

*The difference between a fool and a genius can be stated in
one word—success. And success had not found Gideon Clew....*

Then there was Frank K. Kelly—maybe the brightest of us and the most
gifted, who produced a swift spate of excellent, very human, almost lyrical novelettes, and then vanished, I expect to what he considered better things. Among his
various activities, I've heard that he was later a speech-writer for Harry S Tru-
man....

Then John Russell Fearn, of Blackpool, England who produced a string of
fast-action novelettes. I believe he has been dead for years.

And John W. Campbell, Jr.—then still only a writer, but of sweeping,
cosmic scope—together with his more literary alter-ego, Don A. Stuart....

Enough for now. There were others of equal ability. But as of right now,
these are the ones who come to mind first....

I felt that it was a very good group to belong to, even in my remoteness
from the other members.

We were writing science fiction contemporaneously, which to some will
mean that we belonged to the same school. Looking back from now, I'd say that
our unity was even stronger than that—as if, all together, though separately, we
were on some big, subliminal research and development project.

I shouldn't hurry in explaining this, because I believe that I'm coming up
on a historical truth of considerable importance, and I should approach it carefully,
so that I can make it clear. So let me step back—and away—from my point for a
bit.

You see, the years, 1934 through 1937, were of particular significance and mood to me. It was a *poised interval*; I was at last doing what I most wanted to do. And I was still in my original environment, with all its—to me—defects and advantages, the latter including close contact with woods, earth, and sky, and I was getting ready to bust out—leave, fledge myself. It was hardly an unhappy time for me, but there were shreds of tension and regret mixed in with the heady excitement and purpose.

Beyond just myself—far more broadly—those 1930s were a special interval. Science was getting a better and better hold on understanding the universe, and everything that was in it. And there was a rising ground swell of popular speculation, almost-beliefs, denials, arguments—but anyhow interest. The Great Depression was supposed to be ending, so wasn't an onward surging a necessary part of that? Why, there might even be television before many more years!

Less than a decade before, in 1926, Hugo Gernsback had boosted an old romanticism, that had been quietly endemic for a long time, maybe for ages, and reaching into the future and out toward the stars, he had brought out his *Amazing Stories*. Of course, Jules Verne, H. G. Wells, and Edgar Rice Burroughs, and even Farnsworth Wright, editor of *Weird Tales*, were somewhat ahead of him. But maybe he had sensed a heightened interest, and a potential for much more, in the populace. And now all this was taking a stronger hold.

Imaginative persons, older writers, new ones like myself, and still up-and-coming aspirants, had the luck, whether for good or bad, to be caught in the same timely flow. From our separate views of the same burgeoning outlook in the same world, we did what we were inclined to do—and in almost inadvertent unison. Our primary purpose, I suppose, was to make some extra bucks on which to live. We were the visionaries, the what-if'ers, the glamorizing pointers-out of what just might be—even when it was impossible. And when we wrote about even that, we posed a special challenge—because what can be more thrillingly achieving than to accomplish the impossible?

As I see the situation now, there was considerable fertile ground for the seed of our speculations and imaginings to fall on, and we were part of that ground, and of the amount of seed that was already in it. So, complicating and mixing my present use of metaphors further, what came first: the chicken or the egg? I expect there was feedback and strengthening re-feedback—a kind of heterodyning action. As seed, we developed and multiplied more seed, and more growth.

To begin with, there was a small but sufficient scattering of interest in space, other planets, the whole universe, and the dimly perceived future of the Earth, out there among the population, to viably and vigorously sustain science fiction magazines, if what they presented was attractive enough to fill a need. Their circulation would not be large, but it could expand....

Without these pre-conditions, mostly outside ourselves, we would not have amounted to much as science fiction writers; we would have needed to find bodily sustenance in some other, more ordinary way.

But we were given this chance, and we dived into it with enthusiasm; employment opportunities in other areas were still not very good anyhow, and I suspect that the glimpse of a lighted chink in the lingering gray wall of the Great Depression put a new gleam in our eyes, and exuberantly released our pent-up and frustrated energies. At least this was so with me.

I've suggested that, largely without realizing it, we were engaged in a loosely linked research and development program. For starters, we had to grope our way, and produce almost a new kind of story-presentation, and, in effect, a new literary form, in conformity with necessary, but often experimental magazine policies, trying to hold, and to capture more of, an audience, giving it what it wanted. What we turned out wasn't usually "literature" in the standard, accepted sense. Mostly, it couldn't be that; the people we wrote for wouldn't have cared much for such refinements; their focus was on magnificent Maybes to flesh out and give vision-substance to their optimistic, imaginative capacities, even while we fleshed out our own. To that extent, we were they, and they were we—intermingling parts of the same forward surge.

The opening lines of our yarns had to be quickly attention-grabbing, with the intriging point of the particular story well in mind. Movement and idea-development should be as terse and clear as possible, and there was emphasis on exciting, suspenseful action. With so many notions that were entirely new to explain intelligently to an audience not yet so well attuned to such newness, that was hard to do, without slowing the plot-movement too much. Especially was this so in shorter stories. But we had to find a way, or at least do the best we could. And, at best, there should be a surprise-twist ending, to emphasize our yarn's meaning.

If we borrowed from "pulp" Western magazines—bar-fights, not among good-guy and bad-guy groups of cattlemen and their cow-hands, but among various mixed or separate bands of Earthlings and exotic far-planet beings, that was temporarily all right; for we were writing for pulp magazines, too; besides, it was a perhaps necessary link with the familiar.

And, by reading each other's stories, we leaned on, and borrowed from, each other, in no plagiaristic sense, even while we competed to have our stuff chosen for publication, according to the best judgment of our editors—who might be right or wrong. And we furthered the evolution—*revolution*, rather!—of a whole new set of language-terms, along with our promotion of a widening, general, human awareness, beyond what was known of, and commonly accepted as normal and stable in our humdrum, everyday world:

Space ship. Space suit. Atomic energy. Moon rockets. Relativity. Time travel. Wonder drugs. Robots. Robot brains. Other-worldly beings. Off-Earth settlements. Faster-than-light travel....

And our stories—our dreams crystallized to that extent so that they could be shared with others—were going out among the people. They were touching quite a few thousand minds, most of them young and developing, and at least subliminally searching for what they might do with—and during—the lives that were ahead of them.

Having come this far, I am already deep into the major point I have been trying to make. There will be no message in this book about me—or about science fiction—that will be more important than the one that I am about to write down right now:

> *Science fiction has been a subtle yet dynamic force in recent history. It took hold of a human drive that had already begun, and it reinforced it significantly. It reached those youngsters who would grow up to be actively and creatively involved in the developments of the Space Age...electronics, computers, nuclear physics, advances in medicine, and many other areas. If it did not touch all of them directly, it was nevertheless near them as a suggestive, ambient presence. It helped give them a mind-set and aimed them toward what might be possible and what they might study, learn, and do. For the good that was in it, and whatever bad....*

In making the above statement, I could have a selfish motive, and to a certain extent I must admit that I do: if my life is to have some meaning beyond the mere personal, in which I have done well enough not to feel deprived, my involvement with science fiction will have to carry much of the load.

However, in a detached way, I remain convinced that my statement is correct. Can I prove it? Well—I can try.

I have not attempted to collect any firm statistics about how many well-known scientists read, or have read, science fiction. I'm not temperamentally inclined toward the gathering of such tabular data. Yet I have heard that Wernher von Braun, the top man in our Apollo project to land men on the moon, had *Astounding Science Fiction* sent to him from an enemy country, by round-about means, even while he was working on the *Vergeltungswaffen Eins und Zwei*—V1 and V2—on Penemunde, that island experiment station, just off the Baltic coast of Nazi Germany. Other, similar background hints about other specialists aren't too hard to find.

But back to the mass of the science fiction readership of the 1930s, as represented, for instance and in small part, by the readers' letters appearing in *Astounding*'s "Brass Tacks": quite a few of them later achieved considerable, tangible prominence, either as writers themselves, and thus as direct influencers of many other persons, or as lecturers too, by which they could add a like educating effect. Some of these also have taken part in actual research. And there surely must be others, perhaps sometimes even more effective, though less-known.

More about these letter writers: they were bright, alert kids; many of them could spot a scientific error that some dumb writer made, a light year off! Certainly they didn't all sink into dull conformity to old attitudes as they matured! They couldn't have left their science fiction years entirely behind!

Further, there is some doubt that the letter writers were fully representative of the science fiction readership. Some people like to write letters to magazines; some don't. Which, in self defense, too, I must remark doesn't necessarily make the letter-type stupid or insensitive to exciting notions about what expanded human

56

range in knowledge and know-how should, and probably ought to be, in the future, or to help its development along actively, if given half a chance. I didn't write to the letter columns, either. Though I lack statistics beyond quite a number of individual cases that most anybody can find among his own acquaintances, I have a strong gut-feeling that those silent ones often took part in building our present era.

Yes—there are hazards and regrets. But, on balance, I feel what has happened is good. You don't stop time, or the events that move in it, not so very much in our control, either individually or collectively. It seems we are in a dangerous interim period that has to be gotten past by further forward movement till we reach a more stable plateau, where, hopefully, more problems and needs and yearnings are answered, and there is less threat to our survival. No—I don't too seriously expect an absolutely safe society; anyhow, there has never been one yet....But when a certain number of us move off our crowded Earth, and across space? Maybe then?...Anyhow, I personally find it a very exciting prospect, though I expect considerable disagreement. What are the things we want? What are they even? Freedom, security, simplicity? Better understanding of the universe, and our relationship to it? Or just sex and love and raising families? Somewhere I get lost in all this. But the years and the shifts and changes go on....

* * * * * * *

About us writers of the 1930s again: I don't think we were very aware of our historical significance, as I've stated it a few paragraphs back. I wasn't, anyhow. My conclusions in this are quite recent. Those decades ago, our main object was to feed our insides, and we had a way of doing it that also pleased us—stewing up and feeding ideas and idea-promptings to an eager audience. We might have done other work, more tangible of solid results; some of us managed to do some of that as well. But, for instance, an engineer needed a solid, material, and hence costly base for any job he might get, in order for it to *exist*—to say nothing of being meaningful. And such solidity remained in quite short supply. However, ideas and speculations were the spark even of wonders; they were the intangible, and hence the cheapest, component; and we tried to make them plentiful.

I might possibly have become a physician; I had an interest in living organisms, and, I believe, enough warmth and good will for something better than just a soothing, bedside manner. But what drive in that direction that I had had, still had wavered....And, as for becoming a scientist of any sort, I had known that I lacked the stable persistence to follow through with any particular research; my wits jumped around from this to something else entirely too much. So—no loss to feel there either.

Maybe most of us science fiction writers of my generation were like that; our field was in the presentation of inspirational patterns—others more practical would have to work out the rest. But we played our important part, conscientiously, as later arrivals do now.

Before I go on further, there is something more I should say about our audience. Though I had never yet been face to face with any science fiction fans, I now have a pretty good conception of how they compare and contrast with their present-day counterparts. In a small way, some of them were beginning to organize into groups; but the big science fiction cons, at which "social togetherness" is emphasized, were things yet to come. Perforce the fans were individualists, drawn to science fiction by what it could give them directly, to satisfy a craving that they had for thrilling and romantic adventures, and—yes—intellectual growth too—in a vastly expanded scene, as yet reachable only in vicarious form. To this extent they were lonely purists, more selectively distilled from the general population. They were what they were, and, make no mistake, by their own volition. Persons only very casually interested would soon drop away, bored. For the fans the yet-unknowns seemed near, with *wonder* the keynote.

Big modern cons have their merits, and they can be a lot of fun, from what I've seen of them within the last few years. Present at them are very bright youngsters, very aware of all aspects of space, computer, and other technologies, and of pending possibilities. Many also have a truly astonishing knowledge of old and new stories of both science fiction and fantasy. In short there is a lot of potential for active participation in future ventures among them. Yes—these are far ahead of their forerunners of about fifty years ago, and they are not easily impressed by anything. A loss?...I don't know. Maybe not. *Wonder*—the word that Gernsback pushed forward into a receptive time has lost its punch now; it sounds naive. Because anything was possible.

There is another thing about the cons: many others who attend them appear to be there only for the socializing, the excuse to get together, follow their friends, escape the bugbear of loneliness, and having nothing much else to do. Their interest in, and awareness about, the subject to which the con is supposedly dedicated seems slight. Ask some of these pilgrims to name books they've read, or even looked at, recently, and you draw a blank....Well—to each his own arcane quest.

X.

YARN SEEDS

My final four years in Beaver Dam, terminating just after Christmas, 1937, were, in many ways, the most concentrated of my lifetime. From their beginning, I knew I was going to pull out before long. I felt a constant eager, background excitement in this; I was getting ready for the Big Outer World; there was a tension, and a chilly touch of sadness; yet I can't say that I was unhappy.

Let me coin a phrase. Since wise folks who discuss and write about these matters, seem to like, and require, labels, let's call that time my "Crystal Interlude." Crystal for clarity, and focus, and singleness of aim as far as my outer physical intentions went; no disruptive confusion there; I could shove aside the small, tweaky, frosty doubts; they were slight; that matter was settled, untroubling—a closed book. Thus my mind and nervous system were set free for concentration on the other purpose that was important to me. And the clarity extended to that, as well.

Those years have turned out to be my most active, and productive of ideas, as far as science fiction is concerned.

Nothing changed much, superficially, in the life style of us Galluns. We all knew that it was getting to time to break an arrangement up. The odd old house was no longer much good for any of us. It had been a shelter that had isolated us somewhat from the movement of living. A shabby, decaying place, with, somehow, a protective, in some respects debilitating, cotton-wool atmosphere. But now ma was dead. Sis and I were well-grown. The Depression was gradually fading. Pa, though past sixty, remained vigorous; besides, he had always belonged to outer things. He liked the ladies; they liked him, too.

We still kept the old dwelling neat; we painted the rooms now and then; we patched the leaky roof tentatively, but attempted no extensive repairs of the structure itself. That would have been almost hopeless. The leaky roof bugged me most. Remembering all the toil that it entails, I've had an aversion for house-ownership ever since.

Mostly, I kept on with my usual cannery jobs, in season, and on scattered days, off-season. As for my writing, when the weather was comfortable—neither too hot nor too cold—I had my work table in our bare-raftered upstairs, next to my bed, and in front of the rough shelves I had rigged for my reference books, my favorite tomes about Egyptology, and my more casually piled science fiction mags—what a small fortune in collectors' items were destroyed, when somebody presumably at last threw them out—though who knew, then?...In the bitter winters, I would set up my typewriter on the table in our front room next to the bay window, before which was a bench with our house plants—most of them ma's surviving geraniums. In the far corner our Round Oak heater was there to be stoked with coal and/or wood, in accordance with how cold and windy the weather was. And I'd be sitting on the piano stool—if I got a bit stuck about phrasing a thought, I could swing around on the stool, and pingle out the few notes that I knew, on the old piano which was just behind me—this, while I cleared up the minor problem....In high-summer when the temperature could go to well over a hundred degrees F., I could move my gear out onto our sagging front porch; though, more usually, then, I'd be sweating and toiling vigorously at the cannery. This was my refreshing counterpoise of physical effort.

****

So now I come to a cluster of many questions that any scribe always gets asked: where did I get my ideas? How did I shape them into workable story plots? How did I go at my work? Was it hard or easy? Did I need a lot of scientific information? Did I try to improve my writing style? What do I believe was the overall objective and significance of my work?...The list of queries could go on and on, getting more obscure and esoteric all the way.

I can't succeed fully, but I'll make an attempt at some answers:

About ideas. In the mid-1930s, science fiction was still pretty new—it was a just-after-dawn sort of thing. Many ideas that would be called "old hat" today hadn't even been touched. To that extent, the field was wide open—not like now when you think you've got something original and exciting, only to discover sorrowfully that it has been worked over again and again; so your only chance is to give what is old a fresh slant....However, remember: those "old-hat" ideas still had to be *found* back then, well *before* the term could be applied to them, because they were often scarcely thought of, earlier.

But we writers *did* have an advantage, there; we were digging into an almost fresh lode of possibilities.

Another circumstance that favored us was that there were not too many of us, so the competition was less extensive. We were a second wave of ground breakers—still pioneers. History had been on our side; we had showed up at just the right time! Also, *wonder* was on us, and I suppose we were inspired; anyway, I thought so.

A ways back in this book, I told how "Old Faithful" came to be dreamed up and written. Though the individual cases of various yarns differ, that is a fair example of how the process goes—from idea-conception through to completion—even though that was a particularly special instance. Yet every yarn, if it is any good, has to be somehow special and unique.

Looking eagerly for ideas, I kept roaming around in my dream-universe, where my explorations had begun long before. It had contacts with actualities: the woods, where I had been so often that I could smell it, and feel its shadows, without needing to go there anymore—though I still did. It had become almost part of me. So had the feeling of plowed fields under my shoes. And from looking at them so frequently on clear nights in all seasons, it seemed to me that the major constellations were etched in pale sparks of starlight, on the inner curve of my skull. Up there in the northern sky, Ursa Major and Ursa Minor, including, respectively, the Big and Little Dippers, with Polaris, the Pole Star on which the firmament rotated, placed just at the end of the Little Dipper's handle. The white dots of Draco, the Dragon or Serpent, looping around, and almost intertwining with, the Major and Minor Bears. Usually off to the left when I had looked, Boötes, the Hunter with ruddy Arcuturus its brightest gleam....And a little to the right, the slightly lopsided letter W that was Casseopia. To the south in the winter would be Orion, with the Dog Star, Sirius, brightest of all, close at his undefined hand. In the summer, low down near the southern horizon would be the constellation, Scorpio, featuring the star, Antares, the Red Giant. Silvery Jupiter would be close above the Scorpion....Mars, my favorite Other Planet, when it was visible, would rise out of the east, and move on, quite high up. Looking west into the evening, brightly, enigmatically evident, would often be Venus, close to the crescent moon. And just once or twice, low down in the horizon haze, I think I saw the most elusive of all the naked-eye-visible planets, Mercury, the sun-hugger. Clearly, Saturn could be nearly as hard to find.

Ah, yes—what could be seen in the sky constituted the most prominent reality on which the nebulous region of fact and imagination which I explored for story-seeds was based. Looking up into it, I could sense the truth of the roundness of the Earth, and almost perceive the invisible curved line of its path, called the ecliptic, across the blue evening. But there had to be other tangibles than the skyview alone on which to anchor the mental and emotional simulacra of the universe in which I searched. The mounding of the hills, for instance, were the marks of geological time, the coming and going of glaciers ages ago....Much farther back, there had been other, even more fantastic things. On the ground where I walked every day, had Triceratops and Tyrannosaurus also trod?...This was only one of my speculative wonderings....How about time in the other direction—a hundred, a thousand, a million or a billion years ahead?...And these were only random splinters of possible speculation, and of trying to imagine close and vivid detail, that had at least a semblance of convincing fact—founded on facts as far as they were yet determined.

Yes—if you want to write science fiction, it helps to have the facts pertinent to your story, straight, especially in the area of the physical sciences—and chemistry, atomic structure, astronomy, biology, electronics, nucleonics, and a lot of other fields, areas, and sub-areas. It is good to have a broad fund of information built up in your head; and it isn't a bad habit to recheck. Even now I'm wondering, if in this writing, somewhere, I haven't made a minor booboo which some alert eye will spot, and then aim gleeful claws for a pounce? Anyhow, it used to be that way. Though maybe—I'm not sure that this is entirely good—knowledgeable readers about science-fictional subjects have become more tolerant, and would regard such action as petty?

Stories linked with the social sciences, which are less specific, shouldn't be so tightly bound to facts, though I wouldn't bet on it! Suppose you get some real, historical character of reference-importance in your yarn misplaced in time by a century, and without intentionally meaning to? Ah, well—perhaps all that would result would be another interesting socio-political argument, which seems an ubiquitous hallmark of that field....

Hey—I have a sudden story inspiration! And please note what sort of preceding thought-process it sprang out of: how about bringing, let's see, Abraham Lincoln back, and into our present era? What would he think, or do, about it? I suspect he'd be rather befuddled for a while. How about you, me, or somebody else who knows the ropes, acting as his re-orienting guide, instructor, and protector during his first awful day? Down to the corner, across a busy, trafficky street, into just an ordinary car?...Ah, nuts!—this sounds half good, but doubtless it has been worked over in numerous variant forms before. Still, is there anybody around who wants to try giving it a fresh slant? If so, go ahead....

Wups!—I've slipped a little. I'd better get back on the track I was following: to show *seriously* how, in the 1930s, I hunted down and developed yarn seeds inside a hazy, internal mock-up of a totality of my experience, cluttered with a hodgepodge of all the images, information bits, and impressions that it had gathered. It was an enormous but dimensionless ambience for my wandering, pleasurable quests. It had no appreciable size at all, nor any actual solidity or mass, and its only boundaries were my faulty conceptions of the infinities of time and space.

Let me demonstrate somewhat better how it worked for me—though I'd hardly be so unreasonable as to attempt this for all of my stories. Still—an example:

I'll begin with that silent, yearning, inside appeal of mine, that I could feel strongly at various moments when my attention got itself drawn in any of a variety of directions, to any of a variety of things. It was the initial driving pulse of many of my yarns.

In the case I have now selected, the direction was up into the northern sky, at, I suppose, about ten o'clock on a crisp autumn night. There was a *real* occurrence, though nothing that I hadn't seen the equivalent of often before. But this time it somehow got hold of me harder than usual. There was a sudden dash of greenish, silvery light, almost as long as the Big Dipper. It was absolutely soundless, and I doubt that it lasted for more than a tenth of a second. It was an ordinary meteor-fall, and almost instantaneously it disintegrated into the atmosphere. I'm not sure what special trifle about it got to me with such emphasis. For a moment it left the faintest luminous trail; then there was nothing left with me but the mental image, including the impression of tremendous speed, quickly come and gone, without raising the tiniest whisper. Maybe that was it. Yet a real space ship would have to move that fast, and in airless, soundless space, it would have to be that soundless, too. But there were no spaceships originating from Earth yet, so if any existed, they would have to be from somewhere else.

Of course I was very sure that what I had seen was only a meteor, not a spacecraft—and probably a very small meteor. Yet that recurrent yearning of mine started up in me....All that tremendous velocity, all that inconceivable distance that meteor—meteoroid, more properly—must have travelled, for how many ages! And where had it been—come from?...What if something little like that meteoroid, adrift in space like it had been, wasn't a meteoroid, but something else?

It was then that the familiar appeal truly surged up in me. It became a demand, almost a muted curse or howl; maybe I even muttered it aloud that time. Sort of like this:

Cripes! What all is up there—Out There?...

Yes—if you wanted to grab at the endless unknowns of the stars and the universe, and ease your yearning by filling a few of them in with some believable, imaginary semblance of Reality for yourself—but then to write it all down so that others might share your answer—it helped to be rather passionate about your subject, back in those days of SF pioneering!

Maybe this is still true now, in the 1990s. It seems to me that story writers of any kind have to have an acquaintance with—and hence a capacity for—a wide range of strong emotions, so they can portray and *live* them where they are a necessary part of the yarn. This doesn't mean that they dare be constantly flighty types, since to accomplish anything, their strong feelings must be under cool control. But I suspect that overly bland personalities, only mildly interested in their subject, and working at it casually in a rather forced fashion, shouldn't bother trying to be authors. They wouldn't make it.

I couldn't instantly do much that was constructive with that meteor streak. But the picture of its light and motion lodged in the cluttered region where I collected such stuff. And my fascination with it kept right on. In that instance, I didn't need any will power; the memory had a compulsion of its own for me. And so I mulled and groped, as perhaps only some nut like myself would do. What small objects, like, but different from, meteoroids, *might possibly* have been drifting out there for ages? Very sparsely mixed in, of course—each unique object in the ratio of less than one sand grain contrasted with all the sand and dust grains of all the beaches and deserts on Earth!

But what might the thing be? Sure, the answer, there, was quick: a marvelous device, lost or thrown away by space-roving entities of far-advanced know-how!

Too automatic, simple, and crude a response for so bewildering and enormous a question? Well, maybe. But my limited terran imagination couldn't reach much farther. So I was stuck with it. Let it be.

Next question. *What sort of marvelous device?* Again I hesitated, wanting the best reply, and afraid I couldn't make it good enough....Let the problem slide till later, and go on.

Here was another automatic simplicity: for human contact, somebody had to find the artifact. In this, for realism, I'd better stick with what I knew best. Nobody I was acquainted with could fly into space and get it. So it had to fall to the ground, without being damaged too much. Then it had to catch somebody's eye.

Naturally, and best for me, a young man of the country, rather like myself, would be the person. He could spot the object while crossing a field, much as he might spot a plowed-up Indian arrowhead.

What would the thing look like, since it had to have form and aspect? Well—stay with simplicities for the present. Of a strange metal. Rectangular. A bit fused at the edges from that meteoric fall through the atmosphere. An enigma and a marvel in itself.

But now, what deeper marvel? What was the artifact for? What startling thing of advanced science could it accomplish?...Blow up the world?...Nah— nothing that corny!...So then—what?...

The minute after the discovery, act it through in your mind, and see if anything turns up:

The guy is really wondering, and trying to find out! It is his immediate story's suspense problem. He keeps looking the thing over....Nothing....Maybe he'll have to try to cut into it—but that might ruin its mysterious vitals! Take it to qualified experts, then let them check it out....Maybe....But that would take time. Besides, as finder, he is keeper!

As for myself, I didn't want to slow the story's action all that much. Something remarkable should happen right away! So I play-acted onward a little farther:

The guy holds the artifact to his ear, like anybody might do to a found-watch, shaking it a little, to see if it will tick.

Still nothing came to me that I felt like using.

So still holding the artifact to his head, the guy looks around him. He's a loner. The only other presence that is likely to be with him is his dog; and the pooch is wondering what is going on. Well, perhaps here is a usable, sympathetic point of contact.

The guy begins to get visual, sonic, and thought impressions from his dog. So the thing is a telepathic mind-reading device!

Okay—that should be good enough for a story. One trouble, though, was that you can go an awful lot of different ways with such an apparatus, and in a shortish yarn at least, I'd best hold to one straight, not too complicated line of approach, to avoid a dull bogging down.

So I had to rummage around further in the place where all I had learned and experienced was stored.

The guy would go back to his house. There he would check to see how well the telepathic probe worked. A little guiltily he would find that he could not only read his neighbors' minds, but feel their emotions. The mark of the Great Depression lingered with me as an influence: anger, frustration, need, want....So powerfully did the guy feel these emotions coming to him from not only his neighbors, but from all over the country and the world, that he was naturally forced into trying to do as much as he could to help—though his means were very small.

So he had this intense motivation. *But how could he implement it?* Again, a simple, easily obvious answer. He could, of course, read the brains of the knowing and powerful. Being what he was, new inventions, before they could be patented, would be the things he stole. He would become a Robin Hood of the mind, thus obtaining money to support his altruisms.

But with so much want in the world, *how could anything be enough?* The need was bottomless. Besides, he was getting the waves of such a mass of selfishness among so many.

What to do then?

Take over the world—command it—straighten it out, of course! What other way was there? Still, he hated the thought.

How to become world-dictator?

With a mighty weapon. Based on yet-untapped atomic energy—the most powerful source!

Where to steal its secret?

From beings who already knew it—if the telepathic probe could reach so far?

It could, just barely....So presently the basically gentle, well-intentioned little guy had his super-weapon—swiped from an old alien culture that lived deep in the moon; nobody knew yet that such a circumstance was highly improbable....So the guy built a small, nuclear-powered ship, in which he could fly above all the navies and armies on Earth and destroy them. He won the first battle, and should easily be able to win the few more it would take.

Yes—but *so what?* Somehow, the plot was slipping toward a meandering, blurry extension full of complicated involvements and explanations, not much of it making definite sense....

You know how a story, particularly a fairly short one, is supposed to go, according to the classical pattern:

There is a locale, and a chief character who has a problem which he attempts to solve. But his efforts get him deeper and deeper into more problems and tries at resolving them, until, in the rising tension of suspense—so necessary to sustaining readers' attention if your yarn is going to be successful—he is truly in a jam! Then he makes a last, hopeful play, to win or lose. Here is the toss-up, the crisis! Then the climax—the solution—in its best form, a turn-around, a "twist," a surprise-punch, with some plausible, satisfying meaning.

Those damnable twists! They can be hard to find, and you can't force them; to be believable, they have to come out naturally. And if you're going to use such a twist as your ending, you'd better have it in mind right from the first line of your finished script!

Here I had a plot that went along, and quite easily through, all the phases of locale, character, problem, and successive tries at solution, down to that last element, and there it got stuck! I might have to recast the whole thing in some other form!

But I didn't want to. It felt right, as far as it had gone.

So back once more to that inner place of cluttered records to make a further search. What else might there be about a thought-and-emotion probe? Relax and just sort of drift with it, without trying. Float, and get it all, in a kind of sideways, all-around-ways visualization, nothing missed or neglected. Take a little time; if this is thinking at all, it's *divergent* rather than the usual, *convergent*—answer-seeking—thought.

Emotions....The guy had read happiness in the minds of some of the folks he had helped, even though he hadn't let anybody know from whom his assistance had come. And getting that feedback of happiness, and even un-aimed gratitude, had made him rather happy too, in spite of the short-fall of his efforts against need. Folks in general were pretty good, though less than perfect....But some of them were real bastards....Gentle feelings were supportive, soothing....Healing.... Good....Still, there were other emotions....Rage....Hatred....Also transmittable.... Opposite in effect?...

And there it was—the twist I sought....The wry turn-around, the surprise-jolt, to stir up consideration of a human puzzle, evoking opinions and arguments maybe never quite to be settled, even in some distant, future time, when there was contact with such know-how. The little guy who had found the mind-probe, had always meant quite well...unless he had become corrupted by a human paradox?...

Sure—he won that first battle of a struggle which was meant to fix every-thing. But thousands of service personnel had died....

Right away he raised the telepathic-probe—the accidental gift from the stars—to his head, to find out what the public reaction was. He got no benevolence or thanks. Instead a massive wave of fury and hatred from millions of minds slammed into his brain, killing him instantly. The probe itself became useless, burnt out by the overload.

So this is my demonstration piece of how I cooked up science fiction sto-ries, half a century ago. The method isn't fully applicable to all of my stories of then, of course; but it sort of show how the process went.

That story was "Telepathic Piracy." Checking the record, I see that *Astounding* published it in the March 1935 issue.

Another yarn of the "twist" kind preceded it there in January 1935: "Mind Over Matter." A spaceman's brain is put into a robot-body because the rest of him has been destroyed in an accident. He finds the change horrible and inhuman, so the salvage is a failure. Until his desperate and regretful friend, the surgeon, intro-duces a combination of "adrenalin and something else" into the isolated brain's blood-supply. Immediately the spaceman's mood brightens, reverses itself. He ap-preciates the strength, and the resistance to the harshest of conditions, of his new form, in which he can go almost anywhere. And the stars "beckon like the call of home."

What was I suggesting? The ruggedness and adaptability of the human mind and spirit? Hormonal psychotherapy, scarcely started when the yarn was written? That humans, if they can maintain an adventurous outlook which will incorporate their natural drive to expand as far as they can go, while they employ whatever extra means they can discover or devise, are able to venture anywhere? That, besides the Earth, some of the universe is also their home?...

When I reread a few of my old stories, which I may not have looked at for decades, they *can* seem somewhat quaint—yes. Period pieces. But I have another, sharper impression: that they were written by somebody other than me. Which, when you think about it, has to be so, in a way, of course: time works on us all; even our selves change. I've heard other scribes mention this phenomenon about their early writings.

Back there in the 1930s, we science fiction scribblers kept projecting our notions and suggestions about the possible human future in space—and about cosmology, time-travel, and (who can list everything else?) out to our (I hoped) expanding audience, through our published stories. We might not have been very aware of it, but surely we must have been a force that helped *pull* the present era into being—regardless of the varying and often opposed opinions of the results, nowadays. Even where our ideas were wildly inaccurate, still they must have stirred up thought and discussion toward intent and purpose. I believe we helped broaden and popularize an outlook toward what was on the way, even among people who never read any of our stuff, preparing them to accept the newness. At least, they began to hear of science fiction and the crazy notions it put forth—with the promise that some would come true.

Sometimes I wrote quite easily. Yarns such as "Telepathic Piracy" and "Mind Over Matter," thoroughly figured out in advance, were finished almost first-draft on the typewriter, with few corrections necessary, if I remember correctly. I did, however, pick my way slowly, to get the phrasing just right and in place.

"N'goc"—a weird name for a weird notion of how spiders first arrived on Earth from a tiny natural moon that was about to fall from its low orbit—was finished first draft, too, since its plot structure was complete from the beginning....Little, intelligent *spiders*, though?...Ah, well—why not!...And this small yarn had some points which become more interesting because of parallel events that are quite recent: tiny Earth-satellite—though a natural one—worrisome to primitive Earthmen because it is about to fall? And how the spiders, even with their primitive technology and slight resources, were able to achieve space travel and descend to Earth, propelling their vehicle with only a trivial charge of black gunpowder, because the gravity of—and hence the escape-velocity from—their world was so insignificant....Descending through Earth's atmosphere on a parachute of spider-silk, the voyagers *did* avoid extinction in the fiery crash. Still, they were losers. Primitive men had always feared the little, wobbly moon, for which their name was the title of the story. They killed most of the spider-folk as they landed. Those who escaped forgot their science, and regressed in the terrestrial wilderness. "N'goc" was in the May 1935 *Astounding*.

In the next issue was "Blue Haze on Pluto"—about rather unsubstantial beings made of living plasma—perhaps the fourth form of matter? I suppose that this yarn was a pot-boiler, though easy to write.

However, "The Son of Old Faithful," in the July 1935 *Astounding*, gave me a tussle! My problem there was that it was a sequel, which required that the substance of its forerunner be incorporated into it. It seemed to me that this kept blocking and slowing down its movement. And there were other pile-ups of necessary information. Besides, I was struggling to make it worthy....Well, I finally hogtied it. Number 775, almost a duplicate of his parent, Number 774, who had been Old Faithful himself, extends the Earth-Mars contact with the cooperation of his terrestrial friends. The moon was suggested as a good jumping-off place for interplanetary travel, because of its low gravity and low escape velocity. There was yet to be another "Old Faithful" novelette, "Child of the Stars," in the April 1936 *Astounding*. A little Earth girl and Number 775 become friends—sort of in the mode of *Alice in Wonderland*. I was learning, and the story got written easily enough.

Though there are usually some difficulties—and though every case presents a different set of problems—I've found that if a story resists writing, there has got to be something wrong, either with its components, or in the way they have been put together. For instance, you can't heap up a whole mass of plot-necessary information near the end of your script—not if you want a hard-punching last line or two, anyhow. Nor can you slow the beginning with too many dully-put, straight-forward statements, either, or your audience might get bored before they even get into your yarn. Clotting the action of the middle this way is almost as bad, because the suspense-flow should be firm and continuous....So, before you go on, maybe you should stop, and fiddle around some more, rearranging and re-thinking the whole thing for a better arrangement. It could be that your information could be more tersely presented—less words and more zip—while you distribute—spread it around—more judiciously, without letting it pile up anywhere, but at the same time not causing confusion. There are ways of making the gradual revelation of story data to the reader as strong a factor of suspense as the common threat of death, injury, or other great loss: in *mystery* and emotional shock. For example, if your chief character suddenly finds something that looks like the prints of some sort of *bare, unprotected feet* in snow-cover of frozen air on the surface of some very cold world, where unsheltered humans could never survive for a minute, doesn't that already inform us that that world is not only inhabited by some kind of mobile entities, which, if not robots, must have an exotic and locally compatible metabolism? In science fiction, mystery is used very often in this manner, to supply information *dramatically, as part of the action itself—not separate from it*!

Or a story may refuse to get written because, at critical points, it feels somehow "sour," and never quite as I want it. Maybe the mood, or theme, or philosophy in it, includes something that I have trouble accepting. Those tales I've set aside, or discarded, charging them up to experience.

Maybe this is why I've never completed writing a time-travel yarn, though I've enjoyed many by other scribes. Sure—I've put action and characters into the past and the future, but by more direct means, without involving myself in any variation of that going-back-and-murdering-your-grandmother paradox. And though I used to use the faster-than-light, space-warp, etc. bit, in order to get characters swiftly back and forth across the universe, lately I've tended to shy away from that trick. It may be possible, using a black hole as a gateway, or even by some other means. But the standard scientific denial of this is not my main objection. Instead, there's something too cheap and easy in this kind of facile jumping around, here, there, and everywhere. I find that getting to the stars the long, hard way, has more challenge and appeal—and realism.

But to go on discussing some of those period-piece tales of mine:

"Derelict," in the October 1935 *Astounding*, is particularly significant because it came straight out of a personal jolt. The little Boston terrier we had then was hit and killed by a car. Losing a pet can be as grief-engendering as losing a human friend. And grief for a dog can easily be translated into grief for loved persons. So I visualized this guy who had been setting up a colony on a moon of Jupiter. His wife and child are murdered there. He becomes dazed; he quits his task, and heads homeward, alone. But soon this derelict encounters a huge and very ancient starship, also derelict. He boards it. It is obviously a battlecraft; the mummified corpses of its non-humanoid crew, killed millions of years earlier in some sort of combat, are still there, increasing the man's sense of futility. But triggered by his presence, a strange, serpent-like robot is reactivated, and appears out of the desolation. It attends, serves, and coddles him soothingly, urging him to rest. He does so for the equivalent of many days. He regains enough interest in being alive to think of heading toward the stars in this great ship; though it is damaged, the robot, Khambee, has shown him that it can be repaired. He can spend a lifetime traveling in this enormous vessel, meanwhile studying all that it contains; it is actually a small, complete, artificial world in itself! The work of refurbishing proceeds. But gradually the robot's effort becomes laggard; it no longer continues to be so attentive and solicitous to the man, who, because of this, regains his capacity for anger. Soon, though, he begins to see that everything is turning out for the best. A star-journey would be just a bigger extension of his running away, when morally he is obligated to go back to that Jovian moon to complete his tasks there.

And he sees what Khambee, the robot, was meant to be by its nameless builders—the servant of vigorous beings. Khambee could serve them in peace, and help heal even their mental wounds after disaster. Khambee had done the same for him—and now was urging him back, refreshed, toward his task.

But now, before the man departs for that moon of Jupiter in his little terran craft, Khambee gives him the spatial coordinates of location—so that if he ever wants, or needs, to come back....

I tried hard to do my best in writing that story, because I felt a particular value in its mood and feeling. I liked the story then, and I still do now, except that, at its beginning, on that Jovian moon, where the man has been working till his wife and child are murdered by the local inhabitants, there is a colonialistic tone.

Anyway, as Khambee helped heal the man of his ruinous sorrow, so maybe writing "Derelict" helped me get over losing my dog.

★ ★ ★ ★ ★ ★ ★

Economic circumstances kept getting better for me. So early one winter, I had looked at my shabby old overcoat and decided that perhaps I ought to buy a new one. But a whimsical inspiration blocked this intent. For the same eighteen bucks I could get a Greyhound bus ticket south, and come home in April. A small, preliminary escape!

So I had gone down to New Orleans during two successive winters. The Mardi Gras, with its color and sound, and its chaotic, bacchanalian night!...

Meanwhile, before and after, I was sinking into the mood of the *Vieux Carré*, the Old French Quarter, and its environs: Canal Street, Rampart Street, Marais and Liberty Streets....I settled in at 910 Royal Street—odd how one can remember exact addresses from way back in a time when one's sense of adventure is fresh and uncluttered!

Building-fronts and balconies with antique iron grillwork. Arcaded sidewalks. Individualistic characters....Past Decatur Street and the Market, the river and the docks—and the scratchy hoot of ships—more haunting than far-off train-whistles, up home in the Middle West....

910 Royal Street was, like other houses around it, an Ante-Bellum—pre-War-Between-the-States—mansion, which somebody said had once belonged to a French countess.

I'll draw a veil over some of my adventures and misadventures in New Orleans; after all, a fella must have his privacy—besides, I don't have the word-space to elaborate very much. However, I'm lured into telling a little.

That first winter I came south—mistrusting my penchant for blurred strayings from a sensible path under certain circumstances, and wanting to test my luck at winning my way on the scene—I had brought along not much more than fifty bucks.

Sure, my finances thinned. That can be good for a writer; need builds a fire under his tail; it can make him work harder and better. Contrary-wise, it can also crack him up; he becomes too strained to finish anything!...Well—I found *both* of these things happening to me, simultaneously! I produced good lines and paragraphs that ought to come to something before long, but nothing that I could complete in a hurry.

Back in those bygone times—and this is still true now—when I had a fragment of what seemed to be a good story-germ that hadn't come altogether clear, I didn't waste many hours trying to mull it out just mentally. Instead, with typewriter or pencil, I'd grab hold of the yarn-bit I had, and sort of pull—writing and thinking along in mutual coordination. With words and thoughts focused together like that, a sticky little intimation can—with luck—suddenly pop out into a full-blown plot, with incidents, needed character-types, and scientific concepts, all pretty much in place and matching smoothly, the way they should be for best results—neither character nor plot being more important than its opposite, since they are essentials of the same tale, and have to work together.

But, back then in New Orleans, I wasn't doing quite that well, and my funds were getting down to zero. Besides, even if I did mail in a good, finished script, it would take, at the very least, two weeks for the arrival of a check—or a rejected yarn. So—the scribe's eternal gamble!...Tremaine still had a yarn of mine, sent in from Beaver Dam. Maybe I could have written him a letter, asking him for a loan that I could work off?...Nah—that thought made me shudder! Nor could I pawn my trusty Corona portable....

Broke, I took to the streets, but as a panhandler I had a lot more experienced competition—though people were kind-hearted....And I did have an agreeable grin—which, since I was taking my poverty as a wry sort of lark, didn't get disabled. So I fell in briefly with a fortune teller, whose chief clients were the girls behind the screen doors along Marais and Liberty Streets. "It helps to have a young fella along," he told me. The Great Depression wasn't quite over, yet.

A fact which, long afterward, I saw pointed out in plays by Tennessee Williams, became apparent to me, too: as a professional type, those gals tend to be dreamy, well-meaning romantics—they want to look into the mists ahead, and have their fortunes told. They have hearts, and they are generous. Many of them were good for the handout of a quarter....

But—what the hell!—this couldn't go on! I had my pride!...Emboldened by my experiences, I took another tack on my own. I'd already tried my chances at shipping out, yet being only an inland greenhorn and no sailor, I had known my prospects weren't promising in those still skimpy times. Still, in the evening, I'd go along the docks, and holler up at each successive ship: "coffee pot on?..."

On a couple of occasions it actually worked, though it wasn't exactly a novel approach. Once I got a pretty fair meal. In the other instance, it was coffee and a sandwich. But in neither case was there much outgoing cordiality.

The more common response to my hail was, "Ah—go blow, yuh bum!" Or the equivalent.

Over on the other side of the river—what did they call the place?—Algiers—there were day-by-day jobs, mostly rolling barrels of molasses. I missed out on one morning shape-up, but figured I might make it on the next. But then a check came through from Street & Smith. Seventy-five bucks. Tremaine had had that story of mine, though I don't now remember just which one it was. Then I had trouble cashing the check; the bank said I'd have to wait till it was sent through to New York for collection. Well—I'd shown it to my landlady. She was impressed, and loaned me five dollars.

I hadn't been eating too well, so I thought I'd splurge. I went to the French market and bought a couple of pounds of fresh shrimp, and took them to a friend's place, and we fried the shrimp, and stuffed ourselves. Soon, though, I felt hungry again. I went to a restaurant in the French Quarter where a husky helping of beef stew cost me fifteen cents. I topped this off with a large wedge of deep-dish apple-pie à la mode. I seem to remember having a beer, too. Then I wandered back to the market, and for a nickel, bought six bananas, which I consumed on the spot.

Not much later, however, my recently shrunken, deprived, and over-inspired stomach started to reverse the signals of famishment that it had been sending me, nor did it offer me the least apology for its mistake. This, when I had trusted it; by reputation and the evidence of experience, my gut was of cast-iron. Tums obtained at a drugstore only made my agony worse. I staggered to Royal Street, doubled up and in a cold sweat.

So I wupsed the whole injudicious conglomeration up. By dusk I was comfortable again, except that I felt as limp as a wet mop, and was exhausted. I slept.

I'll recount another anecdote about 910 Royal Street. Though it was clean and comfortable enough otherwise, bats had found a chink somewhere on the top floor, and had taken up residence in considerable numbers between the walls there. At night, they'd creep out from under the mop-board, and flit back and forth in the dim upper hallway, lit only by maybe a fifteen-watt bulb. I suppose the infestation has been corrected now—if the building still exists, as it probably does, since I believe that all of those old houses in the *Vieux Carré* are protected by a landmarks-preservation code, and can't usually be torn down.

Anyhow, an elderly gent had a room on that top floor. His bad habit was smoking in bed. I'll call him Joe. There were rumors that he had almost burned himself up on one or two occasions.

So one night when I was still up, I heard some yells for help. I ran upstairs along with several other persons. Smoke was coming past Joe's partly opened door. We burst inside....

The situation that confronted us surely can't be considered funny. Yet, in spite of that, an element of comedy sneaks into the memory. And that wasn't the whole of the effect, either. Old Joe used his street shirts as nightshirts. Just then there was no light in his room except that provided by the ruddy flames from his bed. And there he was, dancing around with his skinny legs, and slapping away at the fire, and yelling like a sinful soul in hell!...Up near the very high ceiling where the smoke was collecting, frightened bats were flitting to-and-fro, and squeaking....

Somebody quicker than I in such circumstances, grabbed the big pitcher sitting in the old-fashioned wash bowl on the wash-stand, and poured water in coolly calculated dashes onto the little conflagration.

I had been bemused by the—what?—tableau?...Suggestive of Gustav Doré's illustrations of Dante's *Inferno*? Or some voodoo rite?...Yet pathos was there, too....I don't know how much longer after that that Joe lived. To still be alive, he'd have to be well into his second century.

Oh, by the way—I tried inhaling marijuana smoke once, that first time I was in New Orleans. It made me a little floaty and dizzy. The common name for the herb down there then was "tea." But in a curious inconsistency of terminology, if you got high on it, you were a "hay-hop." It hadn't yet achieved a lot of popularity. As for myself, I preferred liquid refreshment, as I still do; though I haven't gone overboard with that, very often. What we had back then, and there in New Orleans, just after the end of Prohibition, was pure, undenatured ethyl alcohol, purchasable at a pharmacy for fifty cents a quart-bottle. Pour some in a glass, add a dash of vanilla extract, maybe a little sugar, and some ice, and you had a nice, smooth, potent potion that was short on hangovers.

XI.

FIRST ENCOUNTERS

At home in Beaver Dam, in the spring of 1935, I finished writing "Davy Jones' Ambassador," which I think has turned out to be my second most anthologized story. Actually, it is another first-encounter yarn, though the alien, and his alien world, are both terrestrial; his place of origin is the bottom of the Atlantic Ocean, about as strange a region as most other planets. A human explorer descends into its pressure and darkness in a small, deep-sea submarine, and, being subject to fearful suspicion as an intruder from a very different and powerful people and culture, is immediately attacked, and captured along with his craft. After an interval of near-unconsciousness, he sees that he and his submarine are enclosed within an oval chamber with pearly walls, containing smelly but breathable air. He comes out of the ship, and finds pairs of eyes looking at him from the black ocean beyond the walls, through observation windows. To these beings of the ocean floor, whose bodies combine characteristics similar to those of octopi, sharks, and crustacea, he is indeed a fearsome curiosity.

The captive man, sure that he is doomed, begins to figure out the technology of these deep-sea-dwelling entities; denied the use of fire in a watery world, they have taken another developmental direction: controlled biological selection, that, over many generations, has emphasized specialized characteristics of various creatures, so that, in living flesh, they can function as parallel equivalents of human inventions—electrical generators, radio-teleprinters....Here is a kind of bio-engineering.

From a distance, the chief scientist of the dominant species of the ocean floor lets the human intruder know of his approach by his version of a teleprintout; yes, he has learned to write English perfectly, by deciphering and studying books from sunken vessels:

> *I am far away, man; but I am coming. I wish to write with*
> *you. Do not die yet. Wait until I arrive. The Student.*

So there is a confrontation, through a clear glass related to pearl, between the outer, pressurized water-world and the small, massively-walled likeness of the upper world of air, where the human explorer is confined. So here, again, I quote from the text:

*Two peoples, two cultures, two backgrounds, two histories,
and two points of view were face-to-face at last, ready for whatever might come of the meeting. The bizarre stood versus the
bizarre from opposite angles. Between them the abyss was wide.
Was there—could there be—any sympathy to bridge it?*

Communicating by printing questions and replies, human and sea-thing
probe each other warily. Being urged to do so, the man demonstrates the miracle of
fire for the student. At last, the student challenges the man to escape, warning him
that he can't, but insisting that humans have many powers, and that he would like to
see them tried.

Employing fire to build up explosive pressure, the explorer manages to
break out of prison with his submarine. But, in making his getaway thereafter, he
begins to realize that he has been assisted.

Up on the sunlit surface of the Atlantic, the man finds to his amazement
that the student has come with him, inside a protective pearly shell that has been
cemented to the submarine. Knowing that the creature had helped him to escape,
the man traces words on the outside of the shell:

Thank you, my friend.
Friend? No. I am not your friend. What I did, I did for my-
self.

The fascinated student continues to observe the fearsome marvels of the
fantastic environment into which he has intruded.

* * * * * * *

I may have regarded the writing of some of my yarns as a routine procedure. However, there were others that truly got hold of me; they demanded and
compelled me to my best efforts. "Davy Jones' Ambassador" was surely one of
these. If I fumbled even just a little bit in getting it written, it would be less than it
could be. So I tried to make it a polished jewel. Something I might manage to be
proud of.

To me it seemed to have everything—and in a matching, coordinated place:
scientific ideas, strong suspense, excellent characters, mood, imagery, and a subtly
convoluted twist-ending. So I was fiercely hopeful about it. Sure? No. When I
send a script to an editor, I find it hard to be that.

The student resembled Old Faithful, the Martian: as different from humans
in form and mind, and with much the same driving will to find out, against dread;
yet, in his way, he was a more developed character. As learned, and maybe
tougher....

While I was shining up "Davy Jones' Ambassador" I also wrote two short
stories.

74

"Nova Solis": If a distant star could explode—go nova—like Nova Herculis, couldn't the same thing happen to Sol, our familiar, stable old sun?...Could the Earth escape being entirely vaporized by such an event? To me, it seemed that it could. Because, if the relatively small bulk of the sun were to expand enough to fill the Earth's entire orbit, its substance would have to become very tenuous indeed. Could people survive by burrowing far underground? Well, maybe....And mightn't some exotic process, which might be called life, have evolved, even on the sun? Again, a speculative maybe.

Then, "Avalanche." If a little space-viable robot, given the capability and the urge to reproduce itself, were turned loose, what would happen? With the mathematical progression of multiples functioning, wouldn't all of the materials in the solar system be swiftly used up in this reproductive avalanche?...A lesson for people?...

I mailed the three above yarns to Tremaine at about the same time in 1935; probably it was early June. Then, immediately, in another preliminary though widened getting away, I bused down to Mexico.

I had prevously suggested to Tremaine that if he ever wanted to put two of my stories in an issue of *Astounding*, he could dream up a pseudonym for me for the second. Well—as it turned out—he gave me a triple appearance in the December 1935 issue. So I became also Dow Elstar and E. V. Raymond.

* * * * * * *

I was knocking around in Mexico all through that summer. My first venture into a foreign land! As temporal orienting points, that was when Will Rogers and—who was it?—Wylie Post, were killed in Alaska when their plane crashed. And that was when the song, "The Isle of Capri," was popular. I heard it everywhere, south of the border.

I got back to Beaver Dam around Labor Day. I was bushed, thin, haggard, and coughing, after all the shoestring-type rushing around and minor mishaps I'd been through on my jaunt. Somebody teased me that I looked like an old tomcat, returned at last after an extended prowl. But I came loaded down with serapes, pairs of huaraches, banderillos, leather belts, and purses impressed with miniature likenesses of the Aztec Calendar Stone, and other tourist truck. But I also had a lot of vivid, new memories. I had really extended my bodily forces to the limit on that venture, propelled by eager enthusiasm. And I swore that someday I'd go back to Mexico, to stay for a while.

Of course I hadn't done any story writing, nor had I intended to. So now I had to get going again—the last long stretch in Wisconsin.

* * * * * * *

"Buried Moon," "Mad Robot," "The Weapon," "The Scarab"....But since I've already done quite a lot of story descriptions, I'd better begin to be selective in touching on my yarns that appeared in *Astounding* during 1936 and 1937. I'll pick only those that seem particularly significant to me.

"A Beast of the Void," in the September 1936 issue, was one of these. In it I isolated a single space-environment-compatible animal, such as Gernsback had removed from my "Revolt of the Starmen" as the *natural*, self-propelling, rideable mounts for the starmen. I took it through its growth-phases to huge maturity, rather in the manner of a detailed, step-by-step nature study of a strange and ominous life form, to make it as convincing as I could. The opening circumstances of the story were perhaps a bit classical-science-fictional, yet, I think, effective. A reclusive scholar, living alone in the country, notices a firm, rubbery spot on the flank of a rock that has been lying at the edge of his garden for as long as he had been around. The spot is exposed because a piece of rusty limestone had just broken away. Puzzled, the scholar examines the rock. It is very heavy—mostly of iron. So it has to be a very ancient meteorite, that may have spent ages submerged in sea water.

When he cuts into it, and accidentally touches the spot with the flame of his acetylene torch, the rubbery stuff doesn't seemed to be harmed at all by the intense heat. When he pokes at it, it opens up like a flower, becoming a flattish, radially ribbed disk that resembles the top of a small umbrella. Circumferentially, at the ends of the radiating ribs, there are sharp claws.

The thing shows no sign of animation. But the scholar knows he has found something truly remarkable. With scant hope, he puts the creature in an open box, and sets it out in the sunshine. Presently, the little beast begins to quiver feebly, as if the solar energy was stimulating it out of its millions of years of vital suspension.

It will eat none of the food he offers it. Instead, with its claws, it draws soil, sand—anything of the sort—toward a kind of mouth at the center of the under-surface of its disk-shaped body, where there is a thickened mass which must contain its vital organs. It assimilates these inorganic materials into its strange flesh, and begins to grow. Its vigor mounts rapidly.

The scholar names the little beast Darkness. He is afraid of it, but totally fascinated by its enigmatic novelty. He becomes secretive, telling nobody about it; but, like any zoologist observing the habits and development of an unusual specimen, he keeps a log.

A day comes when he finds out that Darkness can fly! Its form flattens and stiffens, and it rises straight upward. As it swoops over his head, he feels the thrust of the propelling emanations—ions, perhaps?—being radiated from its ventral—under parts. He thinks it will escape, but it returns to him. Still, he pens it up.

It seems to be angered by this, and when it has grown to a yard width it attacks him. Badly clawed, and fearing it will kill him, the scholar knifes the creature. Now he is afraid it will die, but it has great vitality. Under his solicitous attention it heals, and thereafter is his almost docile pet, though the glinting specks which must be its eyes, randomly scattered over its rough hide, do not suggest that it is harmless.

He contrives a sort of saddle for its back. Thus, it carries him high into the atmosphere. Their successively more extended excursions require that, for his own survival where there is no air for him to breathe, he must construct for himself better and better shelter—first a crude space suit....

Darkness is able to produce a sustained thrust of about one-G. With this, velocities to quickly reach, and return from, the moon, Mars, and Venus, are readily attainable. These exciting journeys of exploration are made.

But Darkness now goes into a lethargic state. In the woods near the scholar's house, the beast begins to dig a great pit, much like a small lunar crater. It absorbs all of the excavated soil, clay, and small stones into itself, and keeps growing more and more enormous.

Though Darkness is now his friend and pet, and will not harm him willfully, the scholar has encountered other ominous signs: the forest around the pit is dying, and he, himself, *is ill*. Radiation sickness—for the beast's metabolic energy-source is radioactive—nuclear.

More threatening: Under each of the creature's claws is a cluster of small transparent globes, each with a tiny likeness of itself visible inside! Darkness was preparing to spawn!...Asexual reproduction.

Because this alien vitality is intrinsically lethal to all Earthly biology, the beast must be quickly gotten as far away from Earth as possible!

The scholar knows that radiation has already doomed him. Still, pleasurably, although rather sadly, he contemplates his greatest adventure of all. A sealable and well-provisioned habitation for himself has been built, and is attached to Darkness's huge back. It seems somewhat odd and wry to the man to be heading into the far, interstellar depths on a glorious spring day.

Readers of *Astounding* seemed to like "A Beast of the Void" well enough. I recall no complaints that it was too fantastic. So, even if Gernsback didn't notice the story, still I had proved something, anyway to me. Though the yarn has never been anthologized in the States, eighteen years and a lot of history later, Georges H. Gallet in Paris remembered it and put it in a Hachette collection called *Escales dans l'infini*, as "La Bête du vide." That was 1954. Years later, still, in 1979, in Brighton, England, I talked to Monsieur Gallet at a world science fiction con, and he told me that, among SF buffs in France, "La Bête..." had created quite a stir as a live flying saucer!

Occasionally I've thought of completing the original intent of "The Revolt of the Starmen" by putting such nomads—with such mounts, too!—into space, and sending them through a book-length sequence of mystery and high adventure. Wild, primitive tribes of the void—what a pleasant, romantic idea!...It might even be a series....Well, so far I haven't done it. What puzzles me, though, is that so few, if any, other SF writers have written anything about creatures and beings native to space itself. To me it is *not* impossible at all.

In October 1936—the next issue after "A Beast of the Void"—"Godson of Almarlu" was printed in *Astounding*. I'd been dreaming this one up happily for quite a while: what if, millions of years ago, there had been a fifth planet in the solar system that had been smashed in a cosmic disaster, its fragments becoming the innumerable planetoids of the Asteroid Belt? What if its high-technology inhabitants, lacking enough time to save themselves, but motivated by altruism toward similar life—the human race yet unborn on Earth—were still able to prearrange their partial survival from a cyclic repeating cause for their own destruction, at its next appearance, ages ahead?

What sort of cyclic cause—or force? Something like a massive comet of a very long period suggested itself. But it couldn't have crashed directly into the fifth planet, Almarlu; because it might have destroyed itself and thus couldn't endanger the solar system again....So I had to mull further....Besides, I wanted a menace that was something new, and different. So I worked the problem out by combining two rather novel ideas.

I began the yarn with a mysterious nocturnal episode, wherein a fragile space-mobile device enters a house, hovers over a baby's crib, and touches the child's head with its filaments; it is implanting information and instructions into the subconscious memory areas of the baby's brain. Then the little robot slips away and hurtles back into deep space to some shelter where it has rested passively since the destruction of Almarlu. All that its extinct inhabitants could prearrange, actively, is now accomplished.

Almarlu's godson, the baby, becomes the man, Scanlon. Since I was a bit tired of big, very righteous and moral heroes, I made him much less perfect; he was just somebody to get a very important job done. So Scanlon is an aggressive loudmouth with a talent for making money, and for inventing remarkable and useful devices which he brags about, but can't seem to explain very well. Having become a world figure of finance, he begins building a huge power plant in the arctic, and boasts that it will provide free electricity to everybody; its energy-source is the inertial rotation of the Earth.

So astronomers now see signs of approaching disaster with their telescopes. The rings of Saturn are pulled askew, the big planet itself bulges lopsidedly. Titan, its largest moon, explodes.

Some huge force is yanking at the Saturnian system. But no cause for this is visible....

I had my explanation. Back in 1936, who had ever heard of either black holes or neutron stars? Nevertheless, there was a theoretical substance—neutronium—consisting of neutrons tightly packed together with no space between. Somebody had calculated that neutronium would weigh sixty-million tons per cubic inch. Any considerable bulk of it, though too small to be visible from any distance, still would have tremendous gravity. So there was the cause of the distortions: my reappearing intruder into the solar system, as I described it—though I did not use the modern term—was surely a *neutron star*.

I had had a bit more prompting in coming up with this idea. White dwarf stars, known of back then, were also known to be more massive than any ordinary matter. But not to anything like this degree.

The little reddish body comes quite close to Earth, but does not touch it. Why then does Earth explode? So my answer to a second riddle: I figured that there would be some neutronium at the centers of all worlds. Being heavier than anything else, it would have fallen right through other substances, accumulating as an ordinarily passive and harmless presence at the centers. But if some great outside force pulls at those massed neutrons suddenly, wouldn't they start oscillating rapidly back and forth, right through the atoms of other substances, tending to break them up, releasing their energy explosively?

So isn't that pretty much what happens in a nuclear bomb blast? Neutrons passing through atoms, breaking them up, and freeing more neutrons in a chain reaction?

Anyhow, Scanlon's power plant turns out to be more then he had known of, at the outset; before Earth explodes, it is the means for siphoning terrestrial air and water to the dry, airless moon. Along this controlled column of moonward-rushing vapors, airplanes in flight are drawn. So a few thousand people reach our satellite for a new beginning. Scanlon, partly through the benevolent ministrations of his cynical though realistic nephew, is humbled into being a better person. And now, responding to some trigger planted in his subconscious when he was a baby by the device from Almarlu, he understands fully at last how it all came about.

Shall I be a little proud of the two rather forward-looking concepts, contained, before their time, in this long novelette? A neutron star? And a hint of the process by which nuclear fission takes place?...

Maybe not too proud. However, there are folks who attribute my relative little-knownness in science fiction history today to my tendency to keep my mouth shut. False modesty and all that. Bad for book sales, too. I think they're right. So I'm trying to make up for a neglect. Quiet scribes take heed.

"Luminous Mine," in the January 1937 *Astounding*, had to do with the idea of drawing rich metals up from the otherwise unreachable core of the Earth by a long-range process related to electroplating. Who knows? Such a thing might someday happen. In this yarn, a greedy crook, trying to beat the method, gets caught in it instead.

The March 1937 *Astounding* gave me a doubleheader: "Fires of Genesis," under my own name, was a long novelette, groping again at the question of how an inanimate substance first became alive. Might a brief emanation from the primal sun have been the cause? What if some solar unbalance caused this creative fire to erupt again? The human hero, born and orphaned on the moon's mysterious far side where the Earth is hidden, grows up to struggle his way to Earth, and out of his primitive condition, and at last defeats a plague of newly created, voracious, and simple bladder-like creatures, the Tegati.

"The Second Cataclysm," bylined Dow Elstar, shows humans burrowing into Earth's crust to escape a threatened noval explosion. They discover refugees of the first nova still living there.

Being short of room, I'll skip comments about "The Path" and "Comet's Captive."

"Dawnworld Echoes." Tremaine put this novelette in the July 1937 issue. During the last ice age, when the oceans were shrunk because so much water was tied up in the glaciers, did civilization begin around the great salt lakes in the Mediterranean basin? Had the Strait of Gibraltar become an isthmus? And when the glaciers began to melt cataclysmically, did primitive engineers try to build a huge dyke there? Was its failure the background of Noah's flood, and of the Atlantis legend?... And if, in our own time, a means could be devised to trace the impressions of light and sound in the atoms of an ancient amulet, couldn't the whole story be recovered in voice and pictures?... This last notion was my substitute for past-ward time-travel.

About halfway through 1937, Tremaine sent me a rough story synopsis by one Robert S. McReady, along with a request that I make what I could of it, and write it up. He never gave me any further explanation of this unusual arrangement. The yarn I turned out was a lot different from the outline. It appeared in the October 1937 *Astounding* as "Stardust Gods," by Dow Elstar with Robert S. McReady.

This story begins with the intentional Earth-fall of a meteorite composed of a sentient mineral; actually it is a cluster of god-like entities. They are so advanced that there is nothing that they really need anymore. So, for entertainment, they engage in curious experiments—almost pranks—on other, less sophisticated beings. They extract a tenuous schematic of an Earthly village, including its inhabitants, move this duplicate to a dangerous world, where they give it full substance and put it into competition with other, similarly derived, though much different, extractions from various planets, to see which will best survive. An old drunk, previously frustrated by an unadventurous existence, proves, under challenge, to be a real, go-getting competent, assisted by his dachshund, Schnitzie.

In that same issue of *Astounding* was also "A Menace in Miniature," under my own name. I think that this was my first go at miniaturized beings. Being very small has advantages, especially when you need to hide!

* * * * * * *

Sometime in late 1937 I heard that John W. Campbell, Jr. had become F. Orlin Tremaine's assistant. I was pleased; I particularly admired John Campbell's Don A. Stuart stories. And now I took his being hired as a sure sign that the science fiction field was getting stronger and stronger. Still, as the weeks passed, I began to miss Tremaine's brief, terse notes of helpful comment. We had had an effective working relationship. On the rare occasions that he had sent a script back to me as unacceptable as was, his remarks were word-efficient, gentle, and to the point. His hints for a rework allowed me plenty of room to choose and operate on my own. Only once had he suggested that any yarn of mine was any better than good. That was when he asked for a picture of me for his office:

"... Certainly you know that, if your stories continue to improve as much in the next two years as they have in the last two, your future is assured...."

This I remember, and can quote exactly, since it was the kind of thing that had to stick in my head. Like others, I hungered for words—as from some oracle—that I was doing all right, and had some probability of going along the upward road. So here it had been—the friendly pat—backgrounding a wise and warning grain of salt, to keep me on my toes. Excuse the multiple mixture of metaphors!

Now there weren't any more short notes from Tremaine. But I pictured him as the man somewhere on top, running the whole show at Street & Smith, by remote control, while all of my contact with *Astounding* was through Campbell. I was happy for F. Orlin; he deserved to rise. I often put "Hello to Mr. Tremaine!" into my letters to Campbell. Among other good men, Tremaine was the best editor I ever had.

John Campbell was a different sort entirely, and it looked as though his takeover was a very propitious event. Conscientious? Wow!... Long, discursive letters about ideas; nothing just terse anymore. There's the old adage about the new broom sweeping clean. Well, that was okay with me; it looked as though John and I were going to get along fine.

With him coaching me somewhat, I wrote "Iszt—Earthman," a long novelette, the idea for which had sprouted from "Something from Jupiter," the novelette I had just written previously. Though very bright, Iszt just wasn't an Earthman at all; to get around on Earth, he has to creep inside his guidable robot disguise of complete, human aspect, even down to the neat business suit and cravat. But he honestly wants to help, not only his kind, but terrans as well, with their overpopulation problems: by breaking up all the planets to make little sealed, artificial worlds to circle the sun in swarms, after the fashion of the countless chunks which form Saturn's rings. Here, then, was a forerunner of the Dyson ring—to me, still, in much more practical and sensible form! Who needs the awesome engineering problems of constructing a *solid* ring around the sun? And what good would it be anyhow? It would even lose the advantage of free movement intrinsic in many separate components....

Campbell eventually put "Iszt—Earthman" in the April 1938 *Astounding*, after using "Mercutian Adventure," and "Thunder Voice" (by Dow Elstar) in the February issue, while "Something from Jupiter" (by Dow Elstar) appeared in March.

Since stories have to be written somewhat ahead of time, let me clear up the possible confusion entailed by mentioning these publication dates. When I wrote "Iszt—Earthman," it was still 1937, and I was still in Beaver Dam.

But it was a time for endings and new beginnings, and, as it happened, Campbell's becoming my new editor, and my intention to finally burst out of seclusion were coincidental. A bit of an emotional overload, maybe?

XII.

A JOURNEY TO MYSELF

I signed the 1931 Chrysler coupe I had over to my sister. Sis kidded me: "London, Paris, Cairo?...Why don't young writers be original for a change, and just go to Halifax?..."

Perhaps she had a point. But against the possible accusation that I was trying to run away from myself, I can still respond that a person can also run *toward something in himself.*

There's a little bit of death in any abrupt and likely terminal shift in scene and lifestyle. As my ham radio friend drove me into town with my gear, I looked back once. I could make a straight face, or laugh and make jokes, pretty much as occasions seemed to demand—which didn't tell all about how a I felt inside. There in the bleak winter scene of January 6, 1938, with grimy snow on the fields, that old house, with the attached barn—the remnants of white paint still clinging—looked eccentric, disowned, pathetic, and forlorn. Yet most of my life, and whatever purposes I had had, were centered here. There was a grimed-in affection. I had enjoyed much contentment, wild dreaming, and satisfying work in the shelter of the odd old place. Would I ever see it again?... As matters have turned out, I never did.

And Annie, pa, sis?...

But to be fair to myself, a person sometimes has to bust away to a fresh start. I turned my eyes and thoughts excitedly ahead.

So I was in New Orleans again for a short while, this time at 1003 Bourbon Street, another more pretentious antebellum mansion. The big front room I had on the ground floor boasted seven mirrors and a marble fireplace. The double doors of that room, if both were opened—which they might never have been since the War Between the States, and belles in hoopskirts and officers in smart, gray CSA uniforms were there dancing—could have passed a full load of hay without even scraping its sides!... At night there I often dreamed of tornadoes because of the screeching whine of the streetcars, passing in the narrow street outside; I could almost have leaned from the windows and shaken hands with the passengers!

It was in these quarters that I wrote what has become my most anthologized story, "Seeds of the Dusk," which Campbell published in the June 1938 *Astounding*. I had discussed its plot with him by letter, and he had urged me to go ahead with it. I was determined to do my damndest!

"Seeds of the Dusk" was—up to then, anyhow—my best developed, totally-alien-culture yarn. My sentient-vegetable entities reach the aged Earth as a single, unnoticeable spore. Propagating surreptitiously, they spread. Being plants, they are rooted to a spot, and what movements they can make are very slow. They can't make much use of fire, or shape metal and other materials, manually. However, they have a profound biological science, aided by an introspective sense which allows them to observe every chemical and vital process within their own substance—where they also have complete and designed control over their tissue growth. Thus, within themselves, they can *grow* their laboratory equipment—for testing and invention. Opposing them are the technologically advanced but cruel Itorloo, the "Children of Men."

On discovering the threatening presence of these spore-plants, the Itorloo, whose cities are underground, decide to destroy all living things still surviving in the harshened surface climate of the senile Earth. These creatures include the crow and prairie dog clans, who, under the pressure of hardships, have evolved to the mental level of primitive men. But the spore-plants defeat them, by developing a subtle and very contagious disease organism, and, with the willing and angry help of Kaw, the Crow chieftain, manage to infect a briefly captured Itorloo individual, who then infects the others. Thus the entire Itorloo race is destroyed. The lesser folk of Earth live on in peace with the new, but unmolesting, masters. I still think the yarn has a nice, slightly wistful, rather legendary mood, perhaps somehow influenced by what had happened in my own life.

Presently I bought passage to Europe on a freighter, the *Leerdam*, which was attached to the Holland-America Line. There were twenty-two other passengers. So I was on my way down river the next morning. The ocean—the Gulf of Mexico—was that kind of vivid blue which I, an inlander, who had never seen such a thing, could scarcely believe!

My first ocean voyage—sixteen days to the Surrey Docks of London—was like a continuous, happy shock of excitement and eagerness, which fairly wore me out, leaving my overburdened nerves and wits a bit frayed. On board, there were people the like of whom I had never before known, including a concert level musician-couple from Belgium. My cabinmate was a mild-mannered Brit on home leave from being overseer in a Central American *finca*; he hung his holstered pistol on the cornerpost of his bunk. One of the things I did, in addition to finishing up a couple of scripts and trying to begin a sequel to "Seeds of the Dusk," was to construct a kite, the inspiration for this springing from conversations with a rather subdued lad of about ten years, whose American mother was taking him to relatives of his English father, a seaman who had died in the States. So the two of us got the cooperation of the genial ship's carpenter and made the kite. We even managed to launch it to perhaps a height of forty feet, before it dived to soggy destruction in the drink. But this much success had still been fun; something Annie had once showed me how to do and had not been forgotten.

* * * * * * *

The ship was docked in London for several days, off-loading and on-loading cargo. I had expected to get off there with all my stuff, but before arriving I had decided to go farther, a girl being one of the reasons for my change of mind. Still, very early in the morning, as soon as we were tied to the pier, I felt compelled to a shore excursion. It was Sunday; a lot of British blue laws were in effect; practically everything was closed. Frustrated and disgruntled, I found my way to the vicinity of the Tower Bridge by the Underground. Before long, a young man with a baby girl on his arm sat down on the bench beside me. A conversational exchange began. He worked in a box factory. Pretty soon we were riding topside in double-decker buses, and I was being shown London—under a sky, somehow, and against everything I had heard, blue from rim-to-rim—and in earliest April! Beautiful!

On a Sunday, the then-biggest-city-in-the-world seemed like a warmhearted village, infinitely extended. Very little traffic. About the middle of the afternoon, the young guy took me home to his little house on Evelyn Street near the Surrey Docks. His good-natured wife, tolerant of his evident inclination to get lost now and then on Sunday rambles, had kept his lunch for him in the warming closet of the small black-with-nickel-plated-trim kitchen stove, which huddled in the corner of an arched niche that looked like the the inside of a huge, medieval fireplace. They made me eat his lunch. There was a gentle Mother Goose quality to the whole adventure. And, at four o'clock, we all went to his mother-in-law's similar habitation close by for tea—and watercress-and-cheese sandwiches. The mother-in-law was Mrs. Scudder. Now, remembering, and still thankful, I dare to salute them all by name, wherever they may, or may not, be: Jack and Bett Watson, and Little Bett, and, of course, Mrs. Scudder.

So—off the ship by about eight in the morning as a lone foreigner, to having tea with a private family by four o'clock—that's fairly quick contact...and something my ma used to say was proven:

"It's only logical, Ray. Lots of people you *don't* know are just as nice as the best you *do* know...."

I've kind of loved London ever since. I guess I was lucky. It wouldn't work for everybody, everywhere—and in *some* places it might not work for *any* strangers, so watch out. But if you have a ready grin, and an obvious interest in the newness around you, plus just the right touch of being from another country, it helps.

During the several days that the freighter was in port, I tried to even the score a little with Jack and Bett. One thing I took them to was a motorbike race. It was more interesting to me than to them. Those bikes had no brakes. But the riders had a steel-soled shoe. On the sharp turns, those soles went down on the gritty track, and the sparks really flew in the evening twilight....

Going ashore, I spent a lot of hours in the British Museum. Cripes, the Rosetta Stone, even!

* * * * * * *

I finally got off the ship at Antwerp. Then the long train ride to Paris—first class, the difference from second being crocheted tidies on the seat backs, and a higher fare. So, a minor chiseling gimmick. Then, in the dusk, a room at the Terminus Nord Hotel, right across from the Gare du Nord station....

The next couple of days were a bit of a muddle. The girl I was with was supposed to know French, but she was worse at it than I was. She had a lot more luggage, and considerably more apparent unworldliness, even, than I....So—innocents abroad—babes in the woods. But she was a sweet little ole thing. She even pinched my socks and undershorts and washed them for me.

The receptionist at the American consulate—a charming, practical lady—helped us solve our immediate problem. So, I was able to unload my friend at a hostelry called *Le palais des femmes*. Meeting her later a few times for lunch, she complained bitterly about the place. Oh, it was clean enough, and everything. Only, there were so many restrictions, and so many locks and keys!

During succeeding months, I saw her around now and then. She interested me strangely....So docile, so simple—how could she pick up such history?...A Frenchman set her up in a place out near Pont de Sevres. Then she was up in Belgium, with a local citizen. She was there during the Nazi invasion, and so she picked up with a handsome Luftwaffe pilot. Much later, I saw her once in the States; she showed me a snapshot of him, and said he was a very nice guy. I guess I had become her brother-confessor, because she also told me, with a chuckle, that she had once cheated on him by skipping to Paris with a Jew. During World War II, she finally got out of Europe by way of Lisbon, where she had lingered for a while. Ah, well....Later on, she married a GI.

As for my own first Paris address, it was *Le Foyer des Jeunes*, 151 Avenue Ledru Rollin, in the eleventh arrondisement. Yes, I suspect it's still there, and in business, though it can't be quite the same as it was! That is one establishment that ought to be monumentalized because, back then, just about every economy-minded young wanderer—be he American, British, Canadian, or whatever—whoever got to Paris seemed to find his way there.

I had a nice student room: a single bed, study table, bookshelf, closet, a window opening like double doors, and a tiny, railed balcony overlooking an inner courtyard, in which, in addition to clotheslines, there were a couple of big chestnut trees. Pleasant....I got a continental breakfast—a roll, a patty of butter, and a bowl—not a cup—of café au lait, no lunch, but evening dinner, except on Sunday, when there was no dinner. All of this cost ninety-four francs a week. The franc was then thirty-seven to the dollar. So the total weekly bill was two dollars and fifty-five cents....Um—such a price sounds like never-never land today, certainly in Paris, but in a lot of other places, too....

So I was set to relax, and to burrow into work, which I did. Campbell may have been startled by my new location, but I kept the scripts coming:

"Hotel Cosmos" appeared in the July 1938 *Astounding*. If contact with other, diverse cultures ever becomes general, there will have to be hostels able to supply widely divergent environmental and comfort requirements. And somebody will have to keep close and cool watch, so that disastrous conflicts among clients who must often see their neighbors as disgusting monsters, don't get out of hand.

Not to mention commercial rivalry and skullduggery. Maybe I was the first to latch onto these angles of an expanded galactic awareness....

Then there was "The Magician of Dream Valley," which turned up in the October 1938 *Astounding*. To avoid polluting the Earth with radioactivity, a spaceship-fuel factory is built on the moon. Its presence there will destroy the tenuous, intelligent Lunarians, the Hexagon Lights. By their mind-science they dupe a man into constructing a device which will blow up the factory. But, close to it, they are weakened by its intense emanations, and lose control of the man. A wonderful people have failed in a valiant effort to survive....Yes—even back in the late 1930s, some folks paid attention to ecological and conservation problems....

"Shadow of the Veil" appeared in the February 1939 *Astounding*. This one is about the exploitation of a primitive, transstellar people by a man—not a cruel, evil sadist, but only acting the part to get rich quick. However, Grud, the primitive protagonist, wins by an adaptation of his kind, gained because their normally tropical planet is periodically rendered extremely cold by passing behind the veil, a swarm of cosmic dust which cuts off the warmth of the local sun. Along with a gathered tribute of pearls, Grud naively contrives to be drawn up into the sky, to wherever the evil oppressor-god of his kind is. Grud's intent is murder, but he knows nothing of space conditions. The man, watching, smiles, because on the way up to his hover spacecraft, he knows that the ignorant creature will be frozen by the spatial cold. What he doesn't know is that Grud has the power of quick thawing and recovery. So Grud kills the man, and though he dies in the crash of the ship, which he can't know how to control, his people are set free....This yarn was perhaps a companion piece for "The Magician of Dream Valley," springing from the same thought and mood linkage: conservation, and sympathy for endangered cultures, attitudes neither of which had yet taken full hold in the world.

Then there was "Masson's Secret," which ran in the September 1939 *Astounding*. This was an "idea reversal" story. If a brain could be salvaged from an otherwise totally demolished human, and put into a robot body, why not the opposite? No, I didn't replace the man's destroyed brain with a computer intellect, but with a remote control device, by which Masson, his friend, sitting at the control console, could direct his still living body in a natural, human way, and thus promote the semi-illusion that he was still alive, and was carrying on good works.

Meanwhile, I had already written a sequel to "Seeds of the Dusk," called "When Earth Is Old." That Campbell rejected it was a signal of various new circumstances. Years later, in the August 1951 *Super Science*, it finally came out. In it, the vegetable culture, using their bioscience, find the mummified body of a twentieth century man, and resurrect him. Parenthetically, I might also add that, in that later time, Campbell also published a similar, though much shorter, story of mine in *Astounding*. Unfortunately, I have forgotten its publication date.

* * * * * * *

While I was writing the aforementioned stories, a lot was happening in the science fiction field, in the world at large, and to me.

Consider my own position: things were coming at me very fast. Suddenly I was in a fascinating foreign city, and trying, among other efforts, to absorb its language. My old patterns of introversion, and of shoving aside most outside distractions, all this rather ideal for the kind of writing I had been doing for years, were getting considerably bollixed by other interests that were crowding at me from all around. I wasn't entirely a dedicated, one-track mind type, but just the same....I still had a lot of simple, human catching up to do....And, over Europe, at shortened range, was the shadow of Adolf Hitler; his Nazi *Anschluss* with Austria, and its annexation, were very recent, and now Czechoslovakia was threatened. At the frontier with Germany, there was the Sudetenland, fortified, but inhabited largely by ethnic Germans, a tempting region for Hitler to pry at.

I was kind of like a kid in a candy shop—one with a frosty, thrilling, but grimly real atmosphere—stuffing myself with strange, new goodies, beyond my best capacity to cope, also—to best advantage—with familiar fare. It was a bit much....

And under John Campbell's conscientious tutelage, competition at *Astounding* was getting stiffer. Erudite L. Sprague de Camp wasn't exactly a new SF scribe, but he was hanging in there. He had had one yarn, about a bear whose brain was stimulated to human level, that had truly grabbed me! Besides my liking it, it was something to gauge my own stuff against, to see if I could still measure up! And there were others! Stanley Weinbaum was long gone, but that was a regret. He had died of throat cancer—damn those bloody cigarettes! When was it? 1936? After a meteoric string of very good, very human stories which had extended, so I had heard, over only ten months of writing time. If Ike Asimov wasn't quite yet on the scene, he was certainly getting close. And there was Lester del Rey...and more....

XIII.

PARIS, REFUGEES, AND CATCHING UP

So let me look at the other side of my mutating life, to see how it fits in: *Le Foyer des Jeunes* was a residence pension, largely inhabited by young Frenchmen—students, or with jobs of various kinds. Shades of my own past—one worked in a shoe factory nearby; another was a meteorologist. But there were a lot of transients too, both short-term and long-term, including a considerable contingent of Americans, Britons, and Canadians, and some refugees from Germany and Austria.

Lacking special documents that were not easy to attain, foreigners weren't supposed to have employment by which they would compete with the French population. Still, there were these guys, not overwhelmed with funds, who wanted to remain for a variety of intertwined reasons: young romanticism, a chance to examine events from closer up, to be somewhat personally involved, altruism....Most of us—see, I now include myself in the group!—had not appeared on the scene with so specific an objective in mind. But there we were, casually...and there was an opportunity to make some sort of living as well. No fortune, but in addition to feeling worthwhile, we might be able to feed our faces. To that extent, we were opportunists.

One of us, however, had been more focused in purpose, right from the start. Since I don't know anything about his present status, views, or whereabouts, I'll just call him "Sid." New York City-born, but with various relatives and friends who had recently come out of, or were still inside, Germany, Austria, and what is now Czechoslovakia. As a child he had gone to school in Vienna for a couple of years. His motive in Paris: to help other Jews get away to new lives.

I remember my first impression of Sid: there in the big *salle à manger* of the Foyer, waiting for dinner, blue and white checkered tablecloths, ditto for the tied back window curtains, baskets of cut up French bread already set out on the table. His quick question:

"You American?"

And, at my nod, "Yeah. It shows."

So we traded a lot of personal information. The father of his favorite girlfriend in New York, though Jewish too, had given him the bum's rush. So he was back in Europe; he came over every once in a while as a workaway on Norwegian ships. Uh-huh—he liked Paris, but used to like Prague better. Maybe he'd write a book sometime.

"The gang'll be straggling in. You'll meet them."

So I did meet them—maybe a half-dozen other English-speaking young men—agreeable types. We collected at one big table, with some French fellows filling it out. Before each of the latter sat down, he insisted on going around the table and shaking everybody's hand.

We had our potage, our salade de laitue, our boeuf bourguignon, or bowl of tripe—honest, the stuff isn't that bad!—or whatever the main course was that first evening after my first full day at the Foyer and my first meeting with the bunch. Then there were tiny, individual stoneware crocks of yogurt, or slices of pastry, or dishes of rubbery Jell-O for dessert.

I recall that right after dinner Sid sat at the battered upright piano there in the dining room and pingled out a few bars of something rather classical, like Schubert's song of love. He followed that with another fragment of the once current abomination of a popular song that had followed me all the way from the States: "Bei Mir Bist du Schön." Sid's obvious intent was to mock the French kid who had picked it up and kept playing it all the time, to the distraction of everybody else.

Sid had replaced his battered, brown porkpie hat on his head. He was a little guy, and he sort of hunched up like a good humored, rather sly elf, full of jokes and put-ons and ribald anecdotes, as well as rambling, whimsical, rather tender bits of philosophy. The first joint of the middle finger of his left hand was somewhat doubled over from the impact of once catching a baseball in not quite the best of form.

At dinner Sid had brought a bottle of *vin rouge ordinaire* to pass around the table, so now I got another bottle to take along with the gang, upstairs, to a big room with three beds in it, where three of the guys roomed, to help enliven a general gabfest.

So they filled me in more about their operation. Lots of refugees had come, and were still coming, out of Germany and Austria by various routes. For those who came to France, Paris was a temporary stopping place prior, usually, to going someplace else that could be induced to accept them—a devious and complicated tangle of processes. For instance, in the States there was not yet any law to help a person enter the country as a political refugee. So, to get a visa, the effective way was to have some citizen of substantial means sign an affidavit guaranteeing support, so that the immigrant would not be on public welfare. Sid had contact with such potential, individual signers in New York, as well as with Jewish organizations there, though most were already overburdened. France had its organizations too, and traditionally being rather liberal regarding refugees, had attitudes to match, although some of its bureaucrats could be rather officious, even when the intended stay in the country was only temporary, as it usually was.

The prearranged or hoped-for destinations for the refugees were, then, the United States, Britain, Canada—all English-speaking countries. They wanted, and would need, some working knowledge of the language. That was where our casual bunch at the Foyer, of which I quickly became a member, came in. There was no fixed daily routine, but in the morning the guys would usually scatter to various addresses of students around the city.

As for myself, wanting to work at my scribble machine early in the day, I regularly didn't care to go very far. But that was more than all right because, in the first place, I had to go somewhere for lunch, and right behind the Foyer a middle-aged couple from Vienna, former pupils of Sid's from an earlier stay of his in Paris, had managed to win French residence permission and had set up a tiny restaurant on a street called Passage Charles D'Allery. So there I could have a nice, thick vegetable soup for lunch, or boiled beef and cabbage, and there my students could come to me for an English lesson. Of course, getting students was easy; Sid just referred people he knew to me.

The two that ran the restaurant were a real cameo pair! He was bald, with a scraggy moustache, and his regular expression was lugubrious and sort of flinty. He had a high, thin voice; it seems he had some throat problem. She was a motherly sort, and sometimes she'd yell at him real good!

I don't think he liked me at first. For one thing, there was my Nordic aspect. For another, here I was, occupying chairs and a table that were intended for paying customers with two or three pupils for several hours at a time, and meanwhile going through some rather peculiar processes of speech and motion, though he should have known the system. I might say, too, that some of my students, remembering their own cultured backgrounds, had an initial distaste for him. But it all worked out pretty well. My clients had to eat, too, and through the shank of the afternoon, when there wasn't much other business coming in anyway, the chances were that they'd want more coffee, tea, or wine, or more of what became the specialty of the house: honest to gosh Viennese *apfel strudel*! Besides, those pupils were repeat customers who often brought their friends. The guys at the Foyer already called the place "Our Strudel Club!"

As to my teaching techniques, and those generally practiced by my colleagues, I suppose you could call them individualized versions of the Berlitz Direct Method. I can't swear to this, because I have never been to a Berlitz school. I remembered enough German to get along okay, but in a lesson you're supposed to speak only the language that is being taught. For example, pointing out objects and naming them distinctly while demonstrating verbal action: "This is a chair. This is a table. We are sitting on chairs. We are sitting at a table. I get up from my chair. I sit down again on my chair."

It can be a tedious, repetitious process. If, as a teacher, you're a bit of a ham, it helps your students, too. When I felt eager about what I was doing, which was most of the time, the ham part came easily enough! Here was a new, purposeful activity for me. Often, all their lives seemed to be concentrated in the facial expressions of my pupils: an earnestness, a puzzled, worried concentration, a fear that they couldn't learn when they absolutely had to. The human instinct, then, was to try to lighten the load: "Take it easy, take it easy! Come on, let me hear you say that....Relax. It's a nice day, the sun is shining. See that patch of sunshine?" Or: "Rain again! Rain in Paris? Rain every afternoon? Oh, well, we are here indoors to learn English. We will not go out in the rain."

Gestures, grins, and obviously make-believe scowls were used to mesh with the vagaries of such free-flowing patter on innumerable topics. Easier, too, to absorb words in strung out clusters and phrases. "You have children, Mister and Missus? A family? Sons and daughters? Tell me about your family...in English or in German/*Deutsch*. I will say the important English words for you to say and remember easily, because they are almost like German, and because they are about your family and friends. *Freund*—friend...*Sohn*—son...."

Most of my pupils knew some English. And, nudged a little toward making use of what they had absorbed, by giving them a lighthearted, easy going mood in which they lost the inhibition about making mistakes, and could laugh at them, many were surprised about how much English they *did* know from school, and that boosted their confidence about learning more. They could laugh at my German, which was considerably short of perfect! Some would have taken over the session to teach *me* Deutsch; but that would have corrupted the basic intent of my stumbling—to build up their assurance about learning English. After all, they were the students, and to be a purist in the method, I shouldn't have been using any German at all. Though a bit of German nursery rhyme, silly, and whimsical, and out of my own childhood, didn't seem to be out of place as a leavening agent for people whose lives had turned grim. For instance: A—B—C—*die Katze lauft im Schnee*...which translated rather directly, and with considerable word similarity, into "A—B—C—the cat walked in the snow, and when it came out again it had white pants on," was good for a mild laugh, and a mutual, increased rapport of memory, even though, in English, the rhyme didn't work out right.

As for getting paid, well, the going rate for teaching was supposd to be ten francs for an hour. At the start, anyhow, I couldn't consider myself a hotshot instructor; if I got my lunch check picked up, I figured I was doing well enough. Very often I ended up paying my students' small bills, too. More than the job, I was interested in the people themselves; they were living, individualized, and detailed extensions into the dark of current history. Names like Auschwitz and Buchenwald, and their full significance, were still well in the future. But there was one old chap who took off his shirt and showed me some deep, new, star-like scars on his back. He told me, with bitter boastfulness, as if I was a dumb kid who didn't know the first thing about life—and I guess he was right!—that he had been beaten with a broad strap in which there were holes, and in each hole a nut and bolt had been fastened. He said that, in some villages where there were still ox teams, such straps were gently used to urge the beasts along, though they were frowned upon for that purpose. He said further that, knowing some corruptable Nazis, he had been able to bribe his way out of Theresienstadt, which was supposed to be one of the milder camps.

The refugees didn't have a lot of money. At one point, back in 1938, they were legally able to export only nine marks, or about one dollar. There were variables, up to thirty or fifty marks depending, it seems, on point and condition of exit, and on who knew somebody in the bureaucracy. Those who got out were the lucky and provident ones who looked ahead, and who had contacts. Then there were valuable items that could be gotten out in one way or another: jewelry, cameras, etc. Much later on, in New York, I knew a fine chap, dead now of a heart attack, who sewed up a lot of Leicas and Kontax cameras in the deep upholstery of some furniture. Awaiting shipment to the States in a lift—a big box—it got caught on the docks when Holland was invaded and, according to a post-war investigation, the furniture had been distributed to the inhabitants of a bombed German city. Ah well, folks in trouble....

But there is more to this man's story! A fantastic bit of luck! He was able to *get out* of a concentration camp and emigrate to the States with his family in 1939 because his wife was able to show a 1917 photograph from World War I to Nazi officials. I have seen that photo; his daughter and her husband live not far from me here in New York, and I see them quite often. In fact, she is sort of an in-law of mine....Well, the picture shows a group of about fifty German soldiers in a rest camp of the Kaiserzeit. Near one end of the rowed up group is her father. A ways to the left—not really close—is none other than Adolf Hitler. Yes, indeed....

Of my pupils, I retain a mass of variant impressions that probably cover a large segment of the spectrum of human possibility.

Some of them considered my rather casual, horsing around method of instruction an utter, clowning waste of their time. But there were others who approved happily, hung on, and brought me more students. I remember a conglomerate of facial expressions and aspects, some refined, intellectual, sometimes maybe a bit fussy, others worldly-wise, practical, no-nonsense types with speech patterns to match. These were professional and business people, gone a little shabby and out of their depth at visible edges, but hanging in there cheerfully. A milliner, too, who was a hat maker, talkative and good-humored. Overall, a good lot; humor and optimism are enduring human traits.

One of Sid's students, whom I visited with a couple of times at a small hotel on the Quai des Grands Augustins near Notre Dame Cathedral, said that he used to have a little office that could move up and down from floor-to-floor in his store in Vienna, because it was built into a lift—an elevator. A wishful bigshot, but able enough to make out again, given the chance. Quite soon thereafter he got away to Britain.

Right now, more or less at random and from out of the grab bag of detailed recollections, I'm thinking of a small, well-shaped, ivory colored hand, writing earnestly in a notebook the words I had pronounced clearly, again, in reply to bubbly chirps and questions, with my attention moving upward to a pair of very grave, very beautiful dark eyes. She was only there once, and with her father or uncle....But I was not yet looking around very seriously.

* * * * * * *

Besides the refugees, there are other things for me to tell about. There at the Foyer, for practically the first time, I had a bunch of friends whom I could relate to. We were all different, and from different places, but we had an anchorpoint of similarity. We were there together, far from our roots; criticisms from such distance couldn't bother us too much. We had come to where we were because we were romantics, alive to many interests. We had a considerable touch of young wildness. Many evenings, those of us who weren't otherwise occupied had an after dinner gabfest, with mixed and mingled moods of whackiness and seriousness, with much philosophizing, yet all edged with a playful tone of nonsense. There were discussions, arguments, recountings of experiences, and the telling of improbable anecdotes. Sid's store of what used to be called "parlor stories" was, to me, incredibly extensive; he could have gone on for days without exhausting it, though for a while there was an English kid, out of London University, who could almost top him, especially with comic, ribald verses and songs. He did, however, have one rather wryly sad song, called "Miralto Marie," which, I imagine, some people who may read this will know, verbatim, along with its rather nice, though wistful, tune. A kind of a classic that matches such specialized literature as "The Prostitute's Curse."

There were some political types among us and, transiently, one young chap from up in the state of Washington who had known a truly unique tragedy. With a mellowed tolerance, he told us about it one evening:

"...My kid brother, eleven-years-old....Around sundown, he wandered away from our place along some fences where there were a lot of bushes. He didn't come back....With flashlights, we found what was left of him about ten o'clock that night. It had to be a cougar that ate half of him. A female with kits, unless she had kits she never would have done that...."

Yes, here was another kind of somber note of sympathy, to mix with our perception of the human condition, and with our contrasting kidding around. I was mildy amazed at the first visible demonstration that ejected bowel wind—farts—would actually burn with a nice blue flame. And it was childish of us—braced as we were by a certain amount of wine—to sit around in our shorts with kitchen matches at hand and a sense of fraternal cooperation, waiting opportunistically to repeat the momentary phenomenon, followed by the loud burst of hilarity. I should have known that that was the way it was; such gas has to be largely combustible methane, only I had never thought about it....

Sid was good at burlesqueing Hitler making a speech. Often enough we tried to figure out the ways and means for blowing up der Führer—almost seriously. How we might get a basement location on some prominent Berlin street, what we might do with the dirt from our tunneling underneath it, where to place the explosive, and then waiting for some big parade. Sure, the requirements were monumentally impossible, as we well knew, but still....

Frequently, several of us would go to the Gard du Nord Station to meet incoming trains. Sid would know the approximate arrival dates of some persons, so we kept watch. But there could be others arriving unheralded. If they got as far as Paris, that meant that they had already successfully passed bureaucratic hurdles on the way out of Germany and then, with some grimness, into France. Thus, they were not entirely helpless, or without resources. If there was simple curiosity, and hope for small gains from paying students, motivating us, there was still at least as much warmth. We would do quite a lot for them without expecting money: directing and assisting them to where they wanted to go if they had a location name or address; or showing them where they might try, if they did not know. If qualified organizational personnel, or obvious acquaintances, had appeared on the platform, we stood aside, but offered grins of greeting and reassurance, and sometimes made a pitch about our services, if that fitted the circumstances.

Of what I suppose many might consider a tense situation—escape and all that—I remember nothing overtly very melodramatic. Refugees were not always easy to spot; among the multinational rail passengers of Europe, they looked much like the others. More strained and wary, perhaps—wary of us, too—because this departure was rougher and more final than past vacations across some frontier. In Germany, throughout the centuries, any stereotyped Semitic traits of features and manner had often become diluted almost to the point of vanishing, except to the conditioned and intuitive. A certain elusive quality existed, much like an American abroad immediately recognizing a fellow American.

I particularly remember the first expectant return to the station, the same one by which I had come to Paris. The train huffed in, slowing to a jerky halt. The long cars looked new and sleekly, though quietly, stylized. In narrow, rather elegant letters, they bore a city's name: *Köln*, for Cologne. Sid was keyed up, intensely alert. Then, as passengers jostled out of it, he made a sudden dash along the platform. There were some squeaks and chirps and exclamatory bursts of laughter from a rather ordinary looking couple in mousy gray. The woman embraced Sid, and gave him a tremendous, smacking buss, followed by a flood of words. The man reached out, trying to shake Sid's hand, while a boy of about nine, with worry in his narrow face, stood uncertainly by.

Two others of our bunch had come along on the Metro. We would have grabbed the three pieces of luggage, but I began to feel benevolently superfluous and intrusive just then. Sid knew the way to the taxis, and the driver would know the way through the evening traffic out toward Porte D'Auteuil. It was Sid's third cousin and family, and they needed a few hours of privacy.

"His show," I said, and the English bloke nodded. We three waved across the small distance, Sid made a funny face at us, and then we faded.

* * * * * * *

Most of our group scattered that summer. Sid, sheltered by his American passport, went into Germany again. Two of our other Americans went along. I wanted to go too, except for what I considered a slightly higher priority—my persistent interest in Arabs. So I took a train to Marseille, then deck passage to Algiers and North Africa. A French flavor and tone mixed in with muezzins wailing out calls to prayer from mosque minarets: *"Allahu akbar!"* For real at last! Some glamor was scraped off by the blunt, uncomfortable edge of reality. Still fascinating, and not too much of the Mediterranean backdoors trots, thanks to my cast-iron gut. I moved east quite a ways. If I'd have had all of my stuff with me instead of a few essentials in a light rucksack, I might have kept moving. But I had work and commitments, and some part of me had struck the treacherous beginnings of roots. So, in just over a month, I was back in Paris.

Sid had returned ahead of me, to that muted, sun-hot, blue-hazed quiet of the season when Parisians who can get away take to the roads, the mountains, the beaches. And maybe now they had more reason. When was the first war scare about the Sudetenland? When was it that Neville Chamberlain, Prime Minister of Great Britain, the gentleman with the umbrella, went, at Hitler's beck, and cheerfully and innocently, as if he had accomplished a great deed, brought back what he called "safety," although Czechoslovakia lost its Sudeten forts? I'm a little hazy about dates, now.

By that strange, sometimes perverse luck to which I seem prone, I once saw Chamberlain up close. I like to take long walks, and so I arrived at the Place de la Concorde. It was very early Sunday morning, with almost no traffic or movement. So, as I crossed the street, heading toward the Rue de Rivoli, I saw a man emerge from the blocky mass of the Hotel Crillon and come my way. Memory details from newsprint pictures matched. I couldn't believe it at first. He was all alone—no guard, no companion—an extremely unusual situation. This had to be a look-alike! He kept coming, and his eyes, under those bushy brows, were on me. His face was lined, and it wore that wary, worried, embarrassed expression of a celebrity who knows that he is recognized by a stranger. I nodded and grinned, not saying anything. He moved past. I was certain it was him, yet how was it possible? Then I looked back, and understood. The American Embassy, 2 Rue Gabriel, was right there at the far corner of the street I had just crossed, and although it was closed on Sundays, somebody was holding the door open for him. The British Prime Minister must have thought, "It's early Sunday, and it's only a few steps, so why fuss?" Right then he had my admiration and sympathy. A brave man with burdens, and a pathos about him.

* * * * * * *

Suddenly and unobtrusively one day, men had started climbing short ladders and putting blue shields around the gas mantles of the streetlamps. So at night the motif was the spooky dimness of a semi-blackout. By then I had signed up for a two-hour morning course at the Alliance Française, less to improve my French than to broaden my acquaintanceships. The Alliance had a charming arbored garden then, where you could get hot chocolate, coffee, and pastries, and sit at tables gabbing with new friends. But in the reading room upstairs there were many newspapers, and a radio usually tuned to the BBC. More than that, it had become a milling, crowded, babbling, smoky funk-hole, with everybody straining to get the latest bit of ominous news. And it was a staging point for bunches of excitable people to set forth again for shipping line offices to see if, by magical chance, they could book passage back across the Atlantic, though one such expedition was enough to prove that things were hopelessly jammed up.

From Germany, Sid had brought back impressions of regular, day-to-day calm there. "No war now," everybody said. "Not until the Fuehrer presses the button." So I had this much additional reason to shrug. I certainly didn't want to head homeward. And the predictions from north of the Rhine proved right; though it might have been better, otherwise. With the relief of a reprieve, it could have seemed that all tensions had been swept away, though this wasn't true. They stayed higher than before the scare, and, with increasing cause, they gradually built up more.

****

Some of the bunch had come back; some had gone home, to resume more regular lives, but, like the refugee/pupils, replacements drifted in, so that things stayed much as they had been. As with any large city, there were many Parises and here was ours, centered at the Foyer, with no particular charm of daubing paint to canvas, or of trying to relive the paths of the great ones in the various arts—unless I was one?...Though I found the thought embarrassing, since everything must be of its own time, not of the past....We were an un-arty clump of guys thrown together in a *pension* in the rather glamorless old revolutionary section, close to Place Voltaire, and just a brisk walk away from the tall pillar marking the site of the Bastille. Along the way was the Rue de Lappe, where we could show newcomers the girls, and where we could all sit at tables with the girls, buy them cheap wine, talk with them, wonder at their numerous ethnic origins and their costumes—frilly and colorful around the shoulders, but absent in front and below, their function being decorative and anti-chill, rather than concealing anything, even coyly. Once, in a nook of the same room and in curious contrast to the atmosphere, I saw a boy of about nine years, oblivious to his surroundings, studiously absorbed with pencil, paper, and book. A school boy studying his arithmetic homework, simple and uncorrupted, perhaps even uncorruptible by—to him—dull commonplaces. A lesson for the puritanical?...Surely, he was the son of one of those damsels.

Of course, the commercial object of these establishments was for clients to withdraw out of sight with a selected female companion—for ten francs plus fifty centimes for the *serviette*. I never saw any of our group do that, though no doubt some came back, alone, when they would not feel self-conscious and exhibitionistic, or when they could overcome mild disdain. These were low-class joints, patronized largely by French soldiers. They were not comparable with the more elegant Sphinx, favored, it seemed to me from a couple of look-ins, by elderly Englishmen recovering, half-vicariously, traces of their youthful exploits, to a large extent just by telling each other about them. And here on the Rue de Lappe there was certainly no equivalent of the House of All Nations, where, for a thousand franc entry fee—and who of us cared to spend that much?—you had full privileges with girls of all kinds, milkmaids, waitresses, shop girls, girls trigged out as harem houris, girls with flagellating whips, etc., plus all the food and drinks you could absorb, and could stay as long as you like. Until—quite soon—cause was found for kicking you out....

****

More characteristic of the spirit of our Foyer bunch were our evening gab sessions, one of which got out of hand from a quiet beginning. Madame Zimmerman, the motherly Swiss directress, recommended gargling with a solution of *gros sel*, coarse salt—fine salt wouldn't do—to medicate a sore throat. From this we moved on to the second part of her prescription for our cold-afflicted patient: two aspirin tablets dissolved in hot wine. One of us had a small cookpot and a tiny alcohol burning stove. Of course we others sampled the remedy, to make sure it was right for our sick colleague. We found the heated wine good, so we decided to send somebody out to bring in more wine for all of us. There were successive excursions to the wine shop, and we didn't bother with the aspirin ingredient. Soon we dispensed with the heating, too....

All this went on in a mingling of vast hilarity, contrasting, from various quarters, with earnest, probing solemnity. Tales were told or retold. For instance, two of our number had crossed back from Germany to France at Kehl and Strasbourg. They were hitchhiking, which the French called "auto stop." Having passed through Strasbourg, the pair were overtaken by a drenching downpour. They ran across fields to the shelter of a barn, where they were immediately seized by French soldiers, who imprisoned them in a potato cellar. There they were kept for several hours, until an officer with good sense let them go, with apologies but with no very clear explanation. Though wasn't it likely that the barn was a blind for a big gun on the Maginot Line?

The topics we discussed and argued about were innumerable: girls—French, English, Dutch, American—What kind of panties did Wehrmacht nurses wear? But the acrimonious high point centered on a speculative historical question that some of us had mulled over before: did Jesus Christ have lice?

A young Scot, ordinarily an agreeable fellow, took instant and glowering exception, especially to the effrontery of such a sacrilegious thought.

My way of calming him down wasn't effective. Saying that whether Jesus had lice or fleas or not had nothing to do with his moral significance. As I pointed out, Jesus, as an itinerant and great evangelist, whose mission was to mingle with even the humblest of the humble, stopping at inns which couldn't be very clean back in the ancient east. So he must have had....

To the Scot, with his strong and purist view about religion—and considering how much wine he had swallowed—this was piling outrage on outrage. Except for the intervention of others, I might have gotten my block knocked off. They managed to soothe him, somewhat. But our noise level had been rising steadily. Those of our co-pensioners who knocked on the door for quiet got invited in to join the party. Finally, though, Madame Zimmerman appeared. If we didn't restore tranquility at once, she would call the police....

We went quiet though, after she had left, there were some titters. Myself—I was well gassed. I had propped myself against the wall. There had to be a closing gesture. I lifted the bottle in my hand and drank the few swallows left in it. Meanwhile, I was slowly sinking, sliding down the wall, and laughing, as at some enormous joke, or glory. As I merged into velvet nothingness—one of the few times in a fairly staid and orderly existence that I have drunk myself into oblivion—I heard gushing, watery sounds, and the Scot's bleary tones:

"Pish on ye bloody fookers!...Pish on the whole bloody fookin' werrrld!"

Slivers of broken glass seemed to float inside my skull the next day. Contrition was on us. Stumbling around in the morning, we cleaned up the mess. At least nobody had been gross enough to vomit on the floor. There were over twenty bottles, not counting several that had been smashed. We traded the good ones back to the wine shop, and added enough to the rebate to make a hundred francs to give to the maid for completing the refurbishing. We apologized to Madame Zimmerman, who ended up rather waspishly tolerant and amused. We hadn't usually been difficult clients. For ourselves, there was a sheepishness and a tendency to chuckle, remembering....For me, it was good at the Foyer, with growth, solidity, and nonsense mixed in a pleasant, warm, and inevitably temporary interlude. Some kind of catching up.

The Osmun House

XIV.

DRIFTING AWAY FROM CAMPBELL

No, I didn't lose contact with science fiction. But I drifted away from Campbell, as I suppose he drifted away from me. I've already touched on some probable reasons. We had been at about equal levels. But he had become *Astounding's* editor—no envy there; I knew I'd make a lousy editor. But my position was to please him with my offerings, and too often I wasn't succeeding. He was shaping his magazine conscientiously his own way, as he had every right to do, particularly as he was good at it. With his long letters he was molding writers, many of them new, to his requirements. I had my own notions, and couldn't quite bend enough. I still had story ideas, but with so much that was new in my existence, maybe my writing went a bit hurried.

Also, from my closer view, with world conflict building toward outbreak, the writing of science fiction—or, in fact, any writing—didn't seem as important as it once had.

Slipping from rapport with Campbell, and practical assurance that *Astounding* would keep on buying my scripts reliably, wasn't too bad a loss. There were other SF magazines, notably *Thrilling Wonder*, of Ned Pine's Thrilling Group, with which I had long been in contact. *Thrilling Wonder* had published my "Saturn's Ringmaster," "Dark Sun," and "Red Shards on Ceres." I would send my stuff to Julius (Julie) Schwartz, the agent, across the Atlantic—always by ship; that was the best way then—and if one magazine didn't take a yarn, there were others. In some ways the stories in *Thrilling Wonder* were better than in *Astounding*: their movement was faster; they were less loaded with science; there was more room for character development; they extended the mystique and mood of the hoped-for Space Age out to a less science-oriented, and perhaps broader, audience. As for my subsistence, I still had my pupils. Up until then, my count of stories at *Astounding* wasn't quite forty, but close.

* * * * * * *

It was time to make more changes. I left the Foyer, but kept contact with the group. For even less than I had paid there, I got a little studio on the top floor of a six-story building at 2 Rue des Grand Degres, just a couple of stone's throws from Notre Dame Cathedral. Not bad! Clean, with a little potbelly stove if I wanted to bring in fuel for heat. Sort of a half-featherbed, like a huge crimson pillow. A primus, if I felt like cooking. A W.C. out in the hall, sure, but a *piscine* a couple of blocks away for a twice-weekly scrub. And an especially attractive feature to my new habitation: a wide, upward slanting window, with a view over the city, centered on the dome of the Pantheon. Yep, my setting and outlook had come to classic, bohemian Paris....And no nocturnal obstacles, such as at the Foyer, where the street doors locked you out at midnight—one a.m. on Sunday—unless you prearranged, for a five franc fee, to have the concierge admit you later. Still, even neglect of such provision could now and then be reversed into an advantage for a bedless, distaff-hungry waif. Don't depend on it, though! Those foreign gals at the Alliance had their discriminations. So, more likely, you'd become the butt of the tolerantly smiling humor of a pair of *gendarmes*, who would stop you and, feigning sternness, demand to know why you were wandering around the eleventh *arrondissement* early in the morning, when they knew perfectly well before they asked you. Then their amused, three-fingered salute, with chuckles, and they would let you go on your disconsolate and dismal way.

Ah, yes, but now such, and other, inconveniences would be ended. Um, maybe....

I kept getting letters from the American consulate, urging me to leave Europe, "unless I had a pressing reason to remain." However, I occasionally had dreams of having returned home—by some incomprehensible error in judgment—and awakening was always a relief. Yes, the United States was the best country in the world; I was proud and grateful to be a citizen; eventually I would return. Still, I had never had things so good, so interesting, so *opening up* as right now, here in rusty, history-charmed and history-cursed old Europe.

Scattered throughout the month were trips. A couple of weeks up into Germany with Sid. Berlin: a bleak, bustling hugeness of red-bannered, swastika-covered power, overtoned with a rattle and tinkle of music to the rhythmed pavement-clump and scrape of heavy shoe soles.

And, for me, silent, pulse-quickening surges of rage. No, we never even glimpsed Hitler or Goering, and treatment of us was, as they say, correct, yet cool. And some glances seemed to suggest that Sid and I were a strange pair....

Walking in the Tiergarten of Berlin, we passed a bench with *Nichts fur Juden* paint-stencilled on its back. Impishly, Sid sat down on it, and I did likewise. But we stayed there only long enough for him to smirk and tease:

"How does it feel to be one-hundred percent Aryan?"

And my reply: "The premise is questionable."

We had been on that topic long before, and I don't know, even now, if Sid acepted fully my version of probabilities. Prejudice is not a sudden phenomenon. Going back several generations, it is clear that, to get along well with neighbors, etc., it is often best to be obscure about origins. Gallun is not a very common name. My father was surely not religious in any formalized sense, and his way of stating this, when any way of kindness or unkindness was under discussion, was to begin his comment with, "I'm not a Christian, but...." Further, not many years ago, I learned that some Galluns, notably in Washington, D.C., are Jewish. To this and similar concerns, there is always the shrugging, slightly exasperated retort, "Ah, bull! What difference does all this ethnic and religious stuff make anyhow?" Still a good question, because to a lot of people on various sides, an easy and emphatic "Nothing!" is not quite the answer.

As for myself, being a romantic, I'd just as soon think that some of my remote ancestors came down into Egypt with Joseph and his brothers; then down into the Sinai, led by Moses.

****

Sid was back in the States briefly, to visit his folks, and to see what he could do about getting more affidavits for refugees signed. So I took another jaunt into Germany—alone. I was prepared, and there was the difference. I wanted to observe the nature of the beast on my own. I looked Nordic, and I was wearing bibbed *lederhosen*, and shouldering a rucksack. If I imagined for fun that I was in disguise, this was true only in a minor way. I was tangibly and frankly American, no bluff there; the only falseness was that, in my costume, I played up my being German-American more than I would have done without a conscious purpose, keeping my deeper thoughts to myself. To that extent, I might have been considered a spy. Well, so be it. Greeted with a "Heil, Hitler!" I would even respond "Sieg heil!" There was no gain in resisting an enormity in such a relatively trivial area; besides, it would lose me a closeness of contact with the others who stopped at the *Jugendherbergen*, the youth hostels. And I knew a lot of old German songs; of particular significance, under the circumstances, was the sentimental and tragic soldier's song, "Ich Hatt Einen Kameraden"—"I Had a Comrade."

It was rather remarkable to me how often even big Wehrmacht trucks gave lifts to hitchhikers like myself, though I suppose my appearance helped. Young Germany moved around a lot, within its own borders, though not beyond it. And the National Socialist policy to assist them in their travels extended to foreign youth as well, no doubt to supply them with favorable impressions to take home, to counteract, to some extent, the grim doubts that were so evident there.

As for the soldiers who manned and drove those Wehrmacht vehicles, my later contacts with State-side GIs revealed, except for the basic difference of the language spoken, a close similarity: the same wry, often laconic cheerfulness; the same tendency for vivid cussing; the same undertoned bitching about regulations and the stiff-necked individuals who administer them; the same gutsy appreciation for the feminine gender and for beer; and the same indulgent cynicism toward the less-knowing.

Among the German youth at the hostels, there were variables of attitude, of course. Against the constant propaganda thrust at them, I particularly remember a bit of impish graffiti, burlesquing the constant Struggle to Save. Its rhyme comes out the same in English: "Wipe thine arse with thine own hand—Save paper for the Fatherland!"

I could sense strong opinions from some around me, but except for a cold and withdrawn hardness, these were seldom indicated beyond that, or pushed toward argument—which I was careful to avoid, too—though there were references to the injustice of the Treaty of Versailles and the burden of reparations at the end of

World War I. *Juden* was a term I seldom heard, and then almost as a kind of thoughtless expletive, past discussion, and injected into a conversation about something else entirely, much as if one exclaimed "Shit!"

Generally—and it is hard to generalize—these young German people were a nice, orderly, polite bunch of kids, though darkly inspired. Their focus was largely on physical competence—sports, and the extensions of sports—and they were justly proud of their hard, agile bodies and their alert, practical wits. And they were trained to know, coolly, what to do about, just for example, a broken leg. At other levels, some were also very bright. One guy, sitting opposite me for, say, five minutes at the most, his *Hitlerjegendsmesser*—his swastika-imprinted knife—sheathed at the left hip of his tan shorts, beat me at chess in....What?...Five moves? Now, admittedly, I'm not much at chess playing, but he made nothing of his easy victory. I was just out of his class. So our conversation drifted to other subjects. He loved opera, and he liked to sing, and I soon learned that he was a whiz at math, physics, and chemistry. He collected fossils....He loved to ski. But the real thing for him was planes; he wanted to become a flyer. When I mentioned Hermann Oberth and Fritz Opel, his eyes lit up. Yes, he knew these rocket experimenters. We talked about space—Weldtraum. Yes, again—maybe, someday....It wasn't my way to tell very many people that I was a SF scribe, nor did I tell him, in part because of my old inclination toward anonymity, especially in Nazi Germany. This, plus my old hangup, left over from Beaver Dam, about the vivid covers. I had not even brought an SF magazine along.

Our conversational subject-matter drifted again. I dared a little. Politics? He shrugged; that was for other people. Freedom? He felt free enough. Somehow, then, I began to hum that old German soldier's song. That kind of tied me in, and when I let slip that my grandfather had served in the Franco-Prussian War, that added a touch.

We went to a *bierstrube* for a couple of beers, which oiled our tonsils and our spirits. That evening, my status as *Unser Amerikaner*—Our American—was pretty well set at the hostel. I was like their somewhat older—yet somehow younger—less apt, brother. I was with perhaps ten of them, several girls as well as fellas, near the Frauenkirche Cathedral in Munich. None of us were drunk; such a thing would have been considerably disapproved of, yet we had a kind of emotional high. The others were supposed to be there, and I was with them as their guest. I was a bit embarrassed, but they locked arms with me, and we sang and marched. So I began to learn the "Horst-Wessël-Lied": *"Die Fahne hoch!...Die Reihen fest Geschlossen...S.A. marchiert mitt ruhig, festen Tritt...."* "The banner high!...The ranks well-closed up!...S.A. marches with peaceful firm tread...."

All of me wanted to react against that kind of stuff. Mostly I did. Still, there was an emotional treachery! There was something about that thumping, jingling music—with tinkles thrown in, as if Rumpelstiltskin's elfin magic was somehow involved, too—that got hold of my guts, as if here I was, arms joined with good friends, and I was not alone. Together in our numbers and in our united purpose, we made mighty, thrilling, and exciting *power*! And I came as close as I ever will to understanding the mechanism of conquest, Hitler's or any other. I would hardly say that this mood is exclusively German; I suspect that the seeds of it are latent in us all, and capable of sprouting, for whatever tense and angry purpose, even if the slogans pretend peace. It's our biological legacy come down to us from a remote and troubled past into our equally troubled present. And who could reasonably call it either wholly bad or good? A device of the human condition....

I had been made into too much of an individualist to be in serious danger of being absorbed by the attitudes of these able young innocents. Their backgrounds were different from mine in too many areas. Trying to clear up their views would have made no sense; there was too much they hadn't been told. As for myself, I had seen too many scared and tragic faces. So I got away when it could be done without abruptness.

But I think now what a strange land Germany was during the Hitler era, as if it were trying to allegorize its folklore: the Pied Piper leading first the rats, and then the children of Hamlin, to destruction; and the Wicked Witch of *Hansel and Gretel*, who baked children into gingerbread, and was herself baked in retribution (this latter tale distorted and gruesomely parodied by the ovens of Auschwitz).

And I wonder how many of these rather nice young folks I knew a little got all the way through WWII and are still alive? I have met a few of their equivalents, grown older. Science fiction enthusiasts, now. One, though his body has become an obvious patchwork of scars, had achieved some of the good life. And those who had been enemies had become friends, with no apparent personal hard feelings. Another paradox?

* * * * * * *

On the way back to Paris, I stopped at Frankfurt-am-Main. There were some people there Sid said I might check up on. I had trouble finding the address he had given me, just going by a city map, since asking might cause them—and me—trouble. I had edgy sensations, fronting on heroics; I wasn't past the grimed in young belief in melodrama. I found them and, actually, there wasn't much to our meeting. At first they didn't want to let me past their closed door, and then they were afraid not to open it when I knocked again; I could be the authorities, countermanding what had been arranged. They lost most of their scare when I said I was Sid's friend from the States. During the few minutes I was with that woman of about fifty-five and her possibly studiedly, plain-looking daughter, the best I did was give them some reassurance that things would turn out all right. And, though they protested, I managed to give them a ten dollar bill, which thus balmed my conscience a little. But what could I do? Lead them past obstacles to escape? I hardly knew enough for that. I heard later that they did get out, but through Holland....What I think I remember most of that short encounter was the household stuff they had piled up in that little room, with one of those twin-belled alarm clocks topping it all off, and ticking loudly....

I left Paris again in the late spring of 1939. Hitler's takeover of the Sudetenland had caused only a minor ripple among the democracies. But when all of Czechoslovakia was gobbled, there was much more of a stir. French soldiers riding the Metro had anxious faces. Many were sent up to the Maginot Line. But again nothing came of this, though there was a last-ditch feeling in the air: so far, no farther. On the map, Nazi-held Czechoslovakia now looked like a hungry dragon's tongue thrust out, lapping at Poland's southern flank.

I hitchhiked down to southern France, to the Côte D'Azur. At Cap d'Antibes the *auberge de la jeunesse*—youth hostel—was called *La Nouvelle Jabotte*. It was a big, rambly, shabby old house covered with climbing roses, and with a bamboo thicket in the back yard. And there, close by, was the blue Mediterranean. As *les ajistes*—youth hostelers—were supposed to assist, though often shirking, I helped the *Mère Aubergist*, Aunt Nanette, the tough old gal who ran the place, with necessary work, peeling vegetables for dinner, etc. No, I didn't willfully try to butter her up, but I guess my enthusiam for the setup fairly glowed out of me. So, pretty soon, I had a deal, even for all winter. There was a *grange*—a barn—with a loft. I could move in a cot and a worktable, and fetch my typewriter down from Paris. I could write and live agreeably for very little.

So, judging pros and cons, I took her up on her offer, dependent on whether I stayed in Europe into another year, as I hoped to. Right then, though, I wanted to take a look at Italy and Switzerland. So I journeyed third class on the train through Ventimelia to Florence. Next was Pisa, then Genoa, Rome, Naples, Ancona, Venice. To me the high point was Pompeii, and the museum in Naples, with all the artifacts of Roman life—and some grim relics of disaster at Pompeii in it. Like time-travel, that town of perhaps fifty thousand inhabitants fairly came alive for me: there were shops, private villas belonging to families with known names; there were even political announcements, red-painted on street walls....I could dream and fantasize alone like I used to do in the woods in Wisconsin....Back to 79 A.D....I extended my ramblings to the low mountain that had buried Pompeii and Herculenium under ash, pumice, and mud flow. I saved the price of the funicular, and trampled upward through a long morning. There was a vast old crater, like a cupped plain, in which locust trees bloomed fragently in the hot sun. Then a zigzag path up the cinder cone. Back in 1939 the condition of the volcano was such that you could step from the end of that switchback path right into the main, active crater. The hardened lava was like coiled piles of great, blue-gray rope, with little plumes of steam coming up here and there. Little concern for burning your shoe soles; the mountain was quiescent. Though off across the rolls of cooled lava was the small final cone, encrusted with sulphur that looked like green moss. And up there, right at the brink, was an enterprising Neopolitan of maybe twelve years. He had a stick about two inches in diameter. Every minute or so, the volcano would give a sleepy, breathy whoosh, and up would fly a gobbet of white hot rock. Watch your head! But when a gobbet of lava plopped down near that kid, he would scramble to thrust the round end of his thick stick right into the middle of it, before it hardened. So he already had a half dozen, irregularly shaped ashtrays—spittle right out of the maw of old Vesuvius!—to sell to tourists.

This was a comic and pragmatic touch, sort of brave....Over all, being up there was more to me, the SF scribe, the visioner of cosmic processes. In the slumberous mutter of the mountain, rather like irregular surf, or the panting of a steam locomotive at rest, and the plume of white vapor rising high, there was a lot of the birth, and the continuing vitality of the Earth, the planets, stars, universe!

In the noon sunshine, I waited and watched a long while, for something I had been told about. Yes—in the brooding, quiet air old Vesuvius blew for me a not quite perfect smoke—a steam-ring, forty feet across....

* * * * * * *

Mussolini's Italy? There had just been another war scare, so I had to evade a lot of aggressive, unemployed tourist guides. Otherwise, I was hampered by a lack of Italian that limited my contact with the friendly, curious Italians, wanting, for instance, to know how many sisters and brothers I had. Even along the railroad tracks, interspersed with adverts for a cooking oil—*Oleo Sasso*—were metal shields bearing triplate, aggressively bulldoggish profiles of Duce, Duce, Duce, Duce!—under scoop helmets. Il Duce's mug was everywhere—except, I noticed, on public bonds, where poor little King Victor Emmanuel's portrait had to stand alone. And the slogans were really crass: *Credere—Obedire—Combattere!*—Believe—Obey—Fight! I suspect that the cynical Italians, in their flowery, beautiful, but rather beaten-down country, never took Mussolini very seriously. But they were history-and-burden-tired, and passive.

* * * * * * *

By way of Switzerland, more than the usual numbers of Parisians were slipping away in the summer doldrums. Citroëns and Peugeots were stacked high with luggage and camping stuff, as if the riders weren't sure of their return. The young Englishman who had taken over my few students had been called home, but he had passed them on to an elderly English woman—a true expatriate—who lived on Rue de la Sorbonne. And at the American consulate I found a letter from Sid, who was still in the States. He doubted there'd be a war, and said he would be looking for a workaway back to Europe in September. I wrote him a response in a like joshing, vagabond tone.

But the summer mood and the frosty feel of events made me easy to persuade into another jaunt. So, very soon, by bus and auto stop, I was on the road again, this time with a companion. European girls were good, rugged, unfussy company; besides, I continued to be pretty well-enamored, which helped. But let me draw a veil over most of such stuff....

Brittany....The pines of Arcachon....Nantes....A tiny, rustic village called Chateau Thebaud....Then, rambling around, to Tours....St. Avertin....To another tiny place of one long street—La Daguenière....France had ordered general mobilization. Poland was invaded....We were the only ones at the little hotel. When we shouldered our rucksacks to leave, the Mère Aubergiste sighed sadly and said, as if some part of her life had ended, "Voici mon travail...."

Though cars, buses, and even bicycles were suddenly subject to requisition, we didn't have too much trouble thumbing back to Paris. Though the word was out to stay away if possible, many departees also had impulses to get home when the chips were down, to look after necessary matters there—though getting out again might not be so easy.

Nobody knew, of course, what the massive bombing of a major city would be like. Though there were rumors, planted as psychological warfare or not, that the first raid would produce half a million casualties, the "phony war" of the next year or so was hidden in the future. So there was a very spooky feeling. The blue-out at night had turned black. Frederic Suter, the chubby, rather fussy little Swiss who operated the building where I lived—no reason not to mention his name, since he is a friend now long-dead—scolded me for not having been around to help him put sandbags on the roof.

The first visitation by Luftwaffe planes came very soon. More application of panic psychology?... Anyhow, the squawk of the alert was supposed to send everybody filing calmly into *abris*—shelters—that were mostly Metro stations. Some scrambled, but for many there was a dare-you-dare-me exchange, feedback, and buildup enhanced by a heady novelty and excitement, already bolstered by considerable absorption of wine. So...a thrilling lark! With several others, I was on a roof, not of my own place but of another small residence hotel near the Alliance Française on Boulevard Raspail.

There was a lot of noise—A-A fire, and the zoom of French fighter planes, which some said came up from the airfield near Chartres. Way up in the dark sky, the swaying, crisscrossing searchlight beams sometimes caught a tiny white fleck. There were, it seemed afterward, just two German aircraft. They dropped dazzling magnesium flares that drifted down on parachutes. Maybe those Luftwaffe men took photographs....The strain lasted after they flew away, but there was no follow-up. That was the whole of it.

* * * * * * *

Freddie Suter laughed at me some, but I laughed back, and told him that my heroes were mostly on paper. Anyhow, there was no percentage in staying in a Paris gone glum and xenophobic, and trying to work there. I waited a couple of days for the rush to die down. Then, standing in line at the Gare d'Orléans, I got two tickets. I wasn't allowed to take my footlocker aboard with me, so I submitted it to the admittedly chancy, wartime prospect of delayed baggage car transport. I never saw it again; so there went most of my magazine tear sheets, and much of my clothing.

It took eighteen hours on the train to get to Bordeaux, much of it spent on sidings, while trains loaded with war materiel rumbled north. My lady and I settled in very properly and separately in the M and F dormitories of a popular pension where there was already an influx of Americans looking for passage home. After food and sleep, weariness dissolved in freshened excitement and anticipation. Hotels had filled up fast, so to help the American consulate we went scouting around for private homes that would accept paying guests.

It was a wacky, cotton-woolish sort of interlude—rather pleasant for many participants, I think; plans were suspended by uncertainty, so you were freed from bothering about them. You had to live for now—well, maybe not *quite* now in the regular sense, but perhaps in some separate and slightly enchanted segment of time that was floating somewhere between the ended past and the uncertain future. You gathered in bunches in cafes in the evening, and there, close by, could be someone you had known a little in Paris....And between and among those unknown, there was the quick and cordial grasping at new friendships that the uprooted feel urged to seek. Already a song had been picked out—who knew how?—to fit the situation, one with a whimsical, child-like fantasy appeal:

> "Horsy, horsy, don't you stop.
> Just let your feet go clippity-clop.
> Your tail go swish and the wheels go 'round.
> Giddy-yap—we're homeward bound!"

Twenty kilometers out of Bordeaux on a Toonerville-type tram was a village called Caillou, a youth hostel whose Pere Aubergiste had a grape farm. Since it was vintage season my companion and I worked there, off and on for a total of about ten days. Monsieur Guerrier would roust me out of the sack before daylight; I forked up manure and pitched hay in the barn for a little while. Then Monsieur Guerrier, having milked his one cow, and talked lovingly to his one remaining big gray horse—the other had been requisitioned by the Army—would lead me on a round of visits to all the neighbors. Every house in the village had electric lights, but everybody cooked at big fireplaces, as if this was still the Seventeenth Century. At every stop we got handouts of food. Along about ten in the morning we'd finally be out among the vines, picking grapes. By then my lady would be long past an ample breakfast with Madame Guerrier.

Monsieur Guerrier also had his tales to tell us. As part of one, he pulled up his pant leg to display the wedged-shaped scar where, during World War I, a German bayonet pierced his thigh.

So, to be further enlightened, I asked him a question. With a mixture of pride and rather histrionic sorrow, he responded:

"Le Boche? Ah, pauvre petit gosse. Il dort...jeune pour toujours!"

"The German? Ah, the poor little lad. He is sleeping...young for all time!"

XV.

BACK TO THE STATES

One of our excursions back to Bordeaux became final, because a ship, the *St. John*, normally a coastline passenger carrier up and down the eastern seaboard, had been rented by the United States Lines and sent over to offer passage home to stranded travelers. It wasn't a free service, though if you lacked funds the consul would take your pledge on the cuff. The ship had just arrived, so right away I applied for workaway passage. The chief steward took me on, along with five or six other guys. We were put to work before lunch, down in stores, sorting fruits and vegetables, throwing out the bad, salvaging the good, a necessary procedure to halt further spoilage because the *St. John* would be in port for quite a few more days, awaiting other strandees.

So, as a crew member, I saved my dwindling money supply for another purpose; when that was taken care of, I wasn't far from broke. Still, I felt good....Besides, for other reasons, something else happened inside me. I hadn't been at all sure that I wanted to head State-side, but now my old intention to drift gradually eastward around the world somehow got blurred. The pungency and opulence of good American grub in the crew mess of that ship was part of the—What?—Treachery? Then the relief and shelter of a temporary job—of working, simply, as I used to, with my hands. Something solved, and a kind of primitive pride....Guys around me, down there with those grapefruits and vegetables, and ice to load. Guys to gab, joke, and philosophize with. An expatriate black musician worrying about what this kind of toil was doing to his pianist's fingers....And the tiered bunks, and the card games and watch changes, down in the glory hole—the crew's quarters....Another facet of life to absorb eagerly....

Evenings I was always ashore and, with those others, gathered at the cafés. In the semi-blackout, they reminisced about New York's lights and the torch of the Statue of Liberty, which I had never seen. The pull in me was powerful—I belonged to that, too! We had impromptu parties in various hotels; sometimes our singing and noise were too loud; once we got a stern lecture from a French Army officer—we were behaving like howling baboons while France was suffering! We were contrite; we apologized.

Most nights I got back to the ship eventually, as I was supposed to do. Anyhow, I soon had a bayonet anecdote of my own to tell. Mildly gassed up, I had fumbled my way through the gloom of the pier, Hangar H, where the *St. John* was tied up. Suddenly there was, not a word, but, rather, a deep-throated grunt, "Rouph-h!" such as you might expect from a grizzly bear that you had blundered upon in a dark forest. At the same instant, a small flashlight was turned on, illuminating the long, gleaming blade of an old-fashioned French bayonet, its point almost prodding my umbilicus! I jumped back, quaking. Looking up, frozen with terror, I beheld, by the reflected dimness of the flashlight beam, a monster that, counting the red fez, towered well over seven feet! He was an enormous Senegalese dock guard, his excellent white teeth displayed in his dark face in a vast smile of prankish amusement.

I had seen him around daytimes, too. Even after that we exchanged grins of remembrance. He'd worked his gag on others.

* * * * * * *

The *St. John* took on almost seven hundred passengers at Bordeaux. Not being a stranded American citizen, my companion had to wait for another U.S. Lines ship. Unlike blacked-out belligerent vessels, the *St. John* voyaged with huge American flags painted on and floodlighted on its flanks. I had an 11 p.m. watch, refurbishing and mopping the public areas, and tying down chairs when the ocean kicked up. One thing: I don't get seasick; maybe the exhilaration of swinging on swings when I was little had immunized me. And, toiling along simply and alone, I could muse. It was fun to think that even Cloe, the mascot cat of the American Students and Artists Center on Boulevard Raspail in Paris, was somewhere aboard.

A stop in Southampton, where more passengers came aboard by tender. And another stop, and brief shore leave, at Cobh, in Ireland. Then onward, swinging south past a cloud-capped sugarloaf island, where the cloth sails of antique windmills were turning....One of the Azores. Though the season was late, the weather along our route stayed mild. There was a report that another ship, the *Independence Hall*, on which I had acquaintances, had picked up survivors of a torpedoed freighter....

So I saw the Statue of Liberty like an immigrant.

Not long after that, I had my first New York City address: a place on West 11th Street that I had been told about. After a good long sleep, I found my way to another, more important business address on East 40th Street.

* * * * * * *

So, my first, actual encounter with the publishing reality of science fiction....That awesome waiting room, its walls covered with floor-to-ceiling blow ups of high adventures. And Mort Weisinger was the first editor I ever met, a big, cordial, genial man. Then dapper Leo Margulies....Chitchat surged back and forth. Then Mort showed me a large and vivid oil painting: several little bulging-browed humanoids floating in midair. Mort said the painting was an intended cover for *Thrilling Wonder*, and that it was a picture still without a story, and did I want to make up and write the yarn?

So that was "Renegade from Saturn," which came out in the March 1940 *Thrilling Wonder*.

I contacted Julius Schwartz, my agent, by phone. So I met a group that regularly gathered every other Thursday at Steuben's on East 47th Street for lunch. Besides Julie Schwartz, there was Otto Binder, whose work included the very popular Adam Link yarns in Fawcett's *Amazing*; Henry Kuttner, still very well remembered in SF; big Manly Wade Wellman, whose writing career went on and on; Malcolm Jameson, retired from the Navy then, whom I remember best for his story "Children of the Betsy B" in *Astounding*....They gave me a fine welcome and, from then on, till I left New York, I was with them at their luncheon gatherings. Only I survive now.

Very shortly after I met the group at Steuben's, I went to that old factory-like Street & Smith place on West 57th Street and Seventh Avenue, and had an hour's conversation with John W. Campbell, Jr. A large, fair-skinned sort, very learned. Then I got him onto the subject of human miniaturization, down to dust grain size, pointing out that, though physical laws would remain the same, the effects would be altered. For instance, a person could float in the air. For such tiny folk, metals would be very difficult to work with. He agreed that they wouldn't be able to hammer them into shape, but thought that pressure might work. Other than being a bit reserved, our contact was entirely friendly. But that was to be the only time I saw Campbell face-to-face.

F. Orlin Tremaine, whom I particularly wanted to meet, was a little harder to find. He was out of S & S then, and was between jobs—not yet editor of *Comet*, briefly, nor, later and much more solidly, with Macfadden. It was good to see him, though! A real good sort, quite a bit older than I. Any rough edges had been long since smoothed off to laconic mildness....I guess he was then thinking of becoming an agent.

The publication of stories done in Paris was catching up with me. "The Lotus Engine," "Terror Out of the Past," "Stepson of Space"....Ask me what yarns such as "Guardian Angel" were about, and darned if I know today! But "Long Winter" was the last tale of mine that Campbell printed for several years. It was in the May 1940 *Astounding*, though, like other stories of mine, since shops that had mags I wanted weren't always within my range, I had to get it later from a back numbers store. "Long Winter" made use of the harsh conditions of the planet Uranus, both for glory-stealing murder and its built-in and unsuspected retribution. I had written it with care, but it wasn't as good as "Stepson of Space"—about a small boy on a farm, his frighteningly super-charged tin can and peach crate "invention," his stern but loving father, and his mysterious, seemingly imaginary friend, Mister Weefles, the Last Lunarian—which Fred Pohl, then editor of *Astounding* in October 1940, and much later—perhaps till 1952?—got a television adaptation of. I missed seeing it, though, because I was in Spain....

But back then, in New York, at the start of 1940, I was writing again: "Nemesis From Lilliput," "Lunar Parasites," "Tangled Paths," "Death and the Dictator," "Achilles Heel," "The Gentle Brain"....

I'll comment on the last of these, which gave me a new alternate identity of Arthur Allport, in the Summer 1940 *Science Fiction Quarterly*. What if an idealistic scientist, trying to artificially construct an *average* member of a violent, barbaric society by secretly inducing all its members to pass through an energy field, which painlessly and harmlessly extracts a few grams of homogeneously-distributed body substance from each individual, and then combines, synthesizes, all these samples into one? What to do, then, if the first experiment was only partially successful, and if these people now threaten truly worldshaking violence, and there is very little time? How to calm them? What the idealist does is to reverse the process, disappearing into, and soothing, the violent mass, by distributing *all* of himself, including the gentle attitudes contained in his brain, among all of these fury-dominated folk.

Thought provoking? Umm...maybe, though, on several levels, I don't seriously believe the idea would work. My first notion, here, was that such a process might be a truly representative, democratic means of creating national leaders—say, a man and a woman? Not long ago, after all these years, I discussed this with an editor. But there was agreement that the result would be a dull, ineffective average....

* * * * * * *

I believe that "Eyes That Watch" was the last yarn I wrote during my brief interlude in New York. Also, it was the one story that Tremaine bought from me in the short time that he was editor of *Comet*. It appeared in the December 1940 issue. Were there beings that watched the experiments of Earthly scientists, ready to take protective countermeasures, if the scientists' probes into natural mysteries were "with too rough a stick," and courted abrupt catastrophes? I liked the enigmatic mood and tension of this yarn.

However, on a personal level, I had gotten knotted up. Eros is often a perverse godling. What had been warmly affectionate in France faded a little in the States. Actually, nothing much happened that hadn't been prearranged. A practical, gifted, eagerly, and justifiably ambitious European girl and me, somewhat of a dreamy fuzz head? It can work, but not always. She went her way, a fair distance south to her own contacts. I guess it jolted us both. But it made me feel wry about New York.

I was urged to go home to Wisconsin. Pa and sis had left the old house to move farther into Beaver Dam. I half wanted to go; but that was just the trouble—another sentimental trap that might tie me up for keeps.

I hadn't seen Sid since Paris, nor had he been back again to Europe. But now I was getting letters from him in California. He'd taken a workaway trip across the Pacific. He wrote with a colorful enthusiasm that, being the way I was—and to some extent still am—couldn't help but stir me up:

"...There's a vast, vast world out there!...Come by plane, train, bus, or thumb!..."

So I got rolling....A lot of it was real good, some of it was less. After a while I reached that infrequent point of mine where enthusiasm, accentuated by too much out of a bottle, used to make me a considerably reckless damn fool. If I didn't draw the veil there, I wouldn't be representing myself quite as I was....To begin with, I'd slipped out of New York without telling anyone there—not even Julius Schwartz, my agent. I had, I suppose, a Saturnine streak—from a psychological scar of childhood?—a tendency to vanish into some other intriguing level of existence.

So Sid and I had more wacky, colorful stuff to remember and laugh about, near the end with skyward-turned eyes and almost a prayer of thanks. Finally, it was too late in the season to immediately implement our next urge: to go up to Alaska and work in the fish canneries. Save our earnings there, and then, in winter, live the life of Riley down on the west coast of Mexico in, say, Mazatlán? Well, maybe next year was what we said. Till then...over the river.

A sort of footnote: the canneries in Alaska thing—which might have been fun—never got around to happening. Years later, I saw Sid once in New York. He was a U.S. Army captain by then, recently a prisoners of war interrogation unit that had been disbanded. We said we'd keep in touch, but it didn't happen either. I guess we'd drifted too far along separate tracks. So, Sid, wherever you may be, all the best. You're okay.

* * * * * * *

Back then, when I was fully in control once more, with matters making better sense, I was in Mexico City—where I had once promised to return. I wasn't broke, but close enough. Rooms for rent were indicated in a rather arcane matter: by tying a wad of newspaper to the top of a streetside balcony railing. It was by following this lead past my first tries, but through a gestured and verbal recommendation mentioned to me at one of my attempts, that I found my way to a better place, one not advertised at all. So I was lodged on the second floor of an ancient house on a street called Articulo 123. The double doors of my quarters opened on a balcony that perimetered a patio alive with potted plants, the chirps of canaries, and the squawks of a parrot. The private family who lived in the house thought it appropriate to put fresh flowers on my table every morning, and to bring me a cup of tequila and a bit of salty cheese on a tray every evening before bedtime. No, it wasn't hard to love Mexico under such conditions. The rent was thirty pesos a month. What was that, back then? Under seven bucks.

To whatever slight extent that I may be considered adventurous, the inclination came in spurts. More regularly, I'm a quiet, studious sort, content to sit with my musings and scribblings. The drama of my existence is largely internal, and that built-up restlessness had recently been knocked out of me. Also, I managed to hang onto my rugged Corona portable. So...back to work.

* * * * * * *

That was how it was for the next year-and-a-half, with local factors crowding gently in. The first awkwardness of communication worked itself out. A secondhand—at least—grammar book, and figuring out ominous world news from newspapers in Spanish. As for speaking, inadvertantly helpful was a dark-skinned, small boy named Facundo, the son of the *criada*—the hired girl. He was always hanging around with questions and remarks. Small-fry always repeat and repeat the same simple words and phrases, and they soak in.

In the neighborhood, on Calle de Dolores, were Chinese restaurants where I took my meals, though the food was more Mexican than Chinese. Yet, often on Sundays, after going to mass with the family—me, the agnostic, though tolerant and interested—I was invited to an enormous Mexican breakfast at home, usually followed, in the afternoon, by a communal, family excursion to the cinema, or out to Chapultepec Park, or to picnic along the canals of Xochimilco. I tried hard to appreciate my adoption. I became *Guero*, which translates to something like "Blondie." Once, I was away for a month, sunning myself on Los Hornos Beach in Acapulco—not yet the opulent resort of today!—in part to cure a persistent, thin cough acquired in the mile-and-a-half-high altitude of Mexico, D.F. But I came back to the city.

* * * * * * *

Once more in contact with my agent Julius Schwartz, I was writing for *Thrilling Wonder, Startling,* and *Planet Stories,* edited by Malcolm Reiss, *Science Fiction Quarterly,* and the Fawcett *Amazing,* whose crusty and admirable editor was RAP—Raymond A. Palmer.

"Secret of the Comet," "Invaders of the Forbidden Moon," "Raider of Saturn's Rings," "Wall of Water," "Gears for Nemesis"....Yes, some titles were slightly...florid? Not all were picked by me.

Since its twist sticks in my memory, I'll comment on "Sarker's Joke Box," which RAP published in the March 1942 *Amazing*: a terrible villain, with great confidence and an impish sense of humor, contrives to avoid a well-deserved punishment by outlasting the time interval dictated by a legal statute of limitations. He does so by sealing himself inside a container made of a substance impervious to all energy, and penetrable only by long and slow grinding. The many months specified by the statute pass, so that when Sarker emerges he will be free. Nobody can legally touch him. But when the unhappy police finally grind their way into his shell, which can't be penetrated by any energy, a fetid, steamy odor assails their noses. Poor Sarker—he had been slowly cooked by the accumulation of his own body heat. Gruesome justice.

"Scientist Disowned," "Space Oasis," "The Eternal Wall"....I'm not sure, but maybe "Hell Stuff for Planet X"—lurid title!—was the last yarn I wrote back then in Mexico. Anyhow, it was the last to get published, in the June 1943 *Startling*, by which time I had been out in the Pacific for most of a year. The yarn was about gigantic weaponry left over from a many-millions-of-years-ago war which wiped out the Martians and blasted their opponent's planet into the fragments which now form the Asteroid Belt.

XVI.

FROM THE WAR TO *COLLIER'S*

Sunday, December 7, 1941, was a beautiful, sunny, temperate day in Mexico, D.F. The radio was giving continuous, though not always clearly defined, news. The Pearl Harbor blitz....President Roosevelt was calling it the "Day of Infamy," and now the U.S. was in the fight.

One of the young men in the family wanted to go up and join the U.S. Air Force right away. So my mere presence as a possible supporting factor for his lusty young enthusiasm put me under a cloud for a while, particularly with the elder, distaff family members, though I tried to stay out of the problem, except to suggest at last that he go see the military attaché at the American consulate, being sure that, though the gentleman whom I had visited myself would be cordial, he would point out certain difficulties about becoming a U.S. fighter pilot, even for a United States citizen. A few years later, this sky-oriented enthusiast did get his wish—flying for a Mexican airline.

It took me four months of inner conflict to pull myself loose from the warm friendliness and other advantages of my home in Mexico. Arriving across the border in Laredo, Texas, I had an easier choice: east or west? Pretty much an indifferent, fifty-fifty proposition. So, by Greyhound to New York, where I tried the Navy. With the war on, I thought I had a chance now. No, but I was steered to an office hiring civilian workers for Pearl Harbor. The medics scowled at the deep scar in my back, but what bothered them most were my nearsighted eyes, even though glasses gave them 20-20 vision. I wonder if the Navy is still so fussy about sight? I was sent to an opthalmologist. Then I was kept waiting....I was, frankly, a little leery about shipping out on a freighter facing U-boats in the North Atlantic, but I got myself a seaman's passport. Finally they got tired of my pestering them at that Navy hiring office and tipped me off about another office in the same building. As I remember it, it was Tuesday; Friday morning I was on the train, a sworn-in civilian employee of the U.S. Corps of Engineers. Ironically, my Navy travel vouchers had come through too, and had to be turned back.

So to Camp Stoneman-does anyone remember it?—near Pittsburg (without an "h"), California. I was lucky; I might have gotten stuck in that desolate scene for most of a month! As it was, I spent only one night there; then, by a troop ship in a convoy, I was headed west.

First I was at a deep, red mud place called Waikakalaua Gulch Camp, fourteen miles from Honolulu. "Some of you guys are supposed to be carpenters," a tough individual told a bunch of us newcomers, "so here's your T-B (prefabbed temporary barracks). All set up nice except for putting on the roof."

With a lot of fumbling and sweat, we got the roof in place and bolted it on. Only we neglected to put in plug boards between the rafters. So the mosquitos swarmed into our dwelling from under the eaves and, that first night, damn near ate us alive. You couldn't even open your mouth to breathe or snore, or they'd be biting your tonsils and choking you....At first daylight we got those plug boards installed, and learned about an electrical gadget which boiled water mixed with an insect killer. No trouble there, after that.

Plenty of us were total greenhorns. No previous training. Application of the old emergency principle of shove 'em in and let 'em find out by doing, if they could. Meat for rugged individualists? Sure, there were guys who bluffed their way into high-paying jobs. One guy had signed on as an experienced riveter. The rivets he knew about were those used in an overalls factory. They busted him down to laborer, same as I was. But he was still employed, which he mightn't have been without his minor prevarication.

First I was loading cement bags into trucks. Then I was deep in tunnels being dug into the mountains, pushing a muck buggy. Then, after the blasting, I was "barring down"—poking at the tunnel roofs to knock loose any unsafe overhead rock masses that might fall and kill somebody. Then I was on a grouting crew, pumping water and cement into the rock strata at fifteen hundred pounds of pressure, to seal the cracks against seepage. The tunnels were for safe storage purposes—ammunition, food, medical supplies. Then I was in a blacksmith shop, whose principle product was drill steels "set up" for the miners and shaped with a screw-type end to accept the cutting drillheads.

I've always kind of liked physical work. It was exhilarating; you felt the worth of your muscles, you knew when the next pay check was coming; and you could see what you had accomplished....To sweat was a good thing.

There were anecdotes around. One grouting crew—not ours—pulled a terrible boo-boo: they hooked the hose of their rig to pipe not intended for grout at all; it was the inlet of a large, buried tank intended for storage of aviation gasoline. So they had to crawl down into that tank and try to dig out all that hardening cement. Then there was the story about how a man who opened a new restaurant in Honolulu acquired the necessary tableware, which was very hard to come by. He put a notice in the *Honolulu Advertiser*: anybody who would bring in a fork, knife, and spoon would get a nice, otherwise free meal. So our mess hall got raided by various characters. And we were reduced to whittling chopsticks out of the wood from dynamite boxes, and learning how to use them. And, well, let the tales go....

I was shifted around with the Corps of Engineers for well over a year. Construction projects got completed. Servicemen, trained in the States, were moving in to take over what work was left. Guys I knew, their contract time completed, were going home to the States. Likely they'd be sent back out to the Pacific again, to do much the same jobs, but in uniform. A ring of power was gradually closing in on the Japanese Empire. But the Pearl Harbor Navy Yard seemed to be working harder than ever. There were many battle-damaged ships to repair.

I went there to ask, and had to go for an opthamologist's okay again, but was hired. So I was there for a year, rated at last as a Marine blacksmith, second class. Life was cleaner and more settled, and more regular. Quarters in Civilian Housing Area Three were, comparatively, almost luxurious. There was still plenty of overtime, but I was off every eighth day—"J-Day." I worked nights and, on the theory that food could replace sleep, to a large extent, I got heavier than I've ever been, before or since—188 pounds—but very little of it fat.

The work? Straightening the bronze blades of ship propellers that had gotten bent and crumpled against the coral reefs in close approaches to enemy-held islands under attack. This was a group job, involving an overhead bridge crane, a chain sling, and a hydraulic press. Then bronze welding to repair the crumples....There were plenty of other tasks, too. Sometimes I speculate about how many thousands of pipe flanges I pounded out under the largest air hammer there in X-23, which was the designation of the Pearl Harbor forge shop.

Writing? Nothing much except some never-finished scribblings vaguely oriented toward big, "slick" magazines such as the *Saturday Evening Post*. Activities for my free daytimes, and for my J-Day off, were going to town or sleeping on the beach. Waikiki had a slight odor, however, because, in order to avoid tracking by submarines, ships dumped garbage not far offshore. Sometimes I would visit an elderly artist-couple whom I'd picked up with. They had a house, with a nice lanai to doze or read on, up Black Point Road. Through them, I tried my luck at sketching at the Honolulu Academy of Arts.

One J-Day when I headed home in the late afternoon, there was a pall of black smoke over the Navy Yard. When I got to work that evening, screens of green canvas were already put up around a couple of piers. The story never got in the papers, but while two ships were being loaded, some ammunition had exploded. Maybe nobody knew exactly how it happened, but I saw a piece of rib cage in the water.

Reading the SF mags, I got better acquainted with Ray Bradbury's stories. The guy had marvelous terseness, imagery, and movement. He could pack an awful lot of feeling and color into a few lines, and end a yarn with a real punch. The result was close to poetry. But some quality he had bugged me from the start. It wasn't that his science was often thin and inaccurate; I could tolerate that much license. There was something else....Too much focus on death? No, not quite that....Rather, an over-sweet, timorous, phony idealism. But a lot of readers obviously loved his writings, and so, in a way, did I.

Somewhere along the line, Hitler's V-1, the flying buzz bomb, was reported in the papers. There was no good in agonizing further over the many deaths in cities—only to end the process as soon as possible. A new bomb, when bombing had become a way of life? But the V-1 was technologically interesting, especially that pulse-motor. It was much simpler, and, in a way, more effective, than the complicated and costly reciprocating engines that turned propellers.

As a weapon, I had much the same attitude about the V-2. But almost at the first words about it, I sensed a lot more. They called it "the ghost bomb" because it was silent. But how? By descending at supersonic speed from some airless

116

altitude where there could be no sound? Then there were photos of the remains of one in London: crumpled pipes, tubes, pumps....And mention in the papers of "some complicated stoking" before such a weapon could be launched. It all added up to one thing, of particular fascination to a SF scribe: a big, liquid-fueled rocket! Cripes, at last! Warfare wasn't even the point. Here was the threshold, the proven possibility...of spaceships! Of space travel!

* * * * * * *

My contract at Pearl Harbor ran out. A bit "rock happy," I returned to the mainland, and then New York. My draft board was in San Antonio, Texas—Bexar County—since I had registered there when I came out of Mexico. My 1-A status was transferred to New York City and I thought, what the hell, the Army could be as good a way as any to get back to Europe, to be on the scene, to be involved in the chaos of the pending peace. Let's see what happens....

In the induction examination, they bounced me. Unfit—4-F. That the Nazis had thrown in the sponge, and that the war in the Pacific seemed to be close to the showdown stage may have raised the standards of selectivity. Also, I was getting into my middle thirties. Anyhow, an expected result. No sweat. Now I had the freedom of an official and final decision. So, for whatever opportunity came next, I marked time for the war's last couple of months by testing the hardness of crankcase forgings for aircraft engines in Jersey.

Some people I had known before wondered why I'd taken dirty jobs like those with the Corps of Engineers. Why hadn't I tried for something with class in Washington? Well, I'd hardly thought of that. No particular appeal, I guess. Anyhow, nobody had come looking for me for such work.

* * * * * * *

Hiroshima, then Nagasaki....I'd fantasized so much and for so long about the power locked in atoms that there was a reverse effect—I had trouble accepting it as a fact. Atomic bombs? Honest-to-gosh? I had supposed, too, that such stuff was still a good ways into the future, but here it was, a science fiction term actualized—the Nuclear Age! Any peripheral horror I felt for all the people who had been killed was mostly submerged by the wonder of a step forward, and in the fact that the long grief of World War II had abruptly ended.

My urge to get back to Europe, possibly with some U.S. Government job, though still strong, got a bit blurred and indefinite. If you have a pre-set purpose, my experience is that you'd better act on it promptly, or you might put down roots where you are, and have difficulty pulling away. That was what was happening to me again, more so than in the past. I had spent a good while without serious distaff companionship. In part to alleviate this condition, and following up on what I'd started when I first tried to draw at the Honolulu Academy of Arts, I'd been going evenings to the Art Students' League on West 57th Street. The place had a mellow, cotton-woolish mood—an excellent counterpoise for the rough factory ambience of my employment.

At the League I got talking to this girl. Auburn hair, amber eyes, gentle but a little mocking. She liked mathematics and travel, but she taught several languages, and knew several more, including Aramaic and Gothic. Such details came out, not as brags, but in response to my prodding. She was wearing a neat, unobtrusive skirt suit, and she was somebody quite a ways out of my sphere. Still, something clicked.

One Sunday before lunch I came to her family's apartment. We had meant to start the day with a walk, but it was raining. She fixed sandwiches for us.

Then she said, "Look, I have test papers to mark before we go out to dinner. And you ought to write...."

She set me up with a typewriter, a table and paper, and left me alone. A challenge.

I thought, okay, humor her. Cook up and pound out some little exercise story. She doesn't know that serious writing is far from easy.

I came up with a story plot quickly enough. Not SF—mainstream. An exotic scene I knew...Acapulco. Los Hornos Beach. A girl, of course. With whom? Her little daughter. The big girl's problem? The general rottenness of the human race. The man she has divorced for running off with somebody else, and a lousy old uncle of her's who keeps sending her daughter cheap wooden dimestore toys, along with, for herself, crude, transparent flatteries—"My niece, so pretty with plenty of money, from a big fashion art job in New York!" All hints to keep her sending him handout checks. All while her little daughter, whom she dearly loves, is also fundamentally a thoughtless, uncaring stinker! Look...she has just gotten that red, wooden firetruck, and already it's smeared with sand and one wheel is broken, while the little brat runs off from it, indifferent.

Time for the handsome, eligible young hero to come on the scene, with whatever corny approach. He picks up the truck, only—surprise!—he puts Big Girl straight about her crude old uncle, people in general, and, incidentally, himself.

"No," he tells Big Girl, "this isn't a cheap dimestore toy at all. Handmade with love. I bet the little man on the seat wasn't whittled out in less than a day."

I completed this short-short in just about four hours, and finished by typing "Bright Message" at the top of the first page.

My friend—her name was Frieda Talmey—read it through quickly, and had me correct a few typos and spelling errors while she searched out a manila envelope from her desk. I went along with the charade. What could I lose? She also had a postal scale and stamps, and a quiet deliberate way. The rain had eased off. We mailed the script to *Collier's*, a big-time family magazine of those days. Then I took her to a good Chinese restaurant, called Gung-Ho, that was in the neighborhood.

I think it was the next Saturday morning that I received a note from John Schaffner, fiction editor of *Collier's*. He had wanted to phone me before leaving the office for the weekend, but could find no number for me, so he was writing.

Collier's was offering five hundred dollars for "Bright Message," and would I please phone him on Monday.

It was one of those extremely rare occasions when a person with a particular dedication ought to want to yell for sheer joy. However, the fact was that my reaction was so extreme I, even with my hardy stomach, came close to vomiting—even though I *was* happy, although mostly bewildered. I had been prepared to spend months of hard and careful work breaking into "the slicks," with no assurance that I would succeed even then. So, on a Sunday afternoon, with no belief and as a joke, I had done it. The mocking irony was almost too much. It was as if a great crack had appeared in the foundation of a certain faith. Five hundred bucks...for four hours of casual amusement! That was damn good earnings back then.

As soon as I had recovered some of my cool, I phoned Frieda. She was very pleased, but she took it in stride.

I spent ten days of effort on my next shot at *Collier's*. Short-shorts are commonly recognized as being very hard to write. I struggled to put every word in exact place. This one, I thought, was better than the first: a merchant seaman, giving up the free and wandering life, being just recently married and with a settled job ashore, is sorting out his few possessions at his casual rooming house, preparatory to moving in with his bride. What to do with the pictures of his old girl-friends? Lingering, friendly sentiment....Just throw the pictures out? What else can he do?.... His bride comes in to help him pack. He is embarrassed and a little truculent when she picks up the bunch of photos, thinking she will be angry.

"Do you want to keep them?" she asks.

"I travel light," he answers.

"But then is it nice just to leave them lying around exposed on the table like that?" she asks further. Then she does something that makes him love her even more. There are some magazines he is throwing out. She puts each picture into a separate magazine. I called the story "Final Rite."

That time the check was for six hundred dollars. The stories appeared in the May 18, and July 6, 1946 issues of *Collier's*.

Twice out of the first two tries. Am I lucky on first attempts? Did I spend too much of my limited allotment of good fortune on them? Hell, that's mystical—not scientific at all! But there's a perversity.

I wrote "Little Knave" with care. Schnaffner's comment: "Original and touching....Unfortunately we receive so many stories about small boys." So the piece wound up at last in the *New York Daily News*.

I persisted with gritted teeth. Was that part of my trouble? Did I get so tightened up that something froze? Did some esoteric taint derived from my SF background handicap me as a writer for the big, mainstream magazines? Fred Pohl was my agent for awhile, not only for SF but for these more popular markets. He deserved an E for Effort, but it was no go. In addition to one more short-short in the *Daily News*, a rather nice, longer piece called "Blurred Barrier" was published in a 1947 *Family Circle*, although the exact date is now out of my reach.

So ended my visible career as a writer for the slicks—although not the trying. Later on, Roger Terrill, previously top editor at Popular Magazines, also tried to market my mainstream short stories. Same result. Now, most of those big-time magazines are either defunct or debilitated. A lost objective, replaced by TV.

But I was showing up again in science fiction.

Fred Pohl got an altered version of an old Paris story of mine, "Stepson of Space," on television. I was in Spain at the time, 1952, and never saw it. Yes, TV—an old SF promise—had become real.

"Operation Pumice," carefully written and intended for the slicks—a narrow miss at *Collier's*—appeared in *Thrilling Wonder* in April 1949. It was about a first flight around the moon.

"A Step Farther Out" (no connection, that I know of, with a later SF column of the same name) was printed in *Super Science* in March 1950. About a favorite subject of mine then—asteroids that, in my version, were fragments of a once-inhabited planet—the yarn was a story-within-a-story. As I was completing the tale in Guatemala City on July 18, 1949, an abortive revolution broke out. The next morning, while I revised a few pages, there was still sporadic gunfire. Shells from the government-held presidential palace were knocking chunks of masonry off the communications building. Pension Torres, the locally styled hostelry where I was lodged, was midway between these two points.

Most of the time, though, I was in the New York City area.

"Coffins to Mars," a long novelette, ran in the June 1950 *Thrilling Wonder*. On an overpopulated Earth, what do you do with the rejuvenated elderly, in part to keep them away from intergenerational resentments? Ship them to Mars, where, after complaints and hardships, they start constructive new lives. "Generation gap" was a term not yet coined in 1950. Foresight?

"Bluff Play," *Thrilling Wonder*, December 1950: if the Russians think they are far ahead in armed spaceship construction, and threaten to attack us, might not we steal mud from the landing wheels of one of their returned explorer ships, develop the seeds in it, and show them a garden of extraterrestrial plants, suggesting that we aren't behind at all, and that they'd better watch out?

"Asteroid of Fear," "The First Long Journey".... Short of room, I'll skip comment. But though I was working on full-time jobs, mostly related to aircraft, and still trying to crack the big magazines, my science fiction comeback was in full swing. Also, F. Orlin Tremaine, with whom I had exchanged friendly letters since Hawaii, and with whom I occasionally went to lunch now, where we enjoyed rambling discussions, had given me tips about getting into technical writing. This kind of work was soon to become my mainstay of employment.

"Prodigal's Aura." Yes, this one got into the April 1951 issue of *Astounding*. With a wry and reminiscent shrug, I sent the script to Campbell, wondering curiously what his response would be. I got just a check, no letter, which, I guess, was the best answer. It was a pretty good yarn, about a freewheeling, improvident space adventurer who comes home for Christmas to visit his sister and her disapproving, square, and very substantial husband and his family. At length, after much trouble and comical conflict, he wins even his brother-in-law over. In writing this yarn I profited a lot from trying for the major, family-oriented magazines. Maybe I thought, too, of my long-dead Uncle Julius, the Navy man.

Regarding Campbell, however, there was something from long before that had put me in a rather bad light. He wrote me a very nice letter, wondering why he never got any stories from me anymore. The missive caught me in one of those situations and moods wherein I have occasionally been perverse and lacking in good judgment. I had often been told of Campbell's very right-wing politics, so, I thought, dammit, I'll bug him! I wrote back that the subliminal purpose of all my science fiction had been to promote communist dialectics, and that he probably wouldn't be interested in any more of my stories, especially since I was a card-carrying Communist.

This was pure put-on and nonsense, of course. Though I may be a little eccentric otherwise, I've always been, politically, a middle-of-the-roader with an aversion for strong leanings, either to the right or the left. So now I have set the record straight.

"Trailblazer," *Fantastic*, Fall 1951: why not an old American Indian, innocent of technological know-how, yet remembering the hunting lore of his youth, craftily follows two hip young engineers he helped rear to get to the moon? There he finds footprints, millions of years old, in the lunar dust and is led to an ancient spacecraft. Aboard it he "presses the wrong button" and winds up as the first human on Mars. In the terrestrial ship that follows in his wake, there is, as it lands, a flash fire. (For what little this note may be worth, didn't a similar tragedy happen once to an Apollo space capsule at Cape Canaveral?) So the tough, nature-aware Indian has to bail a bunch of strandees out of their difficulties.

"The Restless Tide," *Marvel*, November 1951: perhaps my best short story, certainly one I polished with care. I had shown it to Ben Hibbs at the *Saturday Evening Post*. "Interesting, but not quite our dish of tea," was his response. It was about the nature of mankind, first restlessly reaching for adventure, then for comfort, luxury, and peace, and becoming alternately fed up with both conditions. In a culture where a lifetime is centuries long, wisdom dictates cyclic changes from one to the other.

"The Great Idea," *Startling*, January 1952: at about this time somebody called me "The idea man of science fiction." Maybe this yarn presents an example? The predominance of Earth's gravity over the distance between the Earth and moon, plus the fact that things on the lunar surface weigh only one-sixth as much as on Earth, should give metals, or whatever is mined on the moon, potentially ample and intrinsic energy to transport them to Earth—without the need for any extraneous energy at all! The metals are transported by an endless cable looped around a moon-based pulley. The trouble is, among other things, where to get a cable of a substance with sufficient tensile strength? Otherwise, it would break because of its own weight over such a long distance. "But there must be a way," the disgruntled hero moans at the story's end. "Any suggestions?"

Then there was "EV" (for "Escape Velocity"), *Astounding*, February 1952: I got help with this from Jerry Bixby, a multi-talented young guy—musician, painter, and writer—who had been an editor at Fiction House, publishers of *Planet Stories*, along with Mal Reiss. I showed him the first draft of this little story, and he rewrote and improved it. Escape velocity here is both literal and metaphorical, meaning that, at just about the time when terrestrial science had achieved escape from local gravity into space, it should also, in parallel, have achieved escape from other human limitations....Later on, I heard that Jerry was doing very well as a TV script writer out in his native California.

I see that I've inadvertently skipped past "Passport to Jupiter," my first book-length novel, which editors Sam Merwin and Horace Gold published in the January 1951 *Startling*. Some say that the sensipsych—the artificial-dream machine—is very debilitating to the human spirit, and that the bemused populace needs to be jolted back to reality by a solid shot of violence. This somewhat spurious and controversial thought is supported by the discovery of an alien race that has withdrawn into the depths of Jupiter, where, through such dreams, they have decayed to total mindlessness. So where is the sensible, middle ground? While writing this yarn, I was thinking of television as a crude forerunner of the sensipysch.

Right after "Passport...," in the February 1951 *Thrilling Wonder*, came "Brother Worlds": Since there are so many binary stars in the universe, why haven't more SF scribes written about binary planets? The Earth and moon fall short of being a pair. Take two that are of almost equal size, revolving close together around a common center of gravity, and both life-infested. Mix them up with a romantic but lazy young space vagabond, who, in childhood, happened to lose his twin brother. Add a frosty Earth girl and some other extreme hazards, and it makes a fair story.

Then there were "Return of a Legend" and "Big Pill," both in *Planet*, in March and September 1952, respectively. "Big Pill" means a leftover bomb, a relic that was intended to tear a world apart. It is big enough so that, over the ages, primitive life has taken root on its surface. This masks its still-armed, original purpose.

"Comet's Burial," *Science Fiction (#1)*, 1953: if a large comet, composed of ice and frozen gases, can be deflected so that it crashes into the moon, couldn't it bring the moon a viable atmosphere? If it also hit at a calculated angle, couldn't it increase the lunar rate of axial rotation too, so that settlers from Earth would enjoy days and nights of fairly normal length?

"Ten to the Stars," *Science Fiction Adventures*, March 1953: actually, Lester del Rey, the editor, and I had known each other years before, in what was an entirely non-science fiction relationship—since neither of us knew who the other was! Small world....But, though very different, we were kindred beyond just SF, both of us making our individualistic rambles through the byways of life. So, finally, we met during my brief employment at a prominent literary agency, where Lester was an old pro. I was much too deliberate, and much too a slow a typist, to last!

About "Ten to the Stars"....It was a long novelette. Ten young fellows, poorly financed, but operating as a group to build their own equipment in a shoestring fashion, join the rush to develop the solar system, with future individual fortunes varying from death to glory. Judging from readers' letters, it made a fair hit. Later, I expanded this same story idea into a full-length book.

Lester also took "Legacy from Mars" for the July 1953 *Science Fiction Adventures*: a semi-serious "fish story" spoof, featuring a whimsically charming pair of goldfish-like creatures, Marty and Martia, from the polar regions of arid Mars, a young Greek who plays the harmonica, two old spacemen, the daughter of one, and a villainous tomcat.

"Captive Asteroid," *Science Fiction Plus*, April 1953: back with Hugo Gernsback in his new, though to be short-lived, smooth-papered magazine. Back then, though, he was paying promptly.

"Give Back a World," *Planet*, May 1953: a restoration of diminished axial rotation of the planet Mercury by the application of the same principle as that of an old physics lab trick, involving somebody set spinning on a piano stool, while holding a pair of heavy dumbbells extended outward at arms length. When he pulls the dumbbells inward toward his chest, his rate of spin increases.

"Double Identity," *Dynamic*, June 1953: can Earth-folk be forced to exchange bodies with far-off aliens—through a gradual biological transformation—after they have touched an alien apparatus? A scary, folksy novelette, featuring a different kind of space travel.

"Stamped CAUTION!" My only story in *Galaxy Magazine*, August 1953: one of my best first encounter yarns. A non-humanoid infant Martian is found encased in a mudball aboard a crashed spacecraft. Amid much wary speculation and nervously extreme precautions about the hazard he might pose, he is carefully and experimentally raised on Earth, and accompanies the first Earth expedition to the Red Planet. Yep, about Mars again...my persistent fixation!

"The Guthrie Method," *Science Fiction Quarterly*, May 1954: how about treating patients with weakened hearts by hurling them into the benevolent, zero-G environment of space—if prediagnosed to be able to stand the trip—and then advising them to move to a low-G world?

"Dawn of the Demigods," *Planet*, Summer 1954: about the more adventurous portion of mankind transforming itself to a far hardier android metabolism, which gives numerous other advantages. These people are furiously opposed by the less bold—reckless?—members of the species, who must compete unfavorably with them. This long novelette was the last of my post-World War II spurt in the science fiction magazines. I was not to turn up with anything new in the mags for twenty-three years.

XVII.

FRIEDA

One significant event occurred in the science fiction field back in 1946: two *major* book publishers, Crown and Random House, had each published a large anthology of SF magazine stories. Science fiction had gained status and come of age. I had a story in both books; "Davy Jones' Ambassador" was in Crown's *The Best of Science Fiction*, edited by Groff Conklin, and "Seeds of the Dusk" was in the Random House collection, *Adventures in Time and Space*, edited by Raymond J. Healy and Francis McComas.

A lot had happened in my personal life in the years since. Okay, maybe my powers weren't as good as some others', but, anyhow, I seemed to be slipping more and more into a scramble, a real rat race-type confusion: all-day jobs and scribbling at night, or vice versa, making room for honest sentiment; pulling away in summer for a wider, and shared, look at far horizons. Wanting all this, and needing much of it. Trying to keep pace, and still catching up? Scattering myself all around. Something had begun gradually to give, not all at once.

So I showed a rough draft of a novel based on the same concepts as in "Dawn of the Demigods" to Rogers Terrill, the agent. He, in turn, showed it to the editors at Simon & Schuster, and got me a small advance—only two hundred and fifty dollars—to complete the book. This I did in two months, while working for Republic Aviation, and it had a pretty good go as *People Minus X* (my original title was *Of Firmer Flesh*), though the Simon & Schuster hardcover version didn't come out until 1957 and the Ace Double paperback version the next year. One interesting point, the U.S. Army bought a thousand hardcover copies right away.

This novel links up loosely with "Passport to Jupiter," the recorded dream projector, etc. The central idea, though, is the replacement of natural protoplasm in the human body with far hardier, artificial vitaplasm, thus making conversion of humans into android supermen possible, though this change is fearfully and violently opposed by many. These androids are usually of entirely human size and appearance, though replicates can be made, down to the dimensions of airborne dust motes. Many strange adventures thus become possible, including a ride on a small meteoroid from Mars toward Earth. An imminent conflict between the divergent beings is safely resolved when the androids (who are as charitable as their human counterparts) migrate from Earth to the planets of Sirius where there are no intelligent lifeforms for them to disturb.

I packed a lot of ideas into this novel: monsters of vitaplasm, designed on the drawing board and produced by a forerunner of what we now call bio-engineering; how android-humans might disappear into the practical invisibility and shelter of smallness by reducing their size in several stages, rebuilding successively smaller, necessary apparatus at each step; how beings the size of dust grains might successfully defeat a normal-sized man by burrowing into his blood stream, swimming along, and then sabotaging his heart or brain. Maybe I was the first to bring up some of these possibilities.

Frieda had her long summer vacations and, in my jobs, by prearrangement with my employers, and concentrated work, I could usually break away at the same time without too much fuss being made. So we did a lot of traveling. But, since we had centered attention on Latin America, we didn't get back to Europe till 1952.

When we did, I found *Le Foyer des Jeunes* not very much changed. Madame Zimmerman was still in charge. I made a quick excursion to 2 Rue des Grands Degres, and saw that the neighborhood had deteriorated. I went into the little bistro on the ground floor where Freddie Suter used to preside. When I asked about him, I was met with a cold stare, and then a blunt answer: during the liberation of Paris, Monsieur and Madame Suter were *mitrailleusées...collaborationnistes*.

Yes—it was a jolt. A couple in their sixties put up against a wall and machine gunned....Impassioned, street-court justice. Of course, I couldn't know the full background of their case. Swiss people are hotelkeepers in lots of places. Freddie had spoken French, English, Italian, and German. I had never known him to say anything pro-Hitler, and his snorts of derision against the Nazis had been convincing enough. He had been friendly to my students. A few times I had gone out of the city with him, along the extension of the Paris Metro, *la ligne de Sceaux*, to his small villa, and helped him with his garden. Being a hotelkeeper, no doubt he had had to accept German soldiers as guests during the occupation....But who can say? Parisians had had a lot that was jagged and heavy in their memories. It still showed in their faces. And when they had broken free....Yep, part of the human condition....

I had already looked for what our Foyer bunch used to call "The Strudel Club," off of Passage Charles D'Allery. Gone. I wasn't sure I even recognized which doorway it was. If the refugee-pair that had operated it had stayed, as they had intended, likely they had become ashes.

* * * * * * *

In 1952 I met Walter Ernsting—"Clark Darlton"—well-known now as the author of the Perry Rhodan books. He, tickling the bellies of fish while out in a Bavarian lake in a rubber boat. He, with a P-38 in the glove compartment of his VW. "Who knows whom I'll meet on the Autobahn?" He, a Russian-held POW till 1950! Maybe *he* should write his SF memoirs....

Frieda had been in Germany on a Fulbrights Scholarship that summer. I lingered on in Europe for a short while, wandered down to Ibiza, one of the Balearic Islands in the Mediterranean off Spain. That was where I wrote "Captive Asteroid" for Gernsback.

I lingered again in 1955—two extra months shoestringing around Egypt, the ancient land of my particular fascination. I came back home thinned down and weary, but happy.

Then in 1958 I returned to Ibiza to take one more crack at science fiction—a book: *The Planet Strappers*. I didn't get home till December, but I had a novel done. Like in "Ten to the Stars," it was about a group of young people, including one gutsy girl, joining the rush of mankind to make use of the solar system. A variety of characters: two football players; a tough, cool loner; a rich guy; a momma's boy; a black kid whose passion was gardening; an excitable guy who was always getting into fights; a big, cheerful dolt; a Mexican who loved motorcycles; a braggart who chickened out and didn't go; and, in the background, an old man who owned the hobby shop where it all began. Each of these to his particular destiny, and often a surprising one. For instance, in the very low lunar gravity, does a moon explorer really need *two* good legs?

The script made the rounds of publishers. Pyramid Books brought it out as a paperback in 1961. It had a pretty good go for those days—just a few copies short of eighty thousand. But I had made up my mind long before. The advance had been one thousand dollars, rather standard for then, plus a little extra for the sale that went beyond contract requirements. And later some sales in Germany as *Sternenfieber—Starfever*. Still low pay. Did so much of the effort have to be a labor of love? There were easier, faster, less strained, and more reliable ways of making a living. And in SF I'd at least touched on just about every area that I could think of: aliens; exotic mechanisms and variant biologies; far-flung futures and pasts; planetary macro-mechanics; miniaturized human environments. I'd projected outward most of the stock of ideas that had come my way. And the old drive had burned low. Enough, for now. There were plenty of others promoting speculative, and perhaps constructive, ideas about the future. It was high time to stabilize my existence, simplify and regularize it; slow down the scramble; stop being an idiot. And put my marriage into a calmer, more even, and balanced shape.

I don't suppose that any strong bond of affection and mutual appreciation is ever entirely smooth. And quite a lot in Frieda's and my backgrounds and lifestyles didn't mingle so well at the start. She was a native-born member of a New York family with strong cultural traditions; I was from rural Wisconsin, with a scattered hodgepodge of acquired touches from elsewhere....If I went into a corner beer joint to clutch a mug at the bar, she might go along tolerantly amused, yet it was a considerable change of pace. But this example is a small matter, comparatively. Sentimentality—In the past, I'd gotten and given hurt—without wanting either. But now a new page. Stabilize, simplify. Join the populace; let the nine-to-five bit take precedence, job-wise. Let whatever writing you do be unpressured by the freelancer's rat race....Seek peace....

There was another clincher. I went to a doctor. He said, "I don't know what you're doing to yourself, but you're headed straight for trouble." My blood pressure was over 200. But with a change of attitude, it was down to 120/70 within a month.

126

Science fiction had been fun while it lasted. It had given me a lot. Finished now. A relief. As for why I became relatively little-remembered, part of the reason must be that I dropped out completely. Even dead SF scribes have their eulogists. I just vanished quietly from the scene.

I continued to follow tech writing jobs around, depending on which subcontractor picked up the contract. Getting hired was fairly easy. I'd worked on manuals for DEW Line, the Distance Early Warning radar system set up in northern Canada. Then on ground support equipment books for the Atlas ICBM. Ultimately, I got something more settled, with a manufacturer of sonar equipment for submarine detection and tracking, Edo Corporation, at College Point, Long Island. I could get home quickly every night. And extending summer vacations could be prearranged. I was with that company for eleven years.

No, I didn't give up story writing. Does that ever happen? Like other scribes, I had a mainstream novel that I had long wanted to get to. Rogers Terrill had shown tentative samples of its substance to Harcourt Brace, with an encouraging reaction, but I had never gotten around to going on with it. Now I did, working evenings, without strain, when nothing else more immediate intervened. I called the book *Ormund House*, the model being the house where I grew up. To me, the man who had built it, though he was dead by his own hand before my time, was a close relative of mine, not of blood but of environment—a special kind of godfather. His name, written in some of his books from the attic, was not Ormund as I had made it, but a less euphonious Osman. There is no question that, through those books which he left behind, along with rather unusual surroundings and circumstances, he had done much to shape me. So, in basis, *Ormund House* was autobiographical, as perhaps anything real must be, to some extent. It wasn't science fiction—it was about a science fiction writer, and what he was as a person besides that. It was the story behind many stories, but mostly it was a people story. During twelve years I worked through it four times, enjoying the project all the way through. I put all I had learned about writing into it; I wanted to make it the best I could do. And I think I succeeded.

Then I began showing it around to publishers. Comments: "It certainly has pace and color...." "Interesting characters and situations....Strong suspense....Wry humor and philosophical asides...."

Ultimately, the del Reys took a hand in seeing where it might go. But the bottom-line was, "Too long to be commercially viable." 1,450 pages, and even the price of paper was going up. It would have been a prohibitively expensive book and, particularly after my long silence, I was short on the elusive coin of being known to override all that. So, now, *Ormund House* broods in its carton.

Meanwhile, both science fiction and fantasy had gotten *big*. Well...excellent! Still, I wasn't about to get myself all tied up in knots by such a pleasing and tempting development. I'd had enough acquaintance with such knots before. I'd stay placid. In recent years, Frieda and I had had a good life, yet, at last....

Summers we ranged across the world. We were very different people, but long contact had smoothed us so that we fitted each other as a complimentary pair.

Where one had a lack, the other filled in. For instance, her knowledge of languages was extensive, precise, and rule-shaped; mine was from what I could pick up on the scene.

* * * * * * *

In the spring of 1968 we were preparing for another jaunt. We'd been all up and down eastern and southern Africa before, but we had missed Ethiopia. Frieda's right knee was swollen, but she made light of it. "Sinuvitus," the M.D.s said. No sweat—expected to clear up quickly. Only it didn't. So, more x-rays. A "pathological fracture." Hospital.

They installed an "Elliot Bar," an L-shaped piece of stainless steel, the shorter part through the knee joint, and the longer portion fastened in place by eight screws—much like wood screws—through the femor bone. Of course, there was a biopsy, and a multiplicity of tests. The diagnosis: "Undifferentiated metastatic carcinoma, primary site unkown."

So...radiation therapy. The knee problem cleared up and, doggedly exercising, Frieda regained considerable use of its mobility. A dedicated teacher, she went back to work.

But the damnable stuff moved up into the pelvic bones. More radiation and a clearing-up. And so on, in stages. Cytoxan chemotherapy....

Yet those six years weren't all bad. During two of the late ones, except for a stiffness in that knee, her condition was almost normal. She was off all medication.

We made less strenuous trips. Germany again, the "hex" country of the Hartz Mountains. A leisurely summer in the Canary Islands. Western Mexico, around Guadalajara....Even, in 1969, a stop in Tucson, Arizona where we watched on TV that "First Step for Mankind" on the moon.

But then she began to have trouble swallowing, then breathing. These symptoms were relieved by nitrogen mustard, but of course her blood cell-count plummeted. Yet, she improved greatly, and I hoped to take her home.

On a sunny Sunday in spring, all was ready. Her many friends came in to see her. She was an active part of the happy chatter. She walked successive groups to the elevator. Everything looked good.

Coming back to her room, she began to tell another mild joke, about an elderly country character attending a cookout in the backyard of the nice, modern city house of one of his grandchildren. "When I was young," he said, "we used to eat *inside* the house, and go out in the backyard for the opposite purpose. Now it's the other way 'round!"

In the telling, Frieda laughed. But the laughter was just enough of a jolt to rupture the fragility of the cancer-chewed blood vessels in the center of her chest. She went into a spasm. She was gone of internal bleeding within a few minutes. Perhaps, so best....It was May 19, 1974, in New York's Mount Sinai Hospital.

So passed a gallant lady. This is by no means just *my* opinion. She loved life, fought courageously to hold onto it, and lived it to the fullest as best she could, up to the last moment. She was always thinking of others, and trying to help—me, a major beneficiary there. In the same room with her was a woman of some means from South America, who was worried about her own illness, and was scared of the doctors. Frieda had befriended her, and calmed her down.

After the spasm, the woman met me in the hall, and asked me how my wife had come through it. I told her Frieda had died. The woman broke, unbelieving, totally shocked—the way it can happen when somebody you have just seen, happy and in good spirits, no one for you to worry about at all, is suddenly gone, as if in a car crash after a party.

Having been braced by the facts, I stayed glued together. Within a few days I enveloped and mailed out the cheerful, forward-looking letters Frieda had written that Sunday morning.

Frieda was a very bright, energetic person, with wide potential. But she was indulgently a bit scornful of anything like fame, at least for herself. Perhaps there had been too much of such striving within her own family. But every year since her death, for whatever it is worth, there have been prizes in her name for outstanding language students at John Adams High School in Ozone Park, Queens, New York, where she was foreign language chairman. This is not so much a memorial to her, in a minor way, as it is the sort of thing she would want. Her concerns were always for her students.

XVIII.

A BRUSH WITH EINSTEIN

Somewhere here, I should tell about a matter probably of special interest to SF readers. When Frieda's father, Dr. Max Talmey, was an impecunious medical student in Germany, a local family invited him once a week to have a good, solid dinner. As a reciprocal part of this custom, young Talmey brought the younger lad of the host family scientific books, including one about higher mathematics. Thus, he met Albert Einstein. Their friendship lasted through Dr. Talmey's lifetime.

Max Talmey became an accomplished eye surgeon. But his greatest interest lay in languages, particularly in a simplified, universal tongue which would be a composite of all the others. His belief was that such a language, easily learned everywhere, and thus broadening human communication, would be a strong force toward world peace. Dissatisfied with Esperanto, he constructed his own, which, in improving stages, was first Arulo and then Gloro. He was dead shortly before my arrival on the scene. I don't know how many languages he knew, but, at the last, he was learning Turkish. Among other books, he had also written one explaining the Theory of Relativity.

There had been Einstein's visits, the first from Germany in 1922. Later, for years, Frieda's stepmother sent a birthday cake for him down to Princeton every March 14.

Some of Einstein's impromptu sayings are well-known. Of course, there's the one about God not playing dice, referring, I think, to Einstein's belief in the certainty of the interlocking complexity of the chains of cause and effect, making the future just as definite and fixed as the past, down to the finest detail, in spite of any pragmatic Uncertainty Principle.

Then there is that other one, on view somewhere at Princeton: *Raffiniert ist der Herr Gott, aber boshaft ist er nicht.* "Subtle is God, but malicious he is not." The meaning here is elusive; you have to find what you can in it for yourself.

Einstein was a Jew, very concerned for his own people, but I suspect he separated himself from all varieties of formalized religious dogma, becoming largely a very religious agnostic—which is not a contradiction of terms at all—while using metaphorical language.

Although I never met Einstein, I do know more than one person who did, and the place in New York where they did, for it became my home for quite a while.

The large Talmey apartment was on the corner of West 101st Street and West End Avenue in Manhattan. The window of the big kitchen fronted on a light

130

shaft, which looked down on the rear windows of the adjacent Ansche Khesed Temple, two floors below.

It was a Friday evening. Hearing the cantor singing, Einstein looked out of that kitchen window. Then he turned, smiled in his easy, puckish way, and ad-libbed.

"So *sieht der lieber Gott von hinten aus!... Ich habe mich immer darüber gewundert!*" Translation: "So that's what God looks like from behind!... I've always wondered about that!"

That saying, which Einstein broke out with spontaneously and which is hardly known elsewhere, was a particular treasure of Frieda's family.

* * * * * * *

Once, quite early in Frieda's illness, she was very weak, and I had to stay home from work with her about a month. *Ormund House* had been completed for quite a while, and I felt compelled to get back into science fiction. Almost spontaneously, a novel had been stewing, and so I began it. It was one that would reach as far as my wits would go: ultimate Destination of all intelligent life forms in the universe—those of them that could survive to that goal: the Development, Power, and Knowledge Barrier—nothing left to become, achieve, or learn. And it was logical that these diverse, superentities, thinly scattered far and wide, would link loosely together, like-to-like, to maintain an orderly universe. Needing nothing for themselves, they would become totally benevolent, helping other lesser life forms that had advanced far enough technologically, to gradually follow the same route in outward peace, creating no destructive chaos.

How to accomplish this? By replacing real actions and events with artificially induced dreams indistinguishable from the vividness of reality. Dreams are not substance; the most violent events and adventures can take place in them, and no one and nothing is hurt; no scarce resources can be used up in creating their stage props. Ultimately, actual bodies, with real arms, legs, eyes, ears, and sex organs, are not even needed. Individuals are each reconstituted as "personality nodules" the size of a marble. They lie in great bins sheltered far underground and, for sharing emotions and experiences, they are interlinked by a web of filaments. In this way they are practically immortal, and their ultimate control of what they shall experience is only to wish. Anything conceivable is possible. In this situation there is, of course, the certainty of eventual boredom. The answer to that? To wish for complete forgetfulness, then start over. So—the ultimate solution.

Let us say that at some indefinite time long before the first chapters of the story, the basic design of the SES—Sensory Experience Simulator—had reached Earth by electromagnetic communication from far off super beings, for terrans to develop, apply, and accept warily as a good thing.

So far, much of this—artificial sensory impressions fed directly into the mind through sensory channels—were concepts I'd written about before. But now I wanted to deal with them intimately, personally, *from the inside*. Further, for realism, and for contrast with wonders to come, I wanted to start from real, Earth-bound, familiar ground level—a setting, situation, and emotions that I was closely familiar with.

Hero and heroine, Joe and Jennie, have been through the cycle of initial enthusiasm, final boredom, forgetfulness, and starting over many times. But, again, they have erased almost all of this from their memories. So they are reborn and begin growing up in a rural scene, circa 1920. They are eager, folksy, imaginative, life-hungry kids beset by limitations of their reality to battle. Gradually, though, from retained trace-memories, they find out gleefully that what they perceive as so solid and actual is all a dream, that by intense wishing they can do anything they want, become anybody, and go anywhere within a sensory-simulacrum of the wide universe of space and time. There are no limits to their possible range, except those of their imaginations. As desired, natural laws are retained, altered, or suspended.

Eagerly, Joe and Jennie plunge into this miracle of total freedom where nothing is denied; all that anybody could want is within easy reach. Except...what? They even visit other actual eras of history, together and/or separately. They even visit imaginative mock-ups of heaven and hell. They rediscover the nature of the whole SES system, but in their enjoyment, this hardly matters, at first.

But their frustration grows. They are face-to-face with a paradox. With unlimited range, they feel crushed and hemmed in worse than ever by their impenetrable circumstance. They begin to hate the superentities who ask nothing of them and offer them anything—except pride in themselves and their own accomplishments through real effort, danger, and struggle. So is not their safe, limitless heaven also a narrow hell?

Desperate for escape, Joe even wishes to become one of the "Super-supers." Even this is not denied him. But his self is not yet sufficiently evolved and broadened for him to endure the strain of this for more than an instant; he recoils into his human state, remembering the awesome and wondrous experience only dimly—as a dog who had wished to become a man might remember upon returning, after momentary success, to dog-dom.

Jennie and Joe don't want to forget and start again, because that would only be repeating the same falsifying trap. So they take the last option; they wish that their actual, physical bodies be restored to them. Thus changed, they go out into the real Earth, which, not being needed any more as a place for real habitation, has reverted to wilderness. Here they succeed happily for a while, working proudly with their own hands—until primitive hardship and aging affects their real, physical bodies. This time it is Jennie who becomes very sick, and is dying. Through the agency of a Guardian Light, the godlike entities suggest, but do not insist, that the couple return to the SES system. Stubbornly, her mind fading, Jennies refuses. She'd rather die!

Now the critical center of the whole human psyche comes into focus and question: what does mankind *truly* want? What are the bottom-line values and priorities? Freedom....Pride....What is the hidden meaning of life? *Is it better to be dead than to live endlessly without satisfaction?*

132

Pushed to last-minute extremes, Joe gets a more solid, starker grip on truth, stripped of defiant illusions: being dead is not peace—it is nothingness. And it is final. It ends everything that was, and that still might be. Given the option that he has, death would be an arrogant fool's choice. Joe opts for life.

And he struggles to persuade Jennie's death-clouded mind to go in the same direction, reminding her of all the beauty they have experienced. He succeeds.

Never once, though, do these otherwise friendly, good-hearted two feel thankful for all the lives they have been given. This was intended withholding on my part. Another hint about the human psyche?

Joe and Jennie return to the SES, to forgetfulness, and hopefully to somewhat more satisfying self-fulfillments in yet another go around the Eden Cycle. That is what I called the novel.

To me it remains my best long science fiction story yet brought out. The del Reys published it late in 1974 with *The Best of Raymond Z. Gallun*, an anthology of some of my old yarns. Saleswise, *The Eden Cycle* didn't do as well as hoped. Why? My long absence from SF? A too-dark, not eye-catching cover illo? That I stepped lightly on the toes of some fondly-held views, hinting that natural phenomena are not necessarily pollution-free? Or that dreams might possibly be as destructive as nuclear missiles? Some readers also saw the ending as too negative, showing a heaven that was really a hell. I believed that the positive side, a true, valid, ultimate solution, would come through clearly without being pointed out. Here was a true answer with tremendous advantages, if SF readers would only look at them without Joe's and Jennie's bias. Well, so it is when dealing with the elusive factors of the publishing business.

Frieda saw the galley proofs of *The Eden Cycle*, including the dedication to her, but not the published book.

* * * * * * *

Most people find out how losing a loved one goes: suddenly there's a huge, jagged blank right in the middle of your life. Letting yourself enjoy a sunset or glass of beer without your usual companion can seem an affront to all that is right. That's serious grief, even though you don't show it. It was good that I had my sonar job to hang on to for a long time. Also, I had the diversion of writing.

I saw that SF and fantasy books had taken a new turn of emphasis, farther away from hard science. Many of them had a rather medieval tone. So, if medieval, why not some variety, something parallel but of a different era? Why not ancient Egypt? Here I had piled up a lifetime of interest, information, and constructive envisioning. This included a fair knowledge of the hieroglyphic language. Here was a book I had long wanted to do!

So...how about a man born with the brain of an Isaac Newton or a Galileo, but during the Twelfth Dynasty, circa 1900 B.C., when science was at its barest beginnings? That was Gem-i S'Gem—I-Find He-Who Finds—or, more simply stated, Gemi the Finder, named so by old Sheta, the village midwife and healer. He is to become a rebel against an evil lord, a fugitive with an admitted touch of villainy, a protegé of a tainted wiseman of mysterious origin who heads a troupe of itinerant entertainers aboard a river ship called the *Nen-Ren*—the *No-Name*. Then he meets an escaped criminal from Nubian gold mines, imbued with a purpose hypnotically implanted in his subconscious, then a friend and helper of somewhat wary Pharoah Usertsen himself and an idealistic princess. Gemi, ever a searcher, discovers and works his wonders, including the application of the Archimedian Principle as it functions with heated air. And, finally, admitting himself an unwilling trouble-maker who departs as a favor to everybody but his following, is pursued into a far longer sea voyage than he intends, because of the unwanted and embarrassing presence of the insistent princess whom he honors and admires, though his preference is for a hardier lady.

All of the story elements flowed together readily—rollicking humor as a foil for sorrow, happy surprises countering disasters—and the reverse! Contrasting human characters: Kem, the fugitive black chieftain from Nubia; Keftiu, the mad acrobat from Crete—"the most dangerous man in the world"—who is Gemi's instructor in unarmed combat. Ar-en-heka, He-Who-Makes-Magic, the massive, ugly, enigmatic, overwhelming master of the troupe; learned, lame old Seth, who shows Gemi wonders—a fallen star, a meteorite, the fossil of a tiny pterodactyl. Also there are the beast characters such as Aan, the baboon, and Djineh, the uniquely trained falcon.

Finishing the yarn, I was happy with it, knowing that it came out pretty much as I'd wanted: a fast-moving, adventure tale that also was alive, informative, and as historically accurate as I could make it. And I dedicated it to all searchers and sometime-finders, especially those we do not know.

And I started a couple of other novels.

* * * * * * *

Finally, with loose ends taken care of, I flew to Istanbul. There I joined a group, mostly Australians—an unfussy, friendly lot!—and for a leisurely thirty days we were on the road, by bus, across to Gallipoli, on to Troy and Iran, into Afghanistan, down the Khyber Pass to Peshawar, on into India and Delhi and Agra. We had one bad mishap—a tragedy, really—running down two local motorbikers while entering Tehran, for which our main driver was jailed for six weeks. Though the accident was decidedly not his fault, he was finally bailed out by the company.

Then I moved around in the Far East for another month. For me, the world had recovered much of its shine. I came back to New York by way of Tokyo, Honolulu, and Seattle.

* * * * * * *

After looking up some scientific data at New York's Main Library on Fifth Avenue and 42nd Street, I happened to wander into the reading room where there were a lot of telephone directories, world-wide. So I had a whimsically nostalgic inspiration. I looked up some names of old friends.

A little later, Christmasing in Mexico City, I sent out season's greetings. That was how two kids at the University of Wisconsin found each other again, after some forty years without contact. Bertha Erickson Backman was long-widowed; she had lost her spouse to cancer, the same as I. And she had been true to her old vision—to see the world. Also, she was a travel consultant.

There were telephone conversations—New York-to-Milwaukee, Milwaukee-to-New York. I persuaded her to join a thirty-six-day bus jaunt from Rio, down through Uruguay and Argentina, and up through Bolivia and Lima, Peru where, one summer, I had attended classes in Hispanic literature at San Marcos University.

Bert and I met for the first time, after so long, at the Miami Airport at 1:30 in the morning. "Bert?..." "Ray?..."

Something was still the same, and got even better. The two of us finally on the road together at last! Against all probabilities....Arcane destiny, a full circle completed. A bit magical for a pair of aging romantics....

We returned to our respective homes after the trip. I was just in time to accept an invitation to go down to Florida and watch the launching of Voyager I out toward Jupiter. That was...let's see, September 1977.

Bert and I were married the following year. We honeymooned around the world. No other planets have yet opened up for travel, but the Earth remains quite a remarkable place. We spent a month in Kashmir, one of Bert's favorite locations. And it *is* beautiful.

Though neither of us was especially aquatic, we looked in on Arthur Clarke at Trincomolèe on the east coast of Sri Lanka, where he bases his underwater safaris. Later, I visited him at his big house in Colombo. Among other interesting things there, he had two small monkeys who clung to him so affectionately that, in order to divert their attention enough to make them let go of him so that he could put them back in their tree dwelling, he had to give each a flower to eat! And we had a good talk. Arthur Clarke, in addition to his other blessings, has found a nice way to live. He has made himself intimately familiar with the one other, very different world that is as yet within our general range—the undersea. And I thought, with a certain envy and regret, of my own "Davy Jones' Ambassador." It's a little late for me to start venturing under the ocean's surface now. The space shuttle could be something else, however.

In 1979 Bert and I were in Brighton, England where, at Seacon, I received my one SF honor: First Fandom's Man of the Year Award. Arthur Clarke was at the con, and he was wearing one of his underwater safari t-shirts. Talking to him, I remarked that I wished I had one of those. So, right there, in the single, most literal instance that I know of from anywhere, Clarke demonstrated the old truism about a generous man: *He'd give you the shirt off his back!*

* * * * * * *

On our first anniversary, Bert and I were in Peking—Beijing—China. There have been other junkets since. To South Africa and Madagascar, and to Mauritius, in the Indian Ocean....Most recently, in autumn of 1982, we went to Australia and New Zealand again, and to Papua, New Guinea, new territory to both of us. Don Wollheim, who lived only a ten-minute walk from us, might kid Bert and me about our interest in various exotic cultures, and maybe, to some extent, they were a hobby with us, but what's wrong with that? Some people collect stamps, so what if we collect countries visited? For whatever it may mean I've got my hundred made, according to the Century Travel Club listing, and Bert was just about there too. But there is more to it than the counting. Right now I'm remembering a four-week camping trip, Cairo to Khartoum, early in 1981 that Bertha missed out on because of an injured foot. Getting out of a sleeping bag in the brisk dark of all that desert to start the petrol stove and heat up breakfast water for our bunch of twenty-three people of various origins. Not a light on the horizon, usually—desertion, like in outer space. But once there *was* a light—perfectly clear, right at the bottom edge of the sky. What could it be? No, it wasn't any civilized light because it rose. It was the Morning Star. The air was arid and hazeless, right down to the rim of the world! That's just an example of sudden appreciations. Touches of mood. Know what I mean? It can involve anything. The clasp of a big, dark, calloused hand, the shape of a gnarled tree, and thoughts and other memories blending like bits of history. It's like multi-media poetry, tingling the mind and nerve-ends. Old, yet always new and different.

* * * * * * *

Bert liked to quote Omar Khayyam. It would be a shame to lose a memory, but she was another remarkable woman, from close to my roots, though with enough difference, too. She was keen and practical. Now I also have a daughter, Deidre; we two reciprocate a mutual appreciation. She's another trailnut, lively, good-humored, competent, loyal, and fun to be around—a spark plug for enthusiasm. Bob—or Tink—Steinfuhr, her husband, is a big, cheerful guy, spouting jokes and laughter during our Christmas visits out to Pewaukee, Wisconsin. But he's happy with his business, his house on the lake, his speedboat, his tinkering with his TV recorder and other gadgets, his fishing, his wildlife watching; he couldn't care less about the far side of the Earth. So, in good-natured compromise, he let Deidre gypsy around with Bert and me.

Bert had relatives in the U.S. consular service scattered around Germany, Brazil, and Australia, and—here's a bit of name-dropping again—her eldest brother, Dr. Milton Erickson, deceased now for a couple of years, was a psychiatrist—the authority of hypnotherapy. There is an institute established in his name here in New York to carry out his work and, in May 1983, a memorial arbor of purple-blooming foliage was dedicated to him in Central Park. Not so bad for a kid who grew up on a forty-acre Wisconsin farm, meanwhile contracting polio at age nineteen. But his and Bert's folks were genuine salt of the earth.

* * * * * * *

Bert and I were both retired from formal employment. We lived in a three-and-a-half-room apartment in Forest Hills, New York. Space was limited; we were surrounded by a lot of books, and various objects from afar, and we had to coordinate our activities. Yes, I continued to write, doing pieces pretty much in first-draft form on a manual, portable typewriter in the kitchen, close to the tea kettle, where I could keep my many cups of coffee well-laced with hot water.

An average work day went like this: up before seven; a light breakfast—instant oats with milk and a little sugar—then to work till noon. Meanwhile, if she wasn't doing the shopping, Bert was likely to be in our large living room, reading or working on the very nice patchwork quilts she liked to make. A sandwich for lunch. Back to the mill till drinks at five, dinner before six, usually at home, but sometimes out if we felt like it. Quite often in the evening, in agreeable weather when there was no particular urge to go elsewhere, I'd be down in the nearby playground swinging on the swings. There might be mild laughter from around me, sure, but I was benevolently tolerated. I enjoyed the exuberance of the motion which promoted lively, imaginative, mental activity, besides keeping my belly muscles in shape. My waist measured thirty-four inches, same as when I was twenty, even though I was twenty pounds lighter at 155. I was five feet, nine inches tall; once, I was three-fourths of an inch taller. Often I'd see joggers around, and wonder a bit at the set facial expressions of so many, as if they weren't enjoying their exercise at all. So, you see, after some past contacts with chaos, I'd come to a mellow kind of peace.

We weren't rich, yet by benevolences that include those of unreliable, perhaps amused and tricky—though so far benign—chance, plus some prudence, we had enough to live on simply, and to our taste, with something left over for extras. I was grateful, and found it somewhat wondrous. We had lots of friends scattered around hither and yon, and there were jokes that our little place often served as a motel.

* * * * * * *

As for my further SF writing, first I'd like to mention my minor return to magazine pieces. In *Analog*—what used to be *Astounding*—a novelette, "Then and Now," appeared in the December 1977 issue. The inspiration came a while before, when I was visiting out in Tucson, Arizona, and there was a lot of age-group alienation. So I thought of a way to have some puckish fun with that circumstance, including a nice turnabout at the end, which ended up being whimsical, humorous, optimistic, and maybe even a bit disturbing.

A couple of hundred years into the future—of course—the moon, through the introduction of atmosphere and water from the Jovian system, and with a bio-viable spin imparted to it by the calculated, glancing impacts of two asteroids, has been made into the Garden World of the Solar System, with two hundred million inhabitants. An elderly man, who has taken a lifelong part in this transformation, has a luxurious villa on the pine-shagged slopes of the Lunar Apenines, overlooking Mare Imbrium, which is now a real sea with beaches and all the rest. The old man flies his private helicopter to the space port to pick up two surprise guests with whom he has just talked by Visual. The guests turn out to be a couple, both appearing to be about nineteen-years-old. There is an obvious contrast between the man and the pair: he is an affluent, elderly Have, while they are outwardly eager and vigorous Have-Nots who have been out on one of Saturn's frigid moons, training for the first attempt at interstellar settlement on the planets of Barnard's Star, which involves journeying through suspended animation for more than a century. Before starting out, the young couple take a month of vacation leave; and they can't stay on the moon longer than that because lunar law, on guard against population growth beyond the optimum limits, severely restricts immigration.

Right away, between the elderly man and this boy and girl there is something rather startling and wondrous; both sides know exactly what it is, yet, to preserve the special charm of it by not speaking out, the two sides play a whimsical game with each other—and with the readers of the story. Beyond that, the old chap is determined to give these two kids the best thirty-day vacation that he can; with what is behind them and ahead of them, they surely deserve it. The kids, in turn, are very pleased with the easy, rich, and beautiful life on their refurbished moon. Feeling guilty and sentimental, the oldie even offers to help them overstay their legally allowed time. The kids are tempted; yet at the last they tell him no, that their stronger enthusiasms are outward bound, that they are part of the leading edge of a new, human adventure.

The elderly man, as curator of a museum of lunar history, shows his guests underground burrows from before the moon was transformed. There is even the small, compact apartment where, as a young boy, the man made his first long visit from Earth. On being told of life there, the girl shows minor signs of sentiment.

As a final service for his guests, the oldie takes them on an excursion to Earth, and to an old house which belongs to his family. There the three celebrate the winter solstice festival—Christmas—for which the apt girl bakes cookies and the trio exchange gifts. Then the oldie takes the youngsters to where they will be frozen and put aboard the interstellar ship with many others for the long journey out to Barnard's Star. Meanwhile, they ask him what his plans are.

He tells them that he has a few years more of his allowed 111 years in the Solar System and then, conforming to the law intended to counteract local overpopulation, he will no doubt be rejuvenated, and sent out to the system of some other star. Maybe they'll see him again in somewhat more than a century.

The youngsters are a bit nervous—the revival rate for interstellar travelers has been estimated at about eighty-five percent. At the final farewell, the elderly man at last breaks the spell of remarkable changes in the realm of mankind by pronouncing three arcane words, revealing what these kids are to him. He calls them "Gram and Gramps."

The young boy laughs, as at a great and gentle joke, but the girl—the oldie's grandmother—says, "As long as it's true," and kisses him goodbye.

I took the script of "Then and Now" to Bob Mills, my agent. Four days later I got a phone call and acceptance notice from Ben Bova, then editor of *Analog*. I suppose the sudden reappearance, after so many years, of a yarn of mine on the doorstep of what used to be *Astounding*, had a certain impact. Anyhow, I still think that the yarn is a good one. It received a recommendation for the Nebula Award—hardly enough to carry it into serious competition, nor do I care much for the practice of shoving a story under the noses of colleagues. "Then and Now" says what I wanted it to say. I like a yarn that presents ideas at least minimally possible as future realities, to be given some serious thought. Who can say that the moon can't be made into a pleasant place to live, instead of becoming merely a source of material to be used elsewhere, as commonly conceived? Further, I like to take a light jab at some current, popular opinion or attitude, if only to suggest a slightly different way of looking at it. Here, though, there is the risk of treading on the toes of people whose minds have been made up with great solemnity.

I had another novelette in *Analog*, in the February 1980 issue. "A First Glimpse" is another first-alien-encounter-yarn of mine, possibly the best; anyway, the most up-to-date. Here my main motive was to counteract some of the fear that had come into our society—and has since proliferated. For example, the term "future shock," which is several years old, has now become a giant that makes some people scared of anything technological or unfamiliar. Yet, as far as I can see, technology, although admittedly imperfect, is the best, single, and most-needed problem solver that we have. So I made slightly sour fun of a human tendency to panic, while pointing out that its potential tragedy is worse than its so far rather harmless cause.

Incidentally, "A First Glimpse" has an ancient and rather curious history. I wrote it years before as a five thousand-word short story and, somehow, in the process of being read by editors, the script got stuck in a chandelier that belonged to H. L. Gold. There it stayed for about a year. Meanwhile, I had more or less forgotten about it, and neglected to ask. Finally, Gold found it and sent it back to me with profuse apologies. No sweat—he's a good friend and some of the fault was mine. At this time, I believe, he was no longer editing, but he said he liked the yarn, with some reservations. So it laid around till, at last, I updated it for Stan Schmidt at *Analog*. I salvaged its title, its characters, and much of their conversation. But, modernized, and with the point I wished to make, it expanded to twelve thousand words. Overall, the long, erratic course of its story-behind-the-story seems to have made "A First Glimpse" a more effective yarn. Yes, it did get a couple of Nebula recommendations.

I'd like to write more for Stan Schmidt and *Analog*; in fact, more science fiction in general. But really good ideas that aren't just repeats of something are hard to come up with. And what SF magazines are viably able to pay nowadays puts SF writing largely into the labor-of-love category, a factor which is fine, up to a point. As with other scribes, I prefer to concentrate on books, and don't get to the shorter stuff. But, among other things, there have been jolting events in my personal life.

* * * * * * *

With the books, frankly, I haven't done too well of late—as far as getting them published is concerned. Out there, looking for placement, I currently have two book scripts circulating: *Gemi the Finder* and *Legend Seed*. *Skyclimber* was published by Tower Books in 1981. While I did collect their minimal advance, the distribution of the book, and hence its public exposure in stores, was also rather minimal. Then the already shaky company collapsed. Berkley published *Bioblast* in 1985 with very moderate success.

Recession seems to have become the catch-all excuse for any poor showing in the book business. But much more may be wrong. Perhaps current publishing practices, particularly relating to story selection, is manipulating the kind of stories that are written and are *boring* a lot of SF book lovers out of buying books. Perhaps extravagantly written advert blurbs, that fall dismally flat once the book is read, are discouraging and disgusting many regular readers?

A case in point: Bob Heinlein and his stories have always been tops with me. So, not needing all the flashy hoopla and promises of superexcellence to persuade me, I bought his *Number of the Beast* in hardcover at a stiff price. So what did I get for my money? A bunch of improbable, idiotic characters yakking and scrambling around, not with true comedy and humor, but with ridiculous and wearisome slapstick. Still, some readers enjoyed this. Well, okay, I'm hardly the ultimate judge, but, for me—and for others whom I know—getting through this book was a struggle, even though there were a number of good Heinlein quotes.

Except for his fine writings, Robert Heinlein is gone now. But I did meet him once, and liked him very much. In any case, I surely can't get inside his thoughts to find out what his attitudes were while he was writing *Number of the Beast*. But, somehow, I wonder if he wasn't prompted by something out in the book world. It isn't difficult to imagine him thinking, tongue-in-cheek: "Okay, they'll pay me very well, manuscript almost unread....They want crap, so I'll give them crap." (Bob—I wouldn't blame you even if this happened to be so.) But it wasn't Heinlein that was bought; it was the Heinlein namemark which has become very valuable on the bottom-line of sales. And did it matter too much in some quarters if it got corrupted?

Looking around further on the SF and fantasy shelves in the stores, I find much of the stuff there unreadable. I liked Tolkien's *Lord of the Rings* stories. But there was one Tolkien; I don't need a lot of inferior imitations. And—ghosts of King Arthur's court!—there is a lot of bloodied-up, pseudo-medievalism, some of it located way off on planets far out among the stars, often with some current, very Earthly, issues and gripes worked into the story fabric. Frequently, too, there seems to be a mood where vaguely aimed rebelliousness, humorless self-pity, anarchy, and a reversion to superstition are mingled. As for the actual Middle Ages, I've usually thought of them as a dismal, bigoted, louse-ridden epoch—and I am backed up by considerable historial evidence. As alternative possible models, I prefer earlier cultures: Roman, Etruscan, Greek, Egyptian. At least they believed in taking baths!

Some fantasy yarns are very good; an older one, *Silverlock*, comes readily to mind. And I rather enjoy a good dragon story—Hello, Annie McCaffrey!—

though this isn't an area where I have enough enthusiasm to do much as a writer. It's like much of what I see, and have no urge to imitate.

Arthur Clarke, Fred Pohl, Ike Asimov, Poul Anderson, and some others have sufficient proven and present name clout to stick pretty much to their own standards. Lacking some of that right now, I figure on doing the same. I'm not trying to write yarns according to patterns of the 1930s; I keep looking for newness in my own way, and I think that the quality of my writing has gone upward, not downward. I'll keep plugging and if I make it, fine; if not, it's unlikely to be the thing that kills me, nor will it disturb my good nature all that much.

Ray Gallun 1930

XIX.

FINISHED NOVELS, UNFINISHED THOUGHTS

About my recent novels...regarding the Egyptian one, *Gemi the Finder*: notes of regret from editors have contained a lot of heartening comments. But there is a hesitation about a piece that is somewhat outside of what they are used to—and what their book public is used to. Its publication, then, would be a chancy experiment, sales-wise. So *Gemi*...has so far failed to get a chance to compete with the more regular books. One editor said that it straddled two chairs, meaning history and science fiction, and offered to buy it if I would make it more science fictional by expanding at a hinted interstellar involvement by letting aliens and their ships actually appear. That hit me as too much of a misfitting corn-up; I like the story as is, and didn't want to spoil its balanced mood with that much of an incongruous insertion. So I said no, which I have never done before. Not that I won't bend considerably, but that suggestion was over the permissable boundary with *Gemi*...; he could well be a historical character, though his interests and activities are sufficiently unusual to make good science fiction reading as well, as is—my somewhat prejudiced opinion, of course. Unemphasized, non-burdening, historical accuracy should be no obstacle there. The movement of a book script through a succession of publisher's offices can be a long, slow process, often taking several months at a single try.

There is, however, a lot of validity to the cagey attitudes in publishing houses. Idealistic concepts such as the one that science fiction, almost by definition, should be forward, outward, inward, every-which-way-looking, and constantly innovative, often must yield to other considerations, such as the uneven flow of readers' tastes and trends. Book houses, to survive, must sell enough of what they print. I feel rather sympathetic toward editors out front. Even when an editor has total control over what material to accept, he can easily be wrong in what he takes. From my detached point of view, I have the impression of roiled, shifting complexity. Example: what kind of readers out there in the audience will buy what kind of book? How much do publishers lead their readers, and how much are they themelves led by reader feedback? Which comes first—chicken or egg?

Once upon a time the science fiction audience was easier to understand. Its readers were mostly youngsters directly and personally interested in sciences, astronomy, other worlds, the marvels of an optimistically viewed future. The present, much larger audience has become diverse and complicated. Now there are cliques and groups with a variety of political and social attitudes. With the multiplicity and frequency of cons, SF readership has lost much of its solitary aspect and has become far more of a togetherness thing. People deeply interested in hard science are still present, of course, and more knowledgeable than they used to be; I've talked to some of these. But among the book-buying masses, they have become a minority with tastes that publishers might thus tend to disregard as of minor significance at the cash register. And how many of the convention attendees are seriously interested in science fiction, versus how many are there merely for the social getting together?

Here I feel prompted to make remarks that may seem nonsequitur, though they relate to the diversity of the SF audience, and the convoluted complexity of the overall SF situation. Science fiction has been accused of never rising out of childhood. Part of that is, and must remain, true. Clearly, one function of SF, almost inadvertently attained, is to help even very young persons toward better comprehension of the present and pending world and universe. So some SF must be simple; more must follow at increasing levels of sophistication. But there is nothing to prevent some SF from reaching the highest literary quality, measured by any standard. It is likely certain pieces are already there. With any luck, more will come.

But back to my recent novels, less loftily aimed.

About *Skyclimber*, which has been published: at its first submittals, the immediate complaint by editors was that it was "old hat" because it was about Mars. "Trite old Mars," as I pointed out in the story myself. True, I have been a Mars bug during most of my life, but the familiarity of Mars was a major point in this book. It seems to me that the SF switch, from speculations about exciting or dreadful things to come to the dramatization of existing socioeconomic problems, often at some remote distance where nobody can do much about them anyhow, has progressed to where such debate ought to have some competition from solider possibilities, such as getting real space programs out of their slump in public interest. Mars isn't way beyond our present reach among the far stars; it's right there, our neighbor-world, and well within the range of our existing know-how to physically reach, explore, and establish bases for close study, perhaps even to construct a prototype settlement. The two Mars landers, touching down on two tiny spots out of the vast area of the Martian surface—hardly a proper sample—haven't found any intelligent inhabitants, or macro-fauna and flora, nor any presence of microbiology. Yet this prospect remains at least partly open and unresolved, with the answer lying in the curious Martian soil chemistry. But, right away, a lot of folks, hoping for more spectacular developments, immediately got fed up and shrugged. "Nothing on Mars, so forget it."

I have said that, to me, science fiction has been an interim substitute for realities that have yet to come. In *Skyclimber*, it is this even more: it is a subliminal urging to get a possible and fascinating show on the road, as soon as other circumstances, such as public interest, allow. The economics of such a project would indeed be costly. But with the shuttles to help in assembling a Mars-destined ship from somewhere in Earth's orbit?...

Many facts are already known about Mars. It is reachable from here, it is close; it has a solid surface with mountains, valleys, deserts, polar caps, and what are apparently the courses of what once were mighty rivers—equivalent in area to all land on Earth. There is apparently plenty of usable water in the form of ice and permafrost. It is the nearest major planet on which landings can be made with relative ease. Thus it is one of the first stepping stones into space, along with lunar and asteroid explorations, and searching for intelligent electromagnetic signals from the stars. Its temperature ranges are not prohibitive, and it even has a day just over twenty-four hours long!

Whether there is, or ever has been, life on Mars is almost irrelevant. Though wouldn't it be a philosophical triumph toward understanding the mysterious processes of the universe if living microorganisms, native to Mars, or the fossil remains of such, from a former, obviously wetter age, were found during on-scene investigations? The search about that matter, and others, has not truly begun.

In *Skyclimber*, the settlers on Mars are an average and varied crowd, not super-courageous at all. They are just adventurous, pioneering types with practical know-how, of which there has always been plenty among us. My intention was to make them alive and real in their activities and problems, and in their personal interactions.

I wondered what the first children born surreptitiously on harsh Mars would be like. How would they, in their infant fragility, be taken care of? What would the reaction to the news of their existence be on Earth? Are they a symbol of settler irresponsibility, or do they have publicity value for furthering the still-uncertain Mars project? What would their experiences be when, grown to young adulthood, they are brought to Earth as students? In the weak Martian gravity, Tim Barlow and Agnes Frost have both grown very tall; Tim is over seven feet. And the Martian environment has, of course, affected their outlooks and personalities. Will they—can they?—elect to stay on Earth? How will the settlers on Mars survive completely on their own when, for several years, all terrestrial support is removed? Will the human inhabitation of the planet at last be an expanding success?

As I have said before, I finally got past the dogmatic and shortsighted "Mars is old hat" bit, thrown at me by editors. As far as I'm concerned, the "old hat" was already elsewhere! So Tower published the book, then—I'm sure for accumulative other reasons, not *Skyclimber*!—the company went bankrupt. Past distribution problems, the book did get some rather inadequate public exposure. In the Forest Hills area it was in B. Dalton Bookstores.

Apart from and above any intended ego drives in myself, I wanted the messages in that novel to get across. Because it is a point of my passionate belief that the steadily shrinking Earth, alone, is hardly enough room for our kind. For well-publicized reasons, such concentrated presence is not ever safe! But the larger reason is more basic, fundamental and biological: life forms extend themselves; there are successive phases for birth, growth, and fledgling. I believe that this sequencing is impressed in our genes, brains, and guts. For once, I have become a proselytizer....More movements outward should be made soon. The moon, Mars, and the asteroids are present and actual possibilities, the first future steps. The far stars will have to wait until we are competent to reach them.

I wrote an article about all this and, a while back, the editors of a major fan magazine, *Niekas*, were kind enough to publish it. They took its title, "Trite Old Mars," from the text. I hope the article did some good.

Then there was that other novel of mine, *Bioblast*, from Berkley Books, in 1985. Do our bodies have far more knowledge and know-how than our conscious minds? My contention here is that, clearly, they do! We get a free ride through life atop and inside a marvelous bio-machine, about which we have learned a little through indirect research. The evidence of superior bodily understanding and application of natural laws and forces is overwhelming. Within our flesh, as within the flesh of other contemporary animals and their fossil ancestors, a tremendous amount of coordinated activity—chemical, electrical, and physical—is constantly going on, outside of our conscious reach. All just to keep us alive! Almost every possible science must be actively represented there. As a feeble example of preeminent bodily knowledge, the living flesh of beasts, including our ancestors, has known of, and has been successfully fighting off, disease germs many millions of years before Pasteur.

Our bodies are cautiously secretive, as if they mistrusted our conscious mentalities which they make possible and sustain, and which float inside them, like weightless bubbles of brain functions. But our bodies *do* send us a few signals demanding our active cooperation. These messages come to us in the form of sensations of heat, cold, hunger, thirst, pain, sickness, comfort, weariness, sleepiness, sex urgings....

But what if, in a mutation of some child, the nerve channels transmitting such information were strengthened and broadened a little, so that all bio-physical knowledge was opened up for study by the mutant person? Difficult, but possible. In addition, what if motor nerves were similarly strengthened somewhat and broadened, so the mutant would also have much improved control over the growth processes within his body?

Would prudent biological forces even dare to make such an experiment? Would the mutant, fumbling ignorantly and ineptly with the controls of his own being, quickly kill himself? Surviving that hazard, and learning much of what had been made uniquely available to him, what would he become? Above all, what would be his impact on society? Would he become be a great benefactor? How much hatred, fear, and mistrust would he have to face? Would he be the mainspring of a great leap forward? Would he be able to mingle with lesser humans at all?

So that is the premise of *Bioblast*, including some of the questions which its main character, and its other characters, must deal with. Compactly stated, it is about the effects of a much-expanded, yet already existing, rudimentary, introspective human sense.

Bioblast had a brief life in the bookstores, and broke no sales records. Perhaps the idea is too radical and too far beyond the beaten track for enough readers to like it. Maybe they thought it was a put down of the proud human mentality. Or, maybe, it is too complex for some SF readers to absorb....Yes, editors do have problems in choosing.

Then comes the last of my so far completed science fiction novels, *Legend Seed*. Since it is just recently off the typewriter there is, as yet, no editorial reaction. The plot is about the dramatic ending of the latest ice age, ten-to-fifteen thousand years ago, and the struggle of a first, rather primitive civilization, which sprang up around the salt lakes in what is now the Mediterranean Basin, to survive against cosmic disasters and human enemies. It touches on the Strait of Gibraltar once being an isthmus, and on a comet that crashed into Earth, and on legends such as Noah's Ark and Lost Atlantis, with some basis in fact. It is a more conventional SF adventure, a book filled with human conflict and striving. As for its destiny, again I'll have to wait.

There is just one more related and relevant topic that I need to discuss: the present publishing situation. Other scribes have studied it much more closely than I; but I have sat in on their discussions. Their most emphatic complaint is that big, conglomerate companies have bought in publishing houses as possible tax shelters, and that books, including science fiction, of course, are being categorized, packaged, and marketed according to the same mass production principles as detergents, dog food, and sugary breakfast cereals. Little need to look inside any of the packages. Instead, keep judgments simple by looking at the latest, bottom-line, profit-loss figures, for a supposedly identical product.

Do such practices offend the consumer, in this case the SF reader? Or should he or she passively accept what is shoved at him? Maybe a disgruntled-reader revolt would answer some difficulties in the publishing business.

Scripts might again be bought more on the basis of their individual merit, and with room for some well-presented newness, and less by the name-trademark-tag. Some risks would be taken by competent story editors able to judge quality in their own right, without approval from some higher, and not very interested, chief in the Big Office. Past the advert ballyhoo and build-up, and the elegant packaging, science fiction readers might get better yarns to read, and become more interested in buying books. Maybe that will be some of the answer. In hope, we wait.

****

Now for the last part of my spiel, thoughts of mine aimed less at constructing more SF yarns than as statements of my own views, so that I will be better revealed as a person. There might even be some content of philosophical wisdom. I'll begin almost at random:

First: there are sourpusses who moan that humans are no good, that they are inevitably bound for self-destruction. At worst, this is only fractionally true. We contain qualities that are variously termed good or evil, the difference of opinion often being based on a difference in viewpoint. We have struggled our way onward to present survival through ages of competitive environments and circumstances that might have wiped us out. Courage, love, loyalty, gentleness, and sympathy—and, yes, fear and anger, and even hatred—all are biological tools that have been given us, useful to have under appropriate circumstances. Often enough they are held in precarious balance that has allowed us, up till now, to avert final disaster. Overall, I think that we are a rather amiable, kindly intentioned lot, well worthy of continuing on our way, if we can.

Second: we are a product of Nature. *If we accept this as true, then isn't it obvious that everything we produce is also a natural product, with ourselves acting only as more sophisticated tools of Nature?* Some people have the attitude that we stand apart from natural phenomena as a separate and guiding force with an automatic and thoughtless rigidity. But isn't this view also an innocent one? Because even the ego/pride that prompts it, along with our creative brains, is plainly a gift from Nature. The situation becomes more complicated when we realize that such facts give us the option of blaming every error we seem to make on Nature. But this reaction, too, is a *natural*, causative phenomenon in the intricate, onward moving net of cause-and-effect, happening within our *natural* brains. It is another fragment under constant, dispassionate, amoral testing against the realities of Nature. Approval or rejection?

Having come this far solidly, I have to admit that houses, ships, aircraft, cars, computers, space rockets, everything that natural mankind has made or done, are natural phenomena. This would, of course, include books and the thoughts behind books, and every idea, dream, or feeling that has come to us, sensible or not. It goes without saying that the things we decry are not left out: smog, crime, overlenient courts, nuclear missiles, pollution, terrorism. I won't say that we have the power of judgment to straighten everything out—or to mess it up further! I merely say that we will react, depending on the extent and quality of the pressures, and in accordance with how each of us has been made, by the natural forces and factors that have contrived each of us as we are. We will be acceptingly passive, or active, in varying degrees and ways.

It is clear that mankind is a species destined to affect its immediate environment enormously one way or another. But to deflate our natural egos a little more, let me point out that, so far in Earth's geological history, other life forms have already affected it to a much greater extent. A billion or so years back, some tiny, probably single-celled plant stumbled onto the process of photosynthesis within green chlorophyll. So, proliferating itself in its various descendants, it changed the chemistry of Earth. The atmospheric carbon dioxide became largely breathable oxygen, making the whole animal kingdom possible. Among these, too, were the corals, whose dead skeletons inadvertently piled up enormous, ocean current-affecting reefs, far surpassing in size anything built by man.

Of course, what such tiny bits of natural biology have accomplished were jobs of millions of years. Our point of pride or fear could be that we operate much faster. We have come our full course of achievement and error till today in a relatively few millenia, much of it in the last mere century. In us, Nature has contrived quite an invention.

Now the third element: free will. I have approached it pretty closely already. We each have an illusion of possessing considerable free will—to do what we choose to do. I suspect that, for constructive reasons, it is best to hang on to this attitude most of the time. However, for moments of deeper contemplation, let us probe further: *how much free will do we truly have?*

Not much, it seems to me. In fact, even if we accept the Uncertainty Principle, put forth in physics courses, we have, at rock-bottom analysis, virtually, if not totally, no free will.

Look at it this way. We have no choice at all in the genes that are given each of us at conception. The factors of our prenatal growth, our birth, and our early childhood, are likewise beyond our control. The early environment and teaching that our parents or other guardians give us is ultimately defined by these same kind of factors, external to, and unchosen by, themselves, just as in each of our own cases. When we react to any given situation in our individual way—strongly or weakly, or however assessed—it has to be in accordance with how we have *already* been shaped, plus the effects of stimuli that impinge on us from outside ourselves, being equally beyond our choosing. And so we move on through life, as reacting bits of a natural, perhaps locked-in, process.

Do I hear further murmurs of dismay and disagreement, and sounds of arguments and counterarguments surging forth into a pro, con, or middleground contention and discussion? Usually this a good sign of constructive thought, unless somebody gets physically hurt, which can happen sometimes during this sort of thing.

In any case, take it easy. Whatever else it may be, discussion is fun. And what I say in these last pages of this personal revelation I don't pose as any ultimate pundit; I only make use of what wits I have been given to produce my best opinion, leaving room for flexibility, and a certain measure of doubt. If I am right, I still feel no cause for furious regret; it is simply the way things are.

And a fourth area for scrutiny (or should I stop counting?): religion. It has already subliminally intruded. Historically, religion has been maybe the most unreasonably dangerous and explosive of topics. But it is unavoidable, if I want to present my views about the universe. So let's keep emotions in check.

As to my background, the region where molding forces first began working on me....My father's remarks about any religion were minimal and, as far as I know, his references to any divinity took no more than the form of common and popular expletives. My mother divided her attention, unevenly and according to mood, between strait-laced Lutheranism and an appreciation of the writings of Colonel Robert G. Ingersoll, the Nineteenth Century freethinker and lecturer who denounced religious dogma, and was the opponent and contemporary of General Lew Wallace, the author of *Ben Hur—A Tale of Christ*. So—thanks for small favors—no religious education was shoved down my throat. Though I was interested in the various versions of the subject, I was benevolently and neglectfully allowed to develop according to my own inclinations.

Quite a few young people arrive quickly and emphatically at the point of declaring themselves devout atheists. Okay, as with any other opinion that is not bothersome to others, no sweat. The Great Father Figure, enthroned somewhere out there, soon dissolves into the mists of myth, an untrue fantasy. No crutch; we're on our own, to that extent.

Still, for me anyhow, something goes beyond that and hangs out. There's too much mystery and wonder even in a grass blade, and too much capacity ingrained in ourselves for awe and pleasurable interest and curiosity, for that to be the end of it. The universe in which we live, and of which we are infinitesimally tiny parts, is a tremendous aggregation of interlocked marvels and enigmas—and isn't it somehow a reassuring comfort to feel that we belong as a speck of it all?

We may visualize various peoples of history at varying levels of development. At their beginnings, they have no means of learning much solid truth about the often brutal yet miraculous environment in which they live. Danger and death often terrify them; denied access to the facts, they still need answers, and still want explanations of natural occurrences. So they create substitutes for truth, a kind of primitive science fiction, full of benevolent gods of sun and rain to make offerings of prayers and gifts to; full of demons of plague, famine, and other misfortunes to propitiate with sacrifices.

Our sciences have taken us somewhat beyond that condition. There is a much-improved comprehension of what is and what goes on. But the reasons for wonder increase.

Not being particularly partial to labels, I still suppose I can call myself a religious agnostic. I am hardly unique in the implied attitudes. There are surely millions of us who have arrived at much the same tentative conclusions—not to be made rigid by any dogma. I have not seen the actual face of God, though maybe I have glimpsed portions of some metaphorical equivalent? There is an infinity of things I have no grasp of. When I say that there is probably no such thing as free will, that does not allow me to carry this concept to its logical, negative conclusion: since I have no real choice in the matter, I can do no evil. I cannot do so because built into me is the old biological restraint of conscience, which I can't, and don't want to, do anything to weaken. And I am grateful for the external factors to my internal programming that have reinforced this stand because, with what I have to think with, I feel that it is good. No, I have been constructed as no more a saint than innumerable others. There are crude stupidities and unkindnesses that I have done that I am ashamed of. Should I be grateful, or additionally ashamed and regretful, that I have done what I have done out of lack of choice? The philosophical structure, here, becomes more complex, and then suddenly simple and relieving. The last words are: what is done is done—as with other natural events. So I do not brood.

I'm not so sure that I care much for the term "God." Nor do I think that changing its gender to feminine or neuter would help. What should I call it? The Great Presence? It seems unlikely that it demands for itself such an adulatory address, since one suspects that, in its all-encompassing hugeness and intricacy, it would be quite indifferent to vanity or worship—except insofar as mankind, and other similar forms of intelligent awareness, are parts of it. In our scientific circles, it seems commonly thought of as being insensate to itself. Maybe it is just the sum total of all natural laws, functioning in conflict yet in concert, to rule the universe. So, to designate it, I fall back on an old name which I have already used numerous times in this write-up: Nature. But that name automatically broadens to take in everything there is, of material and energy and order, without separation into its components.

So, what makes Nature work? How does it produce miracles? There are people who keep trying to find out more. There is a relatively new kind of clergy or priesthood, more valid, I think, than those who came before. The texts of their bible are the primary sources, as various as billion-year-old starlights or the marks left on film by the impacts of subatomic particles, contrasted with, say, the detailed convolutions of an insect's wing movements while in flight, as captured by high-speed photography. And what they show us is more awesomely beautiful than anything in the old sacred books—which do not lack value as wisdom and literature. These specialists try to translate and interpret correctly the arcane signs or writings left less openly than dinosaur footprints in mud now turned back into stone. They work in proportions of elemental isotopes residual in rocks, in water and air and fallen meteorites, and in innumerable other things such as the ion physics of brain synapses....They may be wrong in their conclusions and theories; they are human, and they may even be motivated by competitive pride in their research. But when data and hard reasoning prove their ideas incorrect or flawed, they are forced to begin again; none of them are too firmly bound by dogma. And so, gradually, over the decades, they have been replacing old myths with reality. Thus they bring themselves, and us, bit by bit, a little closer to understanding the universe, with the added comfort of, perhaps, being better aware that we are a part of it. Do we now approach a finer form of religious feeling? Nature often is blunt, uncaring and insensate, profligate and wasteful in its processes of test or erasure; yet nothing is lost, for the excess that must remain inside the all-containing completeness.

But with such things as warm sunshine and breezes, Nature is also benign. Further than that, it is benevolent in a more feeling way, to the extent that we are humans, and other creatures like us elsewhere—anywhere—are also benevolent, for we all belong....

Whoops....Have I been carried away in these latest paragraphs, by the arrogance of some seer imagining himself possessing a special pipeline for truth from some divinity? Umm...quite a few people have done that before....However, since I've started, let me continue saying my piece in a quieter tone.

In order to attempt some explanation, let me rephrase the central question: *how can complex marvels arise unprompted out of unaware clottings of matter and energy?*

In scientific writings, answers are often implied, but seldom brought out clearly, so I'll have a go at it.

Some primordial processes seem general and inevitable; they have duplicated themselves again and again. Clouds of dust and gas are drawn together by their intrinsic gravity and other forces, and thus stars are born.

Next, matter seems clearly to have an inherent tendency to arrange itself into more and more complex structures. Hydrogen, the simplest atom—an electron orbiting a proton—is transformed into slightly heavier helium in the furnaces of the stars. After successive stellar explosions and the drawing together once more of the scattered materials to form new stars, with the process of complication continuing, eventually all of the common heavier elements are produced.

There then comes the lacing together of compatible atoms to form the simpler compounds. The complication of chemistry has entered the scene: water, carbon dioxide, methane, ammonia....Then, in the warm seas of some primitive, still-lifeless planet or planets, under the impacts of ultraviolet rays and lightening bolts, more and more intricate molecular chains come into being: DNA. Not yet life, but the building-blocks of life, located in the "primordial soups" of those primordial oceans. Most everybody has heard about those parallel, testing experiments.

Then, suddenly, at last, after ages of this, somewhere, somehow, the spark!

"Wait a minute," somebody demands. "This is getting to be too much. How can all this complication continue? Building the intricate bodies of beasts, and even the brains of mankind, without the guidance of a super-intelligent creator?"

Good question. But maybe the questioners are too much hung up on the common conception of intelligence, and its importance, that anything at all complex must be designed and made by an external mind and hands; that there must be planning and manipulation; wood does not of itself become a chair or a table. Quite true on a human level of thought. The neglected point is that the wood has already formed itself into something far more amazing and involved than a chair.

Let's examine what we mean by intelligence as, for instance, it is represented by the logical, inventive, problem-solving portion of the human mind, apart from its emotional components:

It is an analogy device. It sets up internal images of external realities, and checks them against similar mind images of other actual or supposed realities, looking for new and effective combinations in the direction of solving some problem.

Let us be very simple. Somewhere I see two real oranges. A little apart, I see three other real oranges. In my head I have the substanceless, but intelligent, concepts of two oranges and three oranges. My child-like problem is how many oranges do two and three of them make—in reality? I come up with five oranges. But I might make a mistake, saying four or six, which wouldn't check with the measuring standard of solid fact. So the Reality of Nature already has the problem solved beyond any possibility of error. The five oranges are there; they exist. So is insensate Nature intelligent or not?

The above may be regarded as just a ridiculous syllogism, too simple to make an effective example. But I think that the beginnings of understanding are present. Nature can do all that our collective intelligence can do, while our collective intelligence can only mock up concepts of what we think Nature will do under given sets of circumstance. We can only ask if we are right by comparing our notions with reality, which ultimately supplies the true answer.

The process of intrinsic natural intelligence in action has to go far beyond the elementary analogy of two-plus-three of anything, since it must perform functions enormously more intricate than those of mere addition.

First, there are the precise rules forming the framework and boundaries of what can happen in this fundamental forerunner of what we might call logical reasoning. That water freezes at zero degrees centigrade is our human way of ex-

151

pressing one of them, among innumerable others. In *real* existence, presence and participation of these natural laws, then, are all the criteria for what we term *intelligent* judgment.

For intelligence, then, there should be purpose, motivation, objective. In the enormous quantities of dust, gas, and various forms and clottings of energy mixed with a near-infinite volume of space which composed the primordial universe, this could only have been to explore anything and everything that can happen. No thoughtful or conscious decision was required; the action would, unavoidably, have begun of itself.

Given sufficient time—billions of years—it is a mathematical certainty that much of this huge area of search would have been covered and checked for viability, stumbled upon, so to speak. Every circumstance thus reached would be tried, with whatever result or reaction.

Some results would be stable, and some not. Instabilities would be downgraded in the competition for truth. Stable new arrangements would survive and be retained as new, more complex structures, waiting for the next progressive development, mutation, upward step, in turn, to go through trial and tests. Here, then, is proof of intrinsic intelligence, even in insensate things: *judgment.* What so far works and is viable, when judged against hard fact, survives.

So the process must have gone on and on. It still continues forward, with constant testing. In our humanly inhabited region, we usually regard ourselves as Nature's top achievement or invention. Around here, anyhow, I suppose we are its finest tool, to date.

Yes, quite possibly our future is murkier than it has ever been before. But we'll have to try to live with it....

But here is another topic that I would like to touch upon: consciousness. Besides intelligence, we were given that, too. Or, perhaps I should say that, in us, and perhaps in other beings elsewhere, Nature at last achieved consciousness for itself.

Logical, problem-solving, idea-reassociating, inventive intelligence is fairly easy to define. I've already perhaps had an incomplete go at doing so: an analogy device. We have it inside our own heads. If our computers don't yet fully possess this sort of thing, they should have it very soon, and in a better version than we do.

But *consciousness*? In each of us, our consciousness is what most of us are. While we are awake, unless we are in some dazed condition, it is continually with us. If there is anything that we should be able to describe from familiarity, consciousness should be it! Yet, in kernel and essence, *what is it?* Confronted by this question, I find myself not merely frustrated, but mind-boggled. Oh, we can say that it is awareness of self, or, more properly, just awareness; yet these are mere substitute words that loop around the essential center, without truly hitting the target at all. What is it that gives us "self," that lets us perceive and know continually that we exist, that we are wherever we are, that we are comfortable or uncomfortable, enjoying or suffering?

Indeed, there is much that can be said *about* consciousness. That it seems to be the means of feeling all emotion—joy, sorrow, humor, fear, love, hatred, purpose, wanting. So it is from within this, then, that we are propelled. For here, too, is where our egos live, and experience, pride, anger, determination, courage, and curiosity. A computer does not need such biological motivation to bring its logical, but unaware, intelligence into action, for it is programmed from outside itself to solve problems; a switch is turned on, and the energy flow compels it to perform.

But if, for whatever reason, we wanted to give a computer a consciousness, how could we even begin to do this, when we not only lack a proper and complete definition, but don't know of what awareness consists, or what is its mechanism? Anyhow, *I don't know*—or at least not yet. The assumption, common in science fiction, that a computer advanced enough to think, talk, and act like a human in all outward respects would automatically become conscious is, to me, bunk. Though operating with complete, imitative logic, it would be no more aware than the simplest mechanical adding machine, summing two-plus-two. There has to be something else put into it.

Maybe there are people exploring brain functions who already have substantial inklings of what that something is, or might be. Or perhaps we must wait until we are smarter, or until our computers, whose powers are growing faster than our own, become sufficiently smart to help us to success.

Anyhow, it is one of the problems that Nature, in its slow way, solved long ago, and maybe many times. It is fairly obvious that higher animals besides ourselves—dogs, cats, pigs, and chickens, to name a few—are considerably aware; they can manifest convincing evidence of consciousness—pleasure, fear, anger, and affection—all of which are useful biological traits linked to survival of the species. Even lower animals, down to the level of amoebae, can seem to show some signs of knowing what is going on. A fly, dabbing at a bit of food, or basking in warm sunshine, can appear to be enjoying itself.

It may be that a shortcut to making a computer conscious would be to incorporate into it capabilities present in living things. The thought of a bioelectronic interface has been around for some time.

Related to questions and speculations about consciousness are those about the soul. To the traditional religionists, the soul seems usually to be something more or less intangible that resides within a human form during life, but exists as an immortal and self-sustaining entity at death. All this is a rather charming and reassuring concept. And it may be valid, for all I know. Yet there are certain involved factors to examine before giving the idea full credence.

In the first place, from what *is known* of the human body, it is, like other animal bodies, a chemical-physical-electrical machine, conforming, as far as has yet been solidly determined, to natural laws. It is energized by the chemical union of food fuels with oxygen. Its limbs are arranged levers that satisfy common mechanical principles. Its heart is clearly a pump. Its nervous system has aspects of structure and function that are well within the rules governing electrical circuits and ion activity. In its wondrously intricate brain—though much here is still beyond present knowledge—there seems to be ample room and facilities for sustaining delicate processes that can be called a soul—*as long as life lasts*. But when the whole apparatus is stopped by death, are we to suppose that what has been logical and by rule all the way, suddenly becomes supernatural, allowing the soul to live on, unsupported and immortal, all by itself? Well, there could be conditions which earnest but heavy-witted lab folk have failed to come upon. That can always be. But I'm inclined to doubt....

There's another aspect of consciousness which interests and confounds me much more. Really, it is a part of consciousness: identity. Why am I, I? Why are you, you? Why is anybody his or her own, individual self? Am I—or to what extent am I—the same person I was fifty years ago? Obviously any answer to this last question has to be rather hazed up with limiting qualifications, as I think it must be, too, when directed at anyone else. In myself, traces of physical resemblance remain, along with those of attitudes and personality. But I've calmed down a lot; I'm more at ease with things. My bodily substance, except for the considerable number of original teeth that I've kept, has probably changed almost entirely a number of times. My opinions have undergone certain modifications. The only truly tangible link that I can find between what I am now and what I used to be at various phases of my life is a continuity of consciousness extending back through the years; and I am not at all sure that this is entirely the same as memory. During decades of time, memory fades and blurs somewhat. If I suffered total amnesia, would anything remain of my basic identity—my inner, lasting self—that would be unchanged? Oh, there would be similarities to what I used to be, of course; but these casual likenesses could easily be found in some similar stranger, and thus mean nothing at all. Although nobody is entirely identical to anybody else, no one is so unique, either, as not to have, somewhere, quite a number of reasonably close doubles, not only in physical characteristics, but in other qualities, too. Nor in answering the question of lasting identity do I allow such evidence as fingerprint matching, which would identify my physical form, but would not touch my rather metaphysical riddle at all. So I remain somewhat stumped about how much of anybody's inner identity remains fixed over the passage of time.

Occasionally, since my early youth, I have devised other rhetorical questions and circumstances about the subject, to amuse myself, and maybe to help me clear it up: suppose that I, or any other person—by actual or science fictional means—could be duplicated absolutely, down to the precise position and movement of the last ion acting in the filaments of the last brain cell. Then, logically, there should be two of the subject/individual, right? But what is the circumstance then? Which of the pair would be the original person? Why do I keep feeling that there must be something inaccurate about the suggestion that, simultaneously, there could be two persons of the same singular self-identity? Can a singular consciousness, perhaps which a kind of intuition insists must remain singular, as being the nucleus of one individual personality alone, ever split in duplication, and go on separately in separate simulacres of itself?

The idea can be carried beyond this, and argued or rationalized into some kind of practical accommodation easily enough, of course. I've done it myself in

People Minus X. Yet I remain elusively dissatisfied. But at last I shrug. Why strain my limited wits about a storm in a teapot?

Though it does relate to a subject that seems to be of pretty common interest among us mortals: reincarnation. If we don't care much for the old ecclesiastical notion of hopping around on beautiful clouds during all eternity, forever singing praises to worship-gluttonous, insecure, and improbable Almighty God, we can opt for reincarnation, even though it may have no more reality than a pleasant wish. It offers us an agreeably interrupted immortality to fill, for one thing, a common mortal craving. Even though, after a fulfilled life, the desire to be immortal may become slightly suspect. There is a sense of winding down somewhat, of having seen or experienced a lot. Here, at my considerable age, I speak from experience. Two centuries of continuous living—which might become ordinary before too very long—just could get to be a repetitious drag, unless some memory-eraser was introduced.

Here, though, too, reincarnation has an intriguing relevance. Overall, isn't reincarnation an agreeable concept? People as they are are much more attuned to lives of shifting events and surprises in some sort of upsy-downsy material world than in a perfectly beautiful, but at last tedious, heaven. From childhood I've enjoyed fantasies of having lived former lives in distant past eras. Likewise, I've projected forward into imaginings of lives to come.

Of course, I am hardly alone in this kind of projection. For instance, my Bertha used to insist whimsically, though with some seriousness, that, in a former existence, she was a cat. I find this a charming thought. As for myself, I probably could construct, or rationalize, out of certain sleeping dreams, hunches, and so forth that I have experienced, evidence that I have had previous incarnations, particularly in ancient Egypt. Yet, being, I think, more inclined toward logic than toward mysticism, I have refrained from going far in this direction.

But let's look more closely at reincarnation, and try to grasp just what we mean by it. Centered in it is again that insistence on self-identity—our own personal, deep down thing. We know that in the past there probably have been people much like ourselves in an all-around, general way. Likewise we know that such approximate doubles to ourselves are walking around, or doing whatever, in the immediate present. It is possible, too, that there will be others in the future. But none of these people will serve our needs; they are other people; they are not us. They lack our individual core.

What we seem to expect and want from reincarnation is continuity—a little like waking up on any morning and recognizing that we are still we, unchanged in basic essence, and able to go on with lively interest. Maybe what is most wanted out of the thought of the possibility of reincarnation is a denial of our total ego-extinction, which, true or not, can have a rather abhorrent aspect. In reincarnation, we might expect to be changed considerably from what we were before, and even welcome the adventure of differentness—new name, new body and face, possibly reversed gender, or even the form of some beast. But, anyhow, through it all, the special spark of our durable presence remains! With memory removed, except perhaps for traces, I don't know what the link between a person's separate consciousness in separate lives would be, in order to come up with the same awareness and identity. Solidly, I suspect that the whole notion of reincarnation is what it seems to be on the face of it: a charming piece of wishful, wistful fantasy. Yet, of course, I don't know. By some natural means yet untouched by the regular run of human scientists I, or you, may emerge again and again. Meanwhile, reincarnation remains a mildly interesting topic for speculation, and, whatever the odds, I remain reasonably at peace.

I'm nearing the end of this write-up. Still, I haven't stated my views on the meaning of life.

Well, it can have some great—if not always clear—purpose. I suppose. Yet without anything added to what is evident, it already seems to have plenty of worthwhileness. I am, and have been, among the lucky—unlike quite a few, who complain, with considerable reason, about life's pointless, painful, empty futility. For most of my life, I've been reasonably healthy. The various jolts I've taken have not been overwhelming. So the simplicities retain their validity: morning light, the fragrance of coffee perking, sunsets, first snow underfoot, spring's first crocuses, the taste of good food, books to read. Also the presence, and reminiscence, of old friends, including the dead; kidding around with new ones; relaxed meditations over a drink, or without one, looking down on billowy clouds from an aircraft, even if going no farther than Chicago, when once I looked up at such clouds from Wisconsin ground, yearning....So, that is one tiny fulfillment for me.

The list of interesting trifles could go on and on. What better purpose does life need than to enjoy it as much as we can while we try to improve it?

Then comes the question of what happens—what to do—next? Eager excitement there—or anguish. Perhaps a mixture? It ought to be the first of these, though there can be a tense reaction that says, "Hold on a little! Though far from perfect, and afflicted with new stresses, dangers, bewildering problems, and corrupting muddles, the world is, in some respects, a better place than it has ever been before. Many diseases that used to kill millions every year have been largely overcome.

I will hardly insist that all advances have been entirely good. There have been negative side effects and reactions. There is a lot of valid fear in the world, but some of it seems to me considerably overdrawn. For example, there is the fear of nuclear power plants that has been stirred up. When, by all statistics, they have yet to kill, or demonstrably injure, anybody. There is no other power source that has such a record, or offers cleaner energy. And there are other conditions of our culture which we take with scarcely a shrug, because they are familiar and accepted—for instance, the approximately fifty thousand people that die in traffic accidents in the United States every year. But introduce something that is relatively new, powerful, a bit mysterious, and difficult for some to understand, marked by an overload of fright-talk from various quarters, and it is as if primitive superstitions were revived among us. Dread of the unknown! Ah, well...a valid defense of nuclear energy has been stated in detail, again and again, so I won't reiterate it.

Many other matters of concern, interest, and prediction have been aired too often elsewhere to even be mentioned now.

So, at last, I'm here at the need to say a little about the pending future—and not just as a science fiction scribe. No, I don't like the application of nuclear science to bombs and missiles, either. However, I do want space ventures to move on at a quickened rate, in part because I would like to be alive to see as many of them as I can, but more so because I feel that, Out There, is a destiny that has already been stamped upon our lusty, biological genes. This destiny may, perhaps, prove ultimately vital to our survival through the dispersal of our proliferating kind; we are *not* just for the Earth....And, no, I don't think we can go backward or stop; history's awesome, inexorable movement won't allow that. We have to keep going on, as always.

What else do I expect? Well, other people can offer detailed predictions, too. Just now, I happen to be thinking of a fast substitute for going to school or to a university. Or prison....Maybe by means of a miniaturized chip put inside the human cranium, to interface directly and consciously with the brain, becoming an integrated part of the human mentality, giving it the content of whole courses of study or training, while also augmenting its intelligence....Or, with people who have committed crimes, firm restraints might be applied in the same way—pain at temptation, or, more humanely, by personality modification. Ordinary anti-social misdeeds might vanish entirely.

No, in suggesting these possibilities I'm not more than half kidding. More food for thought. But would an education so easily gained seem frustrating and empty? And wouldn't such a method of dealing with crime smack too much of Orwell's controlled society, leaving dangerous room for evasions, and for misjudgments of what is right? Very likely a matter to consider, and to try to counteract. There would be furious protests and counter-protests.

The future may be entirely variant from the hints which I have just offered. So the substance of fearing the unknown is its uncertainty. In a culture that is changing so fast, it is easy to feel lost, bewildered, and unreasonably frightened. Thus, more future shock. But too often, lately, has technology been the scapegoat for defects in human attitudes, when in fact, where wisely used, it has been the benign aid in problem-solving? Never have we lived in an entirely safe environment, and it is doubtful that we ever shall. Ever since a high point in the progression of human accomplishment, when it began to be said, "If we can reach the moon, why can't we...?" An over-extended factor seems to have been injected into the webwork of cause and effect that moves us, so that we have confused a relatively simple engineering problem with objectives that are not so simple, so that good, but flimsily managed, hopes have come too easily to disgruntlement! Give us a chance to get caught up!...

But lately there have been many large personal misfortunes of a kind which touch almost everybody sooner or later.

During 1988 my wife, Bertha's minor illness turned out to be cancer. Almost a repeat of what happened to Frieda, except that this malignancy was much more virulent and swift-moving. And just a few weeks before the diagnosis was made, Bertha's grandson, Jim, age thirty-five, died in a freak mishap, leaving a widow and a baby son, Kit.

Bertha took this disaster like the rugged soul she was. But she died on January 30, 1989.

Meanwhile, incidental to a bad case of bronchitis, I was given a chest x-ray, a CAT scan, and then a biopsy. Once again the Big C. Yes, those darn cigarettes! I had a two centimeter size adenoidal-type carcinoma in the upper lobe of my left lung. In July 1989 that lobe was removed entirely. So I was lucky. I am told that no follow-ups of radiation or chemotherapy will be needed.

And there have been some startling developments in the world. Final end of the Cold War?

Thus is more human vigor freed for better objectives? Preserving and restoring our Earth, its wildlife, its natural beauty, and—yes—its human-made beauty, too? A better, saner, more responsible energy policy, less fraught with quasi-superstitious fears? A renewal and quickening of space exploration?...

Yes, perhaps....Yet it is evident that much more human error will continue. There are even some anachronistic maniacs who might like to dominate and crush us all. We must still be on guard with courage and our best, coolest judgment.

Though far from perfect, and afflicted with new and old stresses and dangers and bewildering problems and corrupting muddles, the world is, in many respects, a better place for humans than ever before. If there are new diseases, still it is true that many old ones that used to kill millions every year have been largely overcome. Just for example....

And now at last shall I restate my old credo? And not just as a now largely retired science fiction scribe?

Yes—I repeat—I want space exploration to continue and to be accelerated, not only so that I can personally witness their discoveries, but also because I feel that, Out There among the local planets and, ultimately—maybe ages hence—the far more distant stars, is the destiny that I have already spoken of. Though we may fall short in the far reaches of such a goal, I find it hard to believe that our vigorous, proliferating, resourceful, cantankerous kind is made only for this tiny, beautiful, but seminal, Earth!

In any case, huddling in a corner in panic and dread, while clutching too tightly to what we think we possess right now, is not the way to go. Such non-action seems to me the mark of the reject and the moribund. Fortunately, most of us are not like that. Our past generations have been refined and tested, so that we are tough and resiliant. And our illusion of having free will is also a good thing. By best available evidence, the moon, Mars, and the asteroids are already within our reasonable grasp. There are enough bold and eager ones among us now to begin. No doubt there will be hazards, mishaps, problems, and disappointments—as always. But with a new frontier established, many of our inner feelings of hesitation and doubt should begin to dissipate, and simple, constructive action begin once again, even for those of us who take part only as sideliners.

No, I have not by any means ever been a paragon of courage, or even of good sense. But perfection is not what is needed here. In the area of nerve, all that is required is a step forward into the reasonable probability of being okay. And there is nothing new in that part of the situation for most of us. I'd eagerly go along if they'd take me, if I were judged sufficiently rugged and skilled to be useful. Here, I could wish to be thirty or forty years younger. There would be novelty and interest for all participants, even those left at home. There would be a rejuvenating, exploratory exuberance. Yes, I'd bet on it.

While I have been writing these final pages, an incongruous image from my youth keeps re-appearing in my mind. A streamlined form; sleek, rainbow-tinted feathers; low-crested, triangular head; steady, alert, coolly-judging golden eyes; a swaggering, tiptoeing walk. The term *chicken*, in the common vernacular sense, doesn't fit this image at all. For here totally innocent courage and confidence is embodied. Let my primary impression of that fighting cock from my childhood (with the violence wisely deleted), be passed from me on to others, and stand as a symbol of both a propelling cause and our natural biological destiny.

I will say no more for now. Good luck! And aim high!...

Bertha Erickson Gallun and Ray Gallun

SELECTED BIBLIOGRAPHY

NOTE: For a complete primary and secondary bibliography, see the companion volume to this book, *The Work of Raymond Z. Gallun: An Annotated Bibliography & Guide* (San Bernardino, CA: The Borgo Press, 1991).

A. Books by Raymond Z. Gallun

People Minus X. New York: Simon & Schuster, 1957.
The Planet Strappers. New York: Pyramid Books, 1961.
The Eden Cycle. New York: Ballantine Books, 1974.
The Best of Raymond Z. Gallun. New York: A Del Rey Book, Ballantine Books, 1977.
Skyclimber. New York: Tower Books, 1981.
Bioblast. New York: Berkley Books, 1985.
Starclimber. San Bernardino, CA: The Borgo Press, 1991.

B. Magazine Fiction by Raymond Z. Gallun

"The Space Dwellers." Nov. 1929.
"The Crystal Ray." Nov. 1929.
"Atomic Fire." Apr. 1931.
"The Lunar Chrysalis." Sept. 1931.
"Revolt of the Star Men." Winter 1932.
"Waves of Compulsion." Mar. 1932.
"The Moon Mistress." May 1932.
"The Menace from Mercury." Summer 1932.
"Flight of the RX-1." July 1933.
"Moon Plague." Jan. 1934.
"Space Flotsam." Feb. 1934.
"The World Wrecker." June 1934.
"The Wand of Creation." Sept. 1934.
"The Machine from Ganymede." Nov. 1934.
"Old Faithful." Dec. 1934.
"Mind over Matter." Jan. 1935.
"Telepathic Piracy." Mar. 1935.
"N'Goc." May 1935.
"Blue Haze on Pluto." June 1935.
"The Son of Old Faithful." July 1935.

"Derelict." Oct. 1935.
"Davy Jones' Ambassador." Dec. 1935.
"Nova Solis." Dec. 1935.
"Avalanche." Dec. 1935.
"Buried Moon." Feb. 1936.
"Mad Robot." Mar. 1936.
"Child of the Stars." Apr. 1936.
"The Weapon." May 1936.
"The Scarab." Aug. 1936.
"The Great Illusion." Sept. 1936.
"A Beast of the Void." Sept. 1936.
"Godson of Almarlu." Oct. 1936.
"The Path." Nov. 1936.
"Saturn's Ringmaster." Dec. 1936.
"Luminous Mine." Jan. 1937.
"Fires of Genesis." Mar. 1937.
"The Second Cataclysm." Mar. 1937.
"Comet's Captive." June 1937.
"Dark Sun." June 1937.
"Dawnworld Echoes." July 1937.
"Stardust Gods." Oct. 1937.
"A Menace in Miniature." Oct. 1937.
"Red Shards on Ceres." Dec. 1937.
"Mercutian Adventure." Feb. 1938.
"Thunder Voice." Feb. 1938.
"Something from Jupiter." Mar. 1938.
"Iszt-Earthman." Apr. 1938.
"Seeds of the Dusk." June 1938.
"Hotel Cosmos." July 1938.
"The Magician of Dream Valley." Oct. 1938.
"Shadow of the Veil." Feb. 1939.
"The Machine That Thought." Mar. 1939.
"Strange Creature." Aug. 1939.
"Masson's Secret." Sept. 1939.
"Terror Out of the Past." Mar. 1940.
"The Renegade from Saturn." Mar. 1940.
"The Lotus Engine." Mar. 1940.
"Guardian Angel." May 1940.
"The Long Winter." May 1940.
"Nemesis from Lilliput." May 1940.
"Tangled Paths." July 1940.
"The Gentle Brain." Summer 1940.
"Lunar Parasites." Summer 1940.
"Stepson of Space." Oct. 1940.
"Death and the Dictator." Oct. 1940.

"A Dictator for All Time." Nov. 1940.
"Achilles Heel." Nov. 1940.
"Eyes That Watch." Dec. 1940.
"Secret of the Comet." Jan. 1941.
"The Wall of Water." Winter 1941.
"Invaders of the Forbidden Moon." Summer 1941.
"The Raiders of Saturn's Rings." Fall 1941.
"Meteor Legacy." Aug. 1941.
"Gears for Nemesis." Jan. 1942.
"Sarker's Joke Box." Mar. 1942.
"Scientist Disowned." June 1942.
"The Eternal Wall." Nov. 1942.
"Space Oasis." Fall 1942.
"Hell Stuff for Planet X." June 1943.
"Bright Message." May 18, 1946.
"Final Rite." July 6, 1946.
"Operation Pumice." Apr. 1949.
"Blurred Barrier." May 1949.
"A Step Farther Out." Mar. 1950.
"Coffins to Mars." June 1950.
"Bluff Play." Dec. 1950.
Passport to Jupiter [novel]. Jan. 1951.
"Brother Worlds." Feb. 1951.
"Asteroid of Fear." Mar. 1951.
"Prodigal's Aura." Apr. 1951.
"The First Long Journey." Apr. 1951.
"When Earth Is Old." Aug. 1951.
"Trail Blazer." Fall 1951.
"The Restless Tide." Nov. 1951.
"The Great Idea." Jan. 1952.
"EV." Feb. 1952.
"Return of a Legend." Mar. 1952.
"Big Pill." Sept. 1952.
"Ten to the Stars." Mar. 1953.
"Captive Asteroid." Apr. 1953.
"Give Back a World." May 1953.
"Double Identity." June 1953.
"Legacy from Mars." July 1953.
"Stamped CAUTION!" Aug. 1953.
"Comet's Burial." 1953.
"The Guthrie Method." May 1954.
"Dawn of the Demigods." Summer 1954.
"Then and Now." Dec. 1977.
"A First Glimpse." Feb. 1980.
"Sort of Like Atlas." Apr. 1989.

INDEX

Raymond Zinke Gallun—Antarctica 1991

www.ingramcontent.com/pod-product-compliance
Lightning Source LLC
Chambersburg PA
CBHW031600110426
42742CB00036B/571